D1191037

Bloom's Modern Critical Interpretations

Bloom's Modern Critical Interpretations

Ernest Hemingway's
The Sun Also Rises
New Edition

Edited and with an introduction by
Harold Bloom
Sterling Professor of the Humanities
Yale University

BLOOM'S
LITERARY CRITICISM
An imprint of Infobase Publishing

Bloom's Modern Critical Interpretations: The Sun Also Rises—New Edition

Copyright © 2011 by Infobase Publishing
Introduction © 2011 by Harold Bloom

Bloom's Literary Criticism
An imprint of Infobase Publishing
132 West 31st Street
New York NY 10001

Library of Congress Cataloging-in-Publication Data
Ernest Hemingway's The sun also rises / edited and with an introduction by Harold Bloom.—New ed.
    p. cm.—(Bloom's modern critical interpretations)
Includes bibliographical references and index.
ISBN 978-1-60413-890-0 (hardcover)
1. Hemingway, Ernest, 1899–1961. Sun also rises. I. Bloom, Harold. II. Title. III. Series.
PS3515.E37S92355 2010
813'.52—dc22

Bloom's Literary Criticism books are available at special discounts when purchased in bulk quantities for businesses, associations, institutions, or sales promotions. Please call our Special Sales Department in New York at (212) 967-8800 or (800) 322-8755.

You can find Bloom's Literary Criticism on the World Wide Web at
http://www.chelseahouse.com

Contributing editor: Pamela Loos
Cover design by Takeshi Takahashi
Composition by IBT Global, Troy NY
Cover printed by IBT Global, Troy NY
Book printed and bound by IBT Global, Troy NY
Date printed: October 2010
Printed in the United States of America

10 9 8 7 6 5 4 3 2 1

This book is printed on acid-free paper.

All links and Web addresses were checked and verified to be correct at the time of publication. Because of the dynamic nature of the Web, some addresses and links may have changed since publication and may no longer be valid.

Contents

Editor's Note

My introduction centers on Hemingway's rhetorical stance, as the point where his style and sensibility come together.

H. R. Stoneback sees the fundamental structure of the novel as based on pilgrimage, while Wolfgang E. H. Rudat explores the therapeutic nature of humor in the book.

Paul Civello turns to Hemingway's naturalistic proclivities, followed by James Nagel's discussion of narrativity as it relates to the figure of Robert Cohn.

Ron Berman considers the religious divisions that informs the novel, while Adrian Bond addresses the moral and emotional ambiguities Hemingway presents.

For Daniel S. Traber, Jake Barnes embodies a privileged whiteness that imposes judgment and division on the novel, while Jeffrey A. Schwarz turns his attention to Prohibition, alcohol, and alcoholism as it touched Hemingway and his characters' worlds.

Donald A. Daiker concludes the volume in asserting that *The Sun Also Rises* is a pedagogical novel and that teaching and learning are central to the philosophy of life Jake Barnes espouses.

HAROLD BLOOM

Introduction

So severely stylized and rigorously mannered is Ernest Hemingway's *The Sun Also Rises* that it continues to achieve a classic status, decades after its initial publication. It is a masterpiece of stance and of sensibility, and like *The Great Gatsby* (which influenced it) *The Sun Also Rises* evades all the dangers that might have reduced it to become another mere period piece. Again like *The Great Gatsby, The Sun Also Rises* is something of a prose poem, emerging from the literary era dominated by T. S. Eliot's *The Waste Land*. Like Eliot himself, who was much affected by Joseph Conrad's *Heart of Darkness*, both Fitzgerald and Hemingway take up a narrative stance that is influenced by Conrad's Marlow, the prime narrator of *Heart of Darkness, Lord Jim*, and (though he is unnamed there) "The Secret Sharer." Nick Carraway in *The Great Gatsby* and Jake Barnes in *The Sun Also Rises* are equivocal narrators, each with a protagonist who is his main concern: Gatsby for Carraway and Lady Brett Ashley for Jake Barnes. There is something feminine in sensibility about both Carraway and Barnes, as there was about Conrad's Marlow and about Eliot's Tiresias, the implied narrative sensibility of *The Waste Land*.

The wounded Fisher King of *The Waste Land*, impotent and yearning for spiritual salvation, is clearly akin to the impotent Jake Barnes, maimed in World War I and so no longer Brett Ashley's lover, though they continue to be in love with each other. Interpreters of Brett take remarkably varied views of her, ranging from a man-eating, Circean bitch-goddess to another lost Waste Lander, stoic and disinterested and essentially tragic, questing for what cannot be recovered, a lost image of sexual fulfillment. It is suggestive

1

that the hidden model for Eliot's *The Waste Land* was the most powerful of all American poems, Walt Whitman's elegy for the martyred Abraham Lincoln, "When Lilacs Last in the Dooryard Bloom'd." Whitman's poem is truly a self-elegy, as are *The Waste Land*, *The Great Gatsby*, and *The Sun Also Rises*. When the funeral procession of President Lincoln passes him, Whitman makes a symbolic gesture of self-castration by surrendering the "tally," the sprig of lilac that was his own image of voice and more ambiguously the image for his sexual identity. Elegy is the literary genre of *The Sun Also Rises* and ought to help determine our attitude toward Brett as well as toward Jake, who mourns not only his lost potency but his largely abandoned Catholicism.

Hemingway's nostalgias were numerous: for God, heroism, a perfect love, and an antagonistic supremacy in Western literature, even against such titans as Melville and Tolstoy. *The Sun Also Rises* profoundly studies many other American nostalgias but above all our longing for innocence, in the Whitmanian sense of an original American destiny, compounded of freedom, hope, and millennial potential. Against that "optative mood," as Ralph Waldo Emerson termed it, Hemingway sets the negativity of Ecclesiastes, the most nihilistic book of the Hebrew Bible. The novel's epigraph, the source of its title, states Hemingway's ethos and also the stoic condition of Jake Barnes and Brett Ashley:

> One generation passeth away, and another generation cometh; but the earth abideth forever. . . . The sun also ariseth, and the sun goeth down, and hasteth to the place where he arose. . . . The wind goeth toward the south, and turneth about unto the north; it whirleth about continually, and the wind returneth again according to his circuits. . . . All the rivers run into the sea; yet the sea is not full; unto the place from whence the rivers come, thither they return again.

All the generations are lost—not just that of Brett and Jake and their friends—in this dark view of mortality and mutability. *The Sun Also Rises*, like Ecclesiastes, does not urge us either to religious assurance or to an absolute nihilism or despair. One of the most poignant of all American elegies, it affirms the virtues of giving a style to despair and of enduring the loss of love with something like a tragic dignity. Hemingway was never again to write so compelling a novel, though his genius for the short story continued undiminished. Lyrical intensity has rarely sustained a novel with such economy or such grace.

H. R. STONEBACK

From the rue Saint-Jacques to the Pass of Roland to the "Unfinished Church on the Edge of the Cliff"

> I want to make the small pilgrimage to see you ... I prayed for you sincerely and straight in Chartres, Burgos, Segovia and two minor places ... Sorry not to have made the home office of Santiago de Compostella [sic].
>
> —Hemingway to Bernard Berenson (8/11/53, 2/2/54)

> In first war ... was really scared *after* wounded and very devout at the end. Fear of death. Belief in *personal* salvation or maybe just preservation through prayers for intercession of Our Lady and various saints that prayed to with almost tribal faith."
>
> —Hemingway to Thomas Welsh (6/19/45).

More than a decade ago, during the course of preparing an essay for the 50th anniversary of *The Sun Also Rises*, I became convinced that for half a century we had been missing much of that novel. If—as my grandfather used to say—I may be allowed to be personal, I will record here the anecdotal and topographical origin of that process of conviction. It was 1974; I was living in Paris, teaching a Faulkner seminar as a Visiting Professor at the University of Paris. (Everyone there seemed to think that Hemingway was passé.) For some time I had been deep in Faulkner studies, having long since dismissed (i.e., misread) much of Hemingway in some of the ways that

From *The Hemingway Review* 6, no. 1 (Fall 1986): 2–29. Copyright © 1986 by the Ernest Hemingway Foundation.

literary criticism had been dismissing and misreading him for decades. I had
not read or thought much about Hemingway for a long time; the last time I
had read a novel by Hemingway I was living in northern Michigan, on the
edge of Hemingway country. (It was 1961—July 3, 1961, to be exact. I had
just heard at a bar in Gaylord the news of Hemingway's death; the bartender
said these were truly the shots "heard round the world"; an old man—who
claimed he knew Hemingway in the old Michigan days—sat at the end of
the bar chanting: "Papa betrayed us, Papa betrayed us." A friend gave me a
copy of *The Old Man and the Sea* that day and I reread it, sitting by a trout
pool on the AuSable River.) In 1974, as a relief from immersion in Faulkner,
and because I was then living among the Parisian scenes Hemingway had
rendered so vividly, I reread *The Sun Also Rises*. From the window of my
apartment on the rue Saint-Jacques, I looked across to the great, heavy
dome of Val-de-Grâce. Sitting at my table at my regular café on the corner,
I brooded the topography of Jake's itineraries; I was particularly puzzled by
Hemingway's description of the rue Saint-Jacques—there, in my winding,
medieval neighborhood—as "the rigid north and south of the Rue Saint
Jacques" (*SAR*, 78). Why would the ostensible master of precision so clearly
distort the actual conformation of a street which he knew well?

I raised this question one day in conversation at the café, with a Saint-
Jacques autochthon, a life-long denizen of that *quartier*. Yes, he knew of
Hemingway; no, he had not read his *romans*. I read to him the "rigid north
and south" passage, and he pondered the matter in silence over his calva-
dos. He said nothing that day. The next day he sat with me at the café and
after some talk of the weather he asked: "Do you know of Saint-Jacques de
Compostelle?" No, I said, what was that? "Do you know, then, Santiago de
Compostela?" he said, stumbling over the Spanish. I said yes, I had heard of
it—it was a place in Spain. "More than a place, my friend. Come, walk with
me." We walked a few blocks down the rue Saint-Jacques. He said I was right,
the street is not rigid—it is medieval, it bends. The boulevards, the creations
of the 19th century, are rigid. He asked me if I knew that Val-de-Grâce was
a hospital for wounded soldiers, that it was a monastery founded by Ann of
Austria in thanksgiving for the birth of her son after 21 years of marriage.
Yes, I knew that. He pointed out the entrance to the famous Convent of the
Carmelites and spoke of the associations with St. Theresa of Avila. He identified the *Institut Des Sourds-Muets*, the National Institute of the Deaf and
Dumb, and made some joke about how it stood in the place where, for many
centuries, there had been an important hospice for the pilgrims to Santiago
de Compostela. (He was not very religious, he said, but he was much in love
with history.) He made some point, which I missed, about the church of
Saint-Jacques-du-Haut-Pas (my mind was wandering to another high pass

in the novel). In rapid succession he showed me the site of the house where Jean de Meung finished the *Roman de la Rose*, the site of the Saint-Jacques gate in the old city wall, the college of Saint Barbara, patron saint of artillerymen, where St. Ignace de Loyola had been a student, and after a drink at a café on the rue Soufflot, he showed me the site of yet another hospice for the pilgrims of Saint-Jacques. I did not know it then—and of course my neighbor-guide did not know this—but I had just been given a tour of touchstones in Hemingway's life and work.[1] As we walked back toward Val-de-Grâce, he said something like this: So, you see, we are walking the ancient route of millions of pilgrims. Saint-Jacques—Santiago—is a place and the way that takes you there is part of the place. This famous rue Saint-Jacques is a sign we can no longer interpret of the vast, secret ceremony of our civilization, now lost, in this age. It is—how do you say?—a *constatation emblematique* of not alone the history, but the art, the beauty, the feeling, the belief—the very spirit of Western Civilization (he spoke this in upper case). It is, then, "rigid north and south" only in the strict light of history, in the suffering and joy of the great *pèlerinage*. Although I have not read him, it seems your Mr. Hemingway knew more history and was perhaps more *Catholique* than most Americans. *Après tout*, he was concerned with much more than the surface of things. Yes, I said, it did seem so. That small lesson in topography and history has led to an unfolding of the numinous sense, the anagogical level of Hemingway's work which has been unceasing, which has brought me, through pilgrimages great and small, back to Hemingway, the Hemingway of the true moveable feast (as the Church calendar expresses the matter). It is a pilgrim's feast, with *The Sun Also Rises* holding the center, and there is never any end to it.

II

I prayed to St. Fermin for you. Not that you needed it but I found myself in Mass with nothing to do and so prayed for my kid, for Hadley, for myself ...
—Hemingway to Ezra Pound (7/19/24).

[The bull fight is] the one thing that has, with the exception of the ritual of the church, come down to us intact from the old days
—Hemingway to Maxwell Perkins (12/6/26).

Unfortunately, much of the criticism concerned with *The Sun Also Rises* over the past six decades, reads as if it had been written by Robert Cohn (or W. H. Hudson, or H. L. Mencken, or other anti-exemplary specimen figures of the novel). Some of it reads, just a bit more felicitously, as if it had been written by Brett Ashley. Still another kind of representative response reads

as if written by the president of the Epworth League or the W.C.T.U. None
of it deals adequately with the Catholic text and subtext of the novel; none
of it deals precisely with Jake's Catholic sensibility, with the moral and
spiritual anguish and joy of the pilgrim, a quite specifically Catholic pilgrim
on a specific pilgrimage route, very much in touch with the history, the
ritual, the discipline, the moral and aesthetic and salvific legacy of the great
medieval pilgrimage to Santiago de Compostela. It seems, most of the time,
that only the part of the "iceberg" that shows is seen, or that there has been
insufficient discipline in the implications of Hemingway's compositional
principle of the "theory of omission," whereby the omitted parts of the tale
may generate the core feeling of the text. Yet it is worse than that, for by
and large Hemingway criticism has not even seen the parts of the Catholic
sensibility, the pilgrimage motif which do show clearly, the allusions and
symbolic landscapes which are evident in the text.

To be sure, some readers have seen a rather vague, generalized pilgrimage
motif; Jake has been seen, for example, as a Fisher King–figure on a redemp-
tive quest, and there is more than a hint of the Fisher King in Jake Barnes. This
mythic thrust, properly understood, may help us to avoid the familiar misreading of the novel which declares that it is all motion which leads nowhere. Yet
the Fisher King motif, insistently and heavy-handedly applied (without, say,
a firm grasp of Eliot's inclusive vision), may lead the reader astray into five-
and-dime pronunciamientos on the waste land, or skewed readings of the role
of Paris, the role of France, in the novel. Hemingway's France, Jake's Paris, are
not wastelands. Nor is France, as Wirt Williams has suggested in the most
recent variation on the mountains-plains pattern, the "low country" (59–60).
There are just as many hills (and they are generally greener) in Jake's France as
in Jake's Spain. I reckon this amounts to a plea, rather late in the day, that we
begin to read Hemingway's text with the care that it deserves, that we remind
ourselves that his texts, all of them, are as layered and complex, as allusive and
subtle as Eliot's. At least as skillfully as Eliot, Hemingway employs the tactics
of allusion, juxtaposition and omission in the service of a strategy of recovery,
of reappropriating the verities, the values—as the Count says—we must "get
to know" (60), the rituals "from the old days"—as Hemingway says—that we
might shore against ruin. (After all, they had the same poet-teacher-editor, on
whose behalf, in 1924, Hemingway was praying to St. Fermín.)

* * *

In Paris, early in the book, Jake says: "I like this town and I go to Spain in
the summertime" (10). This statement suggests the composed deliberation
of Jake's life. Spain is for the summertime, the pilgrimage season, when

he makes his way south to the bull-fights, to fishing, to spiritual renewal, which is accomplished through *toreo*, through fishing, through Jake's participation in the sacraments, through Mass, confession and prayer. All of these rituals hold Jake steady, provide his stay against the irritable and insistent fundamentalist or gnostic urge to immanentize the eschaton. Only if we have some sense of these matters will we be able to understand Jake, especially the Jake of such passages as the following:

> Perhaps as you went along you did learn something. I did not care what it was all about. All I wanted to know was how to live in it. Maybe if you found out how to live in a you learned from that what it was all about. (148)

This well-known and little understood passage has often been taken to be the primary statement of a kind of pragmatic, relativistic, making-it-up-as-you-go-along code. It is nothing of the kind. Quite simply, the "how" of living that Jake is talking about is ritual, ceremony which, if followed far enough, may lead to the "all." It is an exact rendering of the pilgrim's code: "Perhaps as you went along you did learn something."

Pamplona is, of course, a major way-station on the pilgrimage of Santiago de Compostela, as is Roncevaux. Jake does not get all the way to Santiago, and that is as it should be. It would not seem sound strategy to have your pilgrim arrive at his ultimate destination in your first novel. For that, better to wait until later, say, until *The Old Man and the Sea*, where Santiago (whose name, as Hemingway noted in a letter to Brown, 7/14/54, was not an accident) completes the pilgrimage, in a figurative or incarnational sense. Hemingway, however, did complete the pilgrimage on a number of occasions (the first time, in 1927) to what he called "the loveliest town in Spain"—Santiago de Compostela (Baker, *Life* 186). The student of his life will note that the usual "Spain in the summertime" pattern included, after the Fiesta of San Fermín, the fiesta at Valencia, held in honor of Santiago-St. James (beginning on his feast day, July 25) and, then, Santiago for the month of August. Sometimes the pilgrimage included a stop in Zaragoza, another important pilgrimage site and way-station on the greater pilgrimage of Santiago. It is instructive to note that the venerated shrine of the Virgen del Pilar (in the second cathedral of Zaragoza, *Nuestra Señora del Pilar*) plays a central role in the matter of Santiago: this is where, according to tradition, the primary miracle of Santiago's residence in Spain occurred—the Virgin Mary, in the flesh, standing on a stone pillar.[2] When Hemingway went down to Zaragoza with Archibald MacLeish in 1926, he noted that MacLeish—with his "fine legal mind"—attempted to "take away" from Hemingway, among other things, the Popes and the Holy Grail, giving "in exchange a great Yale football team." He noted with pleasure that the next *Sunday* he read that *Holy Cross* ("or some place like that") beat Yale 33–6: "So I wrote Archie a pneu and said I was sending back his great Yale team . . . and would he return me by return post all the Popes . . . the Holy Grail."[3] It signifies immensely, I think, that Hemingway wrote this particular inscription (to Gerald and Sara Murphy) on the inside back cover of the pamphlet publication (1926) of "Today is Friday," which is not centered, as has been said, on the crucifixion of Christ, but on the way Christ's behavior on the cross affects the Roman soldiers, bringing one of them, perhaps, to the edge of conversion. It is clear, all through the 1920s, which team Hemingway is trying out for; he has no desire to play on the Yale team.

III

This small study in promiscuity set against travel scenes in Navarre and a fishing expedition in the Pass of Roland.
—Hemingway's inscription in a copy of *The Sun Also Rises*, cited in *The New York Times*, July 15, 1977.

Ah que cet cor a long haleine.
—Line from *La Chanson de Roland*, cited Hemingway to Breit (9/16/56).

I have argued elsewhere that the fundamental structure of *The Sun Also Rises* is pilgrimage, that the movement of the novel from Paris to Bayonne to Roncevaux to Pamplona follows the route to Santiago de Compostela, and that Jake Barnes, who designs the journey, is the conscious pilgrim of the piece.[4] Much of the emphasis of these earlier studies fell on Roland and the ways in which he serves the novel as an implicit exemplar. The attention of the reader is focused on Roland by the fishing scenes in the Pass of Roland, by the alteration of landscape in which Hemingway engages when he has Jake observe the monastery of Roncevaux from a vantage point where it is not possible to see the monastery.[5] Such interpolations or geographical incongruities focus the pilgrimage subtext of the novel, as did the earlier "rigid north and south of the Rue Saint Jacques" anachronism. (This suggests a hitherto unnoticed Hemingway principle of composition: to wit, anachorism and anachronism are most useful in calling attention to the unstated patterns, the oblique symbols or emblems of a work. The two anachronisms cited here must serve to illustrate the principle, together with the glaring anachronism by which Hemingway has William Jennings Bryan die in June, rather than July 26,

1925, thereby altering the dates of one of the major news stories of the 1920s in order to introduce the religious theme in the fishing interlude.[6])

In my initial attempts at exegesis of the Roland matter, I was working from a hunch. The only surface clue was the setting of the fishing scenes around Roncevaux-Roncesvalles. Surely, since there were many fine trout streams in the Pyrenees that Jake could have fished, the choice of the Irati was dictated by the Roland association, especially since the concerns of the "fishing" interlude were as much—perhaps more so—religious-Catholic as ichthyographic. In addition, once the Santiago pilgrimage motif was discerned, the Roland notion was reinforced, since Roncevaux was the main gateway into Spain for all pilgrims coming from the north, primarily because of the fame and glory of Roland as the chief Christian knight, hero of the best-known Christian epic. Thus I argued that Hemingway (and Jake) were engaged by the *Chanson*, its dignity, as Pound had noted, and the ways it championed Christianity against paganism. Jake seemed to be questing the same qualities of courage, loyalty and freedom from agonizing self-consciousness that, according to Henry Adams, Roland epitomized. Subsequent perusal of Hemingway's papers and correspondence revealed materials which supported these earlier intuitions. For example, Hemingway writes to Howell Jenkins in November, 1924, and urges him to come fishing with "Ernest de la Mancha Hemingway" in the "wildest damn country ... in from Roncevaux"; one month later, he writes to William B. Smith, Jr., inviting him to come over and "drive down all through France and over the Pass of Roland" and fish the Irati with him (*Letters* 130, 136). And Hemingway declares in his inscription in a friend's copy of *The Sun Also Rises* that it is a study in "promiscuity" together with "a fishing expedition to the Pass of Roland."

This strikes me as more than a casual remark since it centers the novel on two key questions: promiscuity, and fishing in the terrain of Roland. Hemingway's use of the word promiscuity should be taken in the root sense ("mixed," from *prô-miscère*, "to mix thoroughly"); that is, Brett Ashley's sexual promiscuity is only the most obvious form of a lack of discrimination, a disorderly mix, or as the OED has it, "carelessly irregular" behavior. Along with Brett, Robert Cohn displays promiscuous behavior, casual, confused, "lacking standards of selection" (*American Heritage Dictionary*). The antidote to this promiscuity is Jake's deliberate pilgrimage, the fishing trip (and Ichthus-quest), the "expedition" (from "expedire," *to extricate*) in the country of Roland which expedites his pilgrim's progress and suggests behavior based on values, on "standards of selection." Roland, then, joins Pedro Romero and Count Mippipopolous as an exemplary instance of behavior informed by values, courage, grace under pressure.

In 1953, when Hemingway made a trip from Paris, through Chartres, and on south to the Basque country, he "amused himself by imagining that he was a medieval knight"; as late as 1959 he retained his Rolandesque medieval sense of the magical landscape around Roncevaux, dreaming one more time in what he called "the last great forest of the Middle Ages" (Baker, *Life* 511, 547). Obviously, from the 1924 image of "Ernest de la Mancha" on his way to the Pass of Roland until the very end of his life, Hemingway enjoyed assuming the role of knight. In a 1956 letter to Harvey Breit he directly quoted the *Chanson*. Set off in a separate paragraph, with no introductory commentary, identification, or immediately apparent connection with the contexts of the letter, he writes the celebrated line, "Ah que cet cot a long haleine" (*Letters*, 870). This line is spoken by Charlemagne when he hears Roland sounding the oliphant, miles away at Roncevaux; as one recent commentator observes, it is "one of the grandest and most celebrated moments in literary history."[7] That famous horn is indeed long of breath, and it reverberates throughout Hemingway's life and work. It may be that in quoting the line without commentary here, Hemingway is engaging in Hemingway code-talk with Breit, referring to some past conversation, some shared passion for the Roland legend that requires only the famous line to evoke an intricate set of feelings. Or since the main business of the letter is concerned with Spain and the bull-fights, there may be a complex allusion to the pilgrimage and Roland combined with a reference to the horn, in its primal sense, the horn of the bull, as well as the primitive and magical hunting horn and the horn which sounds for the various acts of the ceremony of the *corrida* (especially for the death of the bull).

* * *

As Gerard J. Brault has noted, long-established connotations of Roland's blast on the oliphant include "haunting melancholy" (as in de Vigny's famous poem and—we might add—the closing lines of Faulkner's *Flags in the Dust*), "magic associations" (the legends and poems of the Middle Ages are "replete with references to magic horns, capable of causing wondrous enchantments"), evocations of grace (no one may drink from certain horns unless "he is in the state of grace"), and hunting associations (the "staghunt image" in art is associated with Roland) (Brault 214–15, 223). Finally the horn is obliquely connected with the primary miracle of the *Chanson*, the "staying of the sun," granted by God in answer to Charlemagne's prayers for a prolongation of the day. This echoes Joshua 10:13, where "the sun stood still," and, in turn, points to the "miracle of the tumbling walls of Pamplona in the Pseudo-Turpin, unquestionably an allusion to the fall of Jericho."

Brault concludes: "The staying of the sun was interpreted as the postponing of the Last Judgment by Christ to enable sinners to be saved; the blowing of the trumpets and the collapsing walls at Jericho were also viewed as a prefiguration of the final judging of mankind by God. The sound of Roland's oliphant surely triggered similar associations in the medieval audience" (263). These, then, are a few of the things that Roland's horn. might have suggested to Hemingway. The walls of Pamplona do not quite tumble in *The Sun Also Rises*, but, ultimately, the sun "stays" for Jake, who is a "sinner" in the process of being "saved"—and not by any pagan heliophily. Before we leave Roncevaux-Roncesvalles-Rencesvals, that "Vale of Thorns" through which the pilgrim must pass, we might add that in some versions of the legends, Roland experienced his baptism of fire, his first battles, victories and wounds, as a very young soldier in Italy.

IV

This seems to be getting very solemn for the hour which is 0930 but then I have heard Mass at that hour in Santiago de Campostella [sic] . . . I stayed there three summers trying to learn when I was working on my education.

> —Hemingway to Bernard Berenson (10/24/55).

So my name is Jacob Barnes and I am writing the story, not as I believe is usual in these cases, from a desire for confession, because being a Roman Catholic I am spared that Protestant urge to literary production. . . .

> —Discarded Chapter II, *The Sun Also Rises*, *Antaeus*, Spring 1979.

One of the great things about pilgrims is that they have a lively sense of place, a strong devotion to the *deus loci*, the spirits of the places through and towards which they travel on pilgrimage, unlike the mere promiscuous traveller. The nature of one's response to place and the kind of travel plans that one envisions are established as values, or hallmarks of character, in the opening chapters of *The Sun Also Rises*. Robert Cohn, for example, wants to go to South America because he has read a romantic book about it, while Jake wants to go to Africa to hunt, to participate in a ritual activity, a ceremony which makes incarnate a complex scheme of values. The other side of the coin is that the sentimental dreamer who promiscuously projects romantic schemes of travel is not truly alive in the place where he resides while planning the next adventure. "Why don't you start living your life in Paris?" Jake asks Cohn (11). Indeed, most of the expatriate crowd live their lives in the manner evoked by Fitzgerald's memorable phrase in the first chapter of *The Great Gatsby*: "They had spent a year in France for no particular reason, and then drifted here and there unrestfully." The exception to this rule is Jake, who never drifts, who always seems to know exactly where he is going, and why he is going there. He likes Paris; he goes to Spain in the summertime, for the fishing, for the *corrida*, and for all of the reasons conveyed by the pilgrimage motif.

* * *

It is useful to examine in detail neglected aspects of the novel, in the light of this important thematic configuration. In the first chapter we are told briefly about Cohn's travels, his drifting from Carmel to Provincetown, and finally to Paris. Then, in the first rendered scene, Jake and Robert are at the café discussing places to go. Jake makes all the suggestions. The first proposal is a "walk up to Saint Odile" (6). Why Sainte Odile? I suppose most readers assume that Jake entertains a pleasant walk (actually 41 kilometers, one way, from Strasbourg) in the Vosges. Why, given a host of more popular tourist sites for the ordinary traveller in the Vosges, does Jake select the rather obscure Sainte Odile? The answer is easy and firm, once we have the Santiago pattern in hand (in fact, once we have this, everything in the novel falls into place). Sainte Odile—obscure only to the non-pilgrims—has long been a famous place of pilgrimage. Hemingway might have known this from his *Guide Bleu* where he would read that Sainte Odile, the patron saint of Alsace, "was born blind and recovered her sight when she was baptized." Her father, the Duke of Alsace, who had rejected her, at last recognized her vocation and gave her the Hohenburg mountain (now called the Odilien-burg) to establish a convent. Or Hemingway might have read about her in his copy of *The Book of Saints: A Dictionary of Servants of God canonized by the Catholic Church*: "According to tradition St. Ottilia [also Odile, Odilia, Othilia, Adilia] was born blind and cast out for this reason by her family . . . she miraculously recovered her sight. . . . Her life as it comes down to us abounds in extraordinary legends" (London 1921, 452). The pilgrimage to Sainte Odile was immensely popular in the Middle Ages, went through a long period of neglect, and once again became a popular pilgrimage by the early 1900s. One of the primary acts of pilgrims to Sainte Odile is to bathe their eyes in her miraculous spring. She is the patron saint of the blind.

Now it is instructive to see that the first place Jake mentions as a destination is a well-known pilgrimage place. Yet the significance, the reach of this allusion does not stop there, for we are dealing, as always in Hemingway, with precisely coded signals. A survey of the novel reveals an extraordinary number of references to eyes, vision, near-sightedness and blindness, especially in the sense of "blind drunk." In fact, however, the most extensive and explicit reference to the blindness motif occurred in the original opening chapters, just before the Sainte Odile allusion. (In some respects, Fitzgerald may have been right in urging Hemingway to cut these chapters, but many important matters in the book are—shall we say—*seen* much more clearly with the help of those cut chapters.) This is what Jake says about blindness in the discarded Chapter I:

> But when [Brett] had been drunk she always spoke of it as having been blind. "Weren't we blind last night, though?" It was short for blind drunk, and the curious part was that she really became, in a way, blind. Drinking ... real drinking ... affected Brett in three successive stages. Drinking, say, whiskey and sodas from four o'clock in the afternoon until two o'clock in the morning Brett first lost her power of speech and just sat and listened, then she lost her sight. ... (*Antaeus* 9)

This is not the place to consider in detail the eye-blindness-vision image clusters, so it must suffice to say that Jake, for one, is only truly "blind" once in the novel, on the last night of the fiesta, after Brett has gone off with Pedro Romero. Jake is as drunk as he "ever remembered having been." Mike comes in and asks: "Are you blind? I was blind myself." "Yes," Jake says, "I'm blind." Jake listens to the fiesta going on outside and thinks: "It did not mean anything." He pretends to be asleep, and when Mike and Bill leave he goes to the balcony and sees that "the world was not wheeling any more. It was just very clear and bright, and inclined to blur at the edges" (224). A few pages later, Jake is in San Sebastian, swimming, in the first of the scenes which are sometimes styled "baptismal":

> I dove deep once, swimming down to the bottom. I swam with my eyes open and it was green and dark. (235)

From the beginning of the novel, where Jake is contemplating a small pilgrimage to the numinous place of Sainte Odile, whose blindness was healed by baptism, his primary need has been to see clearly his situation with Brett, to deal with it. He has been "blind," in several senses, with regard to Brett; he has taken his dive to the bottom, again in several senses, but in the baptismal swimming scene his eyes are open in the deep, green water, and after he emerges, everything looks very sharp and bright and sunblazoned in the concluding pages of the novel. And, of course, he is seeing very clearly when he is finally able to say in response to Brett's romantic assertion of the good times they might have had: "Isn't it pretty to think so?" The novel, then, is centrally concerned with vision and we should not be surprised to learn that the standard iconographic representation of Sainte Odile shows her holding an open book, with the open pages turned outwards, facing the viewer: one large piercing eye gazes from each open page. It is a powerful haunting image of vision, of eyes that—as Jake says in another context—"look on and on after every one else's eyes in the world would have stopped looking" (26).

Return now to the café scene; after Cohn kicks Jake under the table for mentioning a girl who could show them around, Jake suggests another place: Bruges, the "Venice of the North." Bruges is a fine medieval town, rich in history, and a good place to visit any time of the year. But we must ask why Jake, sitting in a café in Paris in the springtime, suggests Bruges? Quite probably because Bruges is also a celebrated pilgrimage place, and the primary pilgrimage season is in May, when, with the townspeople wearing crusaders' costumes, the very ancient Procession of the Holy Blood occurs. In 1149, the Count of Flanders "received from the Patriarch of Jerusalem a few drops of the blood of Christ. This sacred relic has been conserved in a gold and silver reliquary . . . carried in the annual procession." (Madden 60). Jake may have been thinking of making this, the best-known of several Holy Blood pilgrimages and processions in Europe. Again, it seems, the allusion does more than reinforce the overarching pilgrimage theme, for the focus in Bruges is the blood, just as the focus in the novel is on those arenas of blood-ceremony which emphasize that all knowledge worth having is bought with blood: the bull-fight, the Church, hunting, fishing and war (as in the baptism of fire, the "blooding" of Jake). It should be noted, too, that Bruges was an important staging area for pilgrims to Santiago from northern Europe (and there is a 13th century Church of Saint-Jacques).

Jake next suggests the Ardennes as a place to go. The Ardennes Forest, which stretches over parts of France, Luxembourg and southern Belgium, covers much territory, compared to Jake's other suggestions. Especially around St. Hubert, the woods are—or were, in the 1920s—regarded as among the most beautiful in Europe. It might be that Jake, as a war veteran, has some interest in seeing the sites of the Battle of the Ardennes (known, curiously enough, as "the battle of the two blind men.") But since Jake seems more interested in walking in the woods than visiting battlefields, we must assume it is the St. Hubert-hunting association which leads him to suggest the Ardennes. Precisely. St. Hubert, the patron saint of hunters, is particularly venerated in the village of St. Hubert, Belgium, in the very heart of the Ardennes. The abbey contains the shrine of St. Hubert and there is an annual pilgrimage. The Mass of St. Hubert is celebrated there (and in many forest-area villages in Belgium and France) to the accompaniment of hunting horns. ("Ah . . . cet cot") The well-known legend of St. Hubert, frequently depicted in sculpture, stained glass and painting, tells how Hubert, a very worldly man and an avid hunter, met a great stag in the forest on Good Friday, bearing between its antlers a crucifix, surrounded by rays of light. This event, of course, marked his conversion. The hunt has been one of the richest motifs of Christian iconography, and hunting scenes, often juxtaposed with banquets, represent the life of virtue, and the banquets, the celestial reward. We have already noted the stag-chase motif and hunting horn associations with Roland. St. Hubert, then, the *deus loci* of the Ardennes, with his rich and multiple iconographic associations with horns and great stags, serves to echo—or more properly—to prefigure the matter of Roland in the novel. And it's my guess that if Jake, an avid hunter, had gone to the Ardennes he would have been at one of those splendid huntsman's Masses of St. Hubert, with the long-breathed horns reverberating from the church into the surrounding forest, or he would have participated in the pilgrimage to St. Hubert, with the hunters and the animals gathered within and without the basilica for the blessing of the beasts, the "bénédiction des animaux."

Finally, still in the same passage, Jake says: "Oh, well . . . let's go to Senlis . . . [it's] a good place and we can stay at the Grand Cerf and take a hike in the woods and come home" (6–7). He seems to have given up on the more complicated, longer-distance pilgrimage destinations, and settled for nearby Senlis. He may also feel that Cohn will be bored by the pilgrimage places, as Cohn later fears he will be bored by the bull-fights. Although it is not a specific pilgrimage town, Senlis is one of the oldest French towns, with a rich history. It was a royal residence for the first two dynasties. Jake would, presumably, go to see the Gallo-Roman arena, the magnificent Cathedral of Notre Dame, and the "cabinet de travail" of Saint Louis in the old Chateau Royal (Saint Louis was one of Hemingway's favorite crusader saints). Also, in keeping with the "walk in the woods" theme of the overall conversation, we might assume Jake's lively interest in walking in the *Bois* of St. Hubert, adjacent to Senlis, which has long been a center of vénerie, of *la chasse*, as well as the French center of the Cult of St. Hubert. The hunt motif is further underlined by Jake's indication that they would stay at the Grand Cerf—the Great Stag—hotel. There are many hotels and cafés in France called the Grand Cerf, and popular lore seems to associate the name with the great mystical stag of St. Hubert—at least, that is what I have gathered from conversations in these places, and from the fine panel of St. Hubert meeting the stag with the crucifix that I saw carved into the wood of a bar, in a café named the Grand Cerf, in Brittany years ago, somewhere near the magical Forest of Paimpont. Finally, their hike in the woods from Senlis would most likely take them through the Forest of Chantilly, and a few kilometers down the way to the tiny forest village and Church of St. Firmin, that native of Pamplona who became the Bishop of Amiens. But then we know all about him and his "religious festival," don't we?

All this may seem a bit much to lavish on a brief, allusive conversation in the opening chapter of the novel. Yet three of the four places Jake names are celebrated pilgrimage centers, resonant with imagistic and thematic implications for the novel; all four places are distinctly medieval, vibrant, with a sense of the medieval Church, pilgrims, crusaders, brilliantly evocative of the real old thing that Jake seeks. Put it this way: suppose Jake had referred instead to possible trips to Leningrad, or some closer shrine associated with Marx, say, or the secret venues of Comintern meetings, or French revolutionary sites. If this were the case, several generations of Hemingway critics would have built up by now an exegesis of these allusions as keys to the vision of the work, and they would be part of a *de rigeur* hermeneutics for all students of Hemingway.[8]

Much more could be done, if space permitted, with the pilgrimage allusions in the novel. The primary purposes, for example, of the repeated references to Lourdes are to announce the more obvious pilgrimage motif to readers who would otherwise miss it and to provide contrast of the most popular modern pilgrimage with the vastly different and grand medieval pilgrimage of Santiago de Compostela. We could note, too, that Jake gets off the train in Tours—another important pilgrimage town—and buys a bottle of wine. In Bayonne, he goes into Notre-Dame-de-Bayonne (now Cathédrale Ste-Marie), one of the finest gothic cathedrals in the South of France; Jake likes it, and is, no doubt, aware of the pilgrim associations of the place, though he does not talk about them.

One last pilgrimage place should be carefully considered here, i.e., the Augustinian Abbey at Roncevaux. Typically, one critic reads the scene as follows:

> The Monastery at Roncesvalles is "a remarkable place." "It isn't the same as fishing, though, is it?" For it is in the personal experience of fishing that one discovers what is good and beautiful and trustworthy, not in the monastery. Morality must constantly stand the test of individual experience, and that which is of value in Hemingway's world arises . . . out of the experience of an individual who is essentially alone and far out in a moral no-man's land. (Reardon 139–40)

This isn't the same as reading Hemingway's text, though, is it? Indeed there seems to be an iron law of Hemingway Criticism which reads something like this: the accuracy of the critic's reading decreases in direct relation to the increase of religious significance in the passage under consideration. (Perhaps this is what Hemingway had in mind when he spoke of critics who were afraid to touch religion with a ten-foot pole, and when he recommended to a friend that he look at the *European Catholic* criticism of his work.)[9] Thus we must insist that readers begin by recognizing who says what:

> "It's a remarkable place," *Harris* said, when we came out. "But you know I'm not much on those sort of places."
> "Me either," *Bill* said.
> "It's a remarkable place, though," *Harris* said. "I wouldn't not have seen it. I'd been intending coming up each day."
> "It isn't the same as fishing, though, is it?" *Bill* asked. He liked Harris.
> "I say not"
> We were standing in front of the old chapel of the monastery.
> (128, emphasis added)

Jake, quite clearly, says nothing, as is usual when he differs with what is being said or finds the matter more complicated than the conversation allows (not to see this is to have missed utterly one of the controlling principles of Hemingway dialogue). Bill doesn't seem much interested in the monastery. Harris, who has walked over the Pass of Roland from Saint Jean Pied de Port (an important staging area of the Santiago pilgrimage), stresses that it is "remarkable," presumably because he has a lively sense of history and knows about Roland and the pilgrimage (it would be difficult—it would suggest blindness—to be in Saint Jean and Roncevaux and not know about it). I will not attempt to read Jake's mind, to describe what he felt at this venerated pilgrimage site, although we do know from his "personal experience" (in Reardon's phrase) that he discovers much that is "good and beautiful and trustworthy" in the pilgrimage places he visits, that he is far from being in a "moral no-man's land" (he is, in fact, in everyman's moral and spiritual country), and that, in the anagogical sense of the work, fishing is *exactly the same* as visiting the pilgrim's shrine. Since we cannot read Jake's mind in this passage—we can read his silence, however—we might consider a partial inventory of what he saw here: various objects reputed to be the property of Roland, including hunting horns and swords; a gold reliquary containing two thorns from Christ's Crown of Thorns, gift to the abbey from Saint Louis; a venerated 13th century icon of the Madonna, Nuestra Señora de Roncesvalles, who was also responsible, with Roland, for Roncevaux becoming a pilgrimage center. (In the 9th century, according to tradition, an abbot of one of the monasteries there saw a vision of the Madonna, accompanied by a deer and a choir of angels. Jake had noted earlier that his room at the inn in Burguete contained an engraving of Nuestra Señora de Roncesvalles.) Also in the Church and the abbey, Jake would have seen, and comprehended, objects and motifs in stone and glass evoking the pilgrimage to Santiago. Jake would know, too, that the "old chapel" was built over the rock which Roland split with Durendal, his magical sword, and that Roland and the Paladins were, as tradition has it, buried there.[10] Hemingway doesn't tell us this, as he never renders the rest of the iceberg—but, oh yes, Jake knows it, just as Jake may be the only one of the expatriate crowd who understands that "San Fermin is also a religious festival" (153), celebrating the anniversary of the transfer of the relics of St. Fermín.

Early in the novel, when they are at the *bal musette* on Montagne Sainte Geneviève, Cohn asks Brett to dance and Brett says: "I've promised to dance this with Jacob. . . . You've a hell of a biblical name, Jake" (22). Readers may follow the track in thinking here of Jacob wrestling with the angel, and if they remember that tale well, they think of the "touch" in the hollow of Jacob's thigh, the wound, and Jacob prevailing, after which he has "power with God and with men . . . and as he passed over Penuel the sun rose upon him" (Genesis 32:24–31). This looks very much like a paradigm of Jake's experience. We may think, too, of Jacob's Ladder, with angels ascending and descending, and the dispensation of blessings; if so, we may feel a strong biblical undercurrent in the scenes where Jake climbs up the ladder to the top of the bus for Burguete—and, there is a kind of blessedness and communion on that ride. We may think of the bus-ride back, when Harris climbs the ladder, giving Jake and Bill hand-tied flies, or again the *desencajonada* scene where Jake leads his friends for the unloading, the first sight of the bulls: "A ladder led up to the top of the wall, and people were climbing up the ladder" (137). Jake, however, has no dreams or visions (that we know about) and no angels—just ladders. And blessings. Clearly, it was part of Hemingway's design to suggest to the reader certain Old Testament associations with Jacob; yet they do not carry very far since there is no Esau, and Jake is anything but a "supplanter." Rather, the primary point of the dancing scene involving Brett, Cohn and Jake is to contrast the old and new dispensations, testaments (in the etymological and the biblical sense). Cohn, who when he sees Brett in this scene looks "a great deal as his compatriot must have looked when he saw the promised land" (22), does not have a "biblical name," but he is more the "supplanter" than Jake. The primary thrust of Jake's "biblical name," then, is to lead us to the following conclusion: Jake is a *jacquet* (the common term for a pilgrim to Santiago), we are on the pilgrimage of Jacob (the older English form of the name), i.e., Santiago, Saint Jacques, Saint James, Sancti Jacobi—all one and the same, just as Jake, every bit as much as Santiago in *The Old Man and the Sea*, is named after the patron saint of Spain and the pilgrims. Hemingway's first "travel" book, *The Sun Also Rises*, is Hemingway's *Liber Sancti Jacobi*, to use the proper name of the famous 12th century *Pilgrims' Guide*, often regarded as the first European travel book.[11] Replete with references to French and Spanish rivers and mountains, forests and shrines, foods and wines, fiestas and dangers, it tells the pilgrim what to expect on the long road to Santiago de Compostela. Eight centuries later, Hemingway's variation on the *Liber Sancti Jacobi* tells us that not much has changed on the great way, although there are not as many pilgrims.

V

We climbed up through the gardens, by the empty palace and the unfinished church on the edge of the cliff. . . . (*SAR* 240)

Lady Brett knew the code: "It's sort of what we have *instead* of God."
—*The American Tradition in Literature*, Vol. II
(emphasis added, unacknowledged, by editors).

There is another kind of symbolic landscape, or *paysage moralisé*, which shapes *The Sun Also Rises*. This type, which does not depend primarily on allusion, on specific topographical and historical knowledge brought to the text by the reader, proceeds through organic metaphor, through exoteric symbolism which informs the poetic texture of the work. The first epigraph above illustrates this kind of symbolic landscape. It serves as the coda, the culmination of a sequence of lyrically and thematically related scenes. Here is the first:

The taxi went up the hill, passed the lighted square, then on into the dark, still climbing, then levelled out onto a dark street behind St. Etienne du Mont, went smoothly down the asphalt, passed the trees and the standing bus at the Place de la Contrescarpe, then turned onto the cobbles of the Rue Mouffetard. . . . We were sitting apart and we jolted close together going down the old street. Brett's hat was off. Her head was back. I saw her face in the lights from the open shops, then it was dark, then I saw her face clearly as we came out on the Avenue des Gobelins. The street was torn up and men were working on the car-tracks by the light of acetylene flares. Brett's face was white and the long line of her neck showed in the bright light of the flares. The street was dark again and I kissed her.

> Our lips were tight together and then she turned away and pressed
> against the corner of the seat, as far away as she could get. (25)

Arriving at a sense of the importance and effectiveness of this passage from
quite another angle of vision, Wirt Williams writes of the "incandescence"
here, which shows in one flash "many faces of the book's truth." About the
incandescence, I agree absolutely, and about *some* of the truths. Williams
continues: "The acetylene torches—hard, bright, and unnatural—are both
connotative, perhaps, of the harshness of the new external world and metaphorical of Jake's personal universe, which is also broken," like the "torn up"
stretch of the Avenue des Gobelins (54–55). He concludes that the "total
image" suggests that Jake and Brett are in hell. This is on the mark, as the
ensuing dialogue confirms when Brett says it's "hell on earth" (27).

But there is a good deal more to this passage, which illuminates and is
illuminated by the pilgrimage motif. First of all, there is the climbing movement, which is part of a pattern of insistent verticality, a rising-hesitance at
the edge-falling action which pervades the book. We note that the hill they
are climbing is the Montagne Sainte Geneviève, sacred site of the patron
saint of Paris, and that the church they pass, St. Etienne du Mont, is the
holiest place of pilgrimage in Paris, where the relics of Ste. Geneviève are
venerated. Then they are on the Place de la Contrescarpe, poised on the scarp,
the steep face of the hill, before turning sharply down the rue Mouffetard, the
ancient road to Italy. This information, which Jake (or Hemingway) would
know from reading any good guidebook, suggests the place of Jake's wounding, the source of his anguish; moreover, it suggests he chose the wrong route
for this ride (it is always Jake who tells the drivers where to go). As the scene
continues, once more they go up, to the Parc Montsouris, from which there
is a fine view dominated by Val-de-Grâce (Vale of Grace, prefiguration of
Ronces*valles*, and, since it is a hospital for wounded soldiers, evocative of the
military sense of coup de grâce—Roncevaux, of course, was also famous as a
hospital for wounded and weary pilgrims); they arrive at the Parc Montsouris,
where there is a pleasant restaurant by a small waterfall where they have,
as Jake says, "the pool of live trout" (27). But it is "closed and dark." Jake is
denied his optative trout, deferred until Roncesvalles. This taxi ride, then, is a
microcosm of the larger action, the journey, hell, and hope of the book. They
leave the Parc, feeling very much in hell, and go *down* to the place Denfert-
Rochereau (the ancient name of which is Place D'Enfer). The ride ends at the
Café Select (and in which circle of hell is it located?).

The next key scene in the sequence occurs when Bill and Jake leave the
Ile Saint Louis, in the shadow of Notre Dame, and walk up the rue du Car-
dinal Lemoine:

> It was steep walking, and we went all the way up to the Place
> Contrescarpe. The arc-light shone through the leaves of the trees
> in the square, and underneath the trees was an S bus ready to start.
> Music came out of the door of the Negre Joyeux. . . . We turned to
> the right off the Place Contrescarpe, walking along smooth narrow
> streets with high old houses on both sides. . . . We came onto the
> Rue du Pot de Fer and followed it along until it brought us to the
> rigid north and south of the Rue Saint Jacques and then walked
> south, past Val de Grâce. . . . (77–78)

I have discussed this important passage in detail in the essays cited above,
though not in the context of the sequence here being considered. As in the
first scene, there is climbing involved. Again, he is on the counterscarp,
but here he makes the *right* turn, which leads not to the ancient road to
Italy, but to the ancient road to Spain, the rue Saint-Jacques, the route of
the pilgrims. We have already stressed the importance of the deliberate
topographical distortion of this "rigid north and south." We should note
yet another anachorism in this scene: it is quite impossible to get to the rue
Saint-Jacques by following the rue du Pot de Fer. At the least, three—and
on Jake's probable route (the most direct) four—streets intervene between
the rue du Pot de Fer and the rue Saint-Jacques. When we know this we
may conclude that Hemingway is a) careless (doubtful), b) anxious to stress
the rue Saint-Jacques, to get Jake there, on the pilgrim route, c) concerned
to call our attention to the symbolic name—Pot de Fer, iron pot—which
occurs in a sequence involving the mention of food and eating fourteen
times in less than two pages (76–77). In fact, just before they turn on to
the rue du Pot de Fer, Jake observes, on the Place de la Contrescarpe, a
girl ladling food onto the plate of an old man—from "an iron pot of stew."
Now Carlos Baker may find it "hard to discover" the purpose of this entire
scene, may find the ostensibly pointless facts "excessive," but it strikes me
as one of the indispensable scenes of the entire novel, a brilliant piece of
symbolic landscape, and a skillful adumbration of the pilgrimage south and
the nourishment and sustenance Jake will derive therefrom (*Artist* 52). Thus
this second Contrescarpe scene, where Jake has made the right turn toward
Spain (his departure is imminent), contrasts sharply with the first: Brett
is not with him, the light is cheerful not infernal, the streets are not torn
up, there is music in the air, the cafés are open and bright (not "closed and
dark") and Jake does get food (the most detailed meal in the book), and he
is feeling, all in all, rather good. And yes, we know the actual route of that
literal bus, "ready to start," but can we resist seeing the symbolic legend on
that "S" bus: South, Santiago, Spain, San Fermín.

The next related series of scenes occurs in Chapter X, where there is plenty of rising and falling as Jake and Bill and Cohn pass through the Pyrenees into Spain, where Jake and Bill (Robert is asleep) see "ripe fields of grain" and a river "shining in the sun" and Pamplona, "rising out of the plain, and the walls of the city, and the great brown cathedral, and the broken skyline of the other churches" (93–94). That first night in Pamplona, Jake feels the "impulse to devil" Cohn, when he does not let him see the telegram from Brett and Mike. He admits for the first time that he hates him. Then they "took a little walk out to the bull-ring and across the field and under the trees at the *edge of the cliff* and looked down at the river in the dark" (99 emphasis added, as in all following "edge" scenes). By this point it seems clear that the rising and falling, the climb-and-descent pattern and the pause on the scarp—here called, for the first time, the "edge of the cliff"—portend major movements in Jake's heart and soul: the rise is essential, and the descent may lead either to hell (e.g., the Place d'Enfer, with Brett) or to the *locus amoenus*, the good place. In this scene, being at the "edge" suggests all of the tension that will explode, that must be purged, in the fiesta.

In the next chapter Jake and Bill, without Cohn, are on the bus which climbs steadily up toward Roncevaux: "As we came to the *edge of the rise* we saw the red roofs and white houses of Burguete . . . and away off on the shoulder of the first dark mountain was the gray metal-sheathed roof of the monastery of Roncesvalles" (108). This, one of the key passages of the novel in a variety of ways, is crucial to the present sequence as well, for when there is no tension, no Brett, no jealousy and hatred, no Cohn, the climb to the edge leads to a descent into the *locus amoenus*, and Jake is there, safe in the good place. The pattern is repeated in the next chapter when Jake and Bill take their long walk to the fishing site, climbing to the top of the hills, walking along the ridge, before going "down the steep road" to another good place.

Even back in Pamplona, with the fiesta going full blast, the pattern recurs. Jake and Brett walk out to the fortifications (another counterscarp), to the edge of the city walls:

> Below us were the dark pits of the fortifications. Behind were the trees and the shadow of the cathedral. . . . We looked out at the plain. . . . There were the lights of a car on the road climbing the mountain. Up on the top of the mountain we saw the lights of the fort. Below to the left was the river. It was high from the rain, and black and smooth. Trees were dark along the banks. We sat and looked out. Brett stared straight ahead. Suddenly she shivered. (182–83)

This scene gathers in most of the elements of the foregoing rise-edge-fall scenes. Again, Brett is with him in this scene, so it is night, the river is black, not "shining," and it is the dangerous edge of things. Williams, who examines this passage in another context, observes that "the universal attempt to attain one's aspiration is compressed into the car ascending; the fort on the top suggests that the goal, romantic happiness, is formidably defended" (61). (I'm not at all sure what this means, though I am sure Hemingway did not write: "On top of the mountain one saw the lights of the fort," as Williams misquotes the passage.) What we do have here once again is a pattern of ascent, of a fortified position on the *edge* (both the fort Jake looks at and the edge of the fortifications where he is sitting), and the tension which precedes the precipitous fall. This is the scene just before Jake delivers Brett to Romero; Jake is at the edge of the abyss, the "dark pits" below him, and as he prepares to betray the code of the aficionado things are "dark" and "black," and only the "shadow of the cathedral" which emblematizes his ultimate code is behind him. In brief, Brett falls, Jake falls, and there is no more rising motion until the fiesta is over, though Jake is seen drunk at another edge, his hotel-room balcony, at the end of the fiesta.

Finally, the fiesta is over, everyone departs, and Jake is alone; in Bayonne, he climbs onto the train for San Sebastian, resumes the direction of Santiago, and rests in another good place, on—or literally within—the Concha, the flawless shell-shaped beach and harbor of San Sebastian. The shell is the universal symbol of the Santiago pilgrim. This is why Jake must go to the Concha, why he does not stay in Biarritz or Saint Jean de Luz, both of which have fine beaches but do not have the Concha, nor would they indicate so clearly the resumption of the pilgrim's route—this time, the coastal route to Santiago.[12] (Jake doesn't tell us what he eats in San Sebastian, but it would be nice to think that he sat at a café by the Concha and ate Coquilles Saint Jacques, the gourmet's iconographic gesture in the direction of Compostela.) At any rate, Jake's main business at the Concha is to enact a variation on the theme of baptism. Let us not make critic-speak nonsense here nor indulge in the vague rhetoric of renewal. Jake is a Catholic; he was baptized long ago, one would assume; at most, the San Sebastian swimming scenes symbolize a quasi-sacramental reenactment, or a confirmation of his pilgrim status; at least, they suggest, at every level, a ritual cleansing after the fiesta. (They most certainly suggest more than a washing away of "hangovers."[13]) We remind ourselves that, according to the Catholic rites (of the 1920s at least), the necessary elements for baptism are water, salt ("the salt of wisdom"), and a baptismal shell (a real shell or a silver shell maybe used in the ceremony). Jake, then, has all three elements, in the salt water of the Concha. In the first swimming scene, although the text is somewhat ambiguous, it appears that Jake dives three times (the required three effusions or immersions "in the name of the Father and of the Son and of the Holy Ghost"). After the first dive, he comes to the surface with "all the chill gone" (235). Then, after some time in the sun, he dives deep, "down to the bottom," swimming with his eyes open, and then dives again and swims ashore.

The next day, he swims again. He looks at the high headlands on either side of the harbor, floats in the quiet water, sees only the sky. The water is "buoyant": "It felt as though you could never sink" (237). This is charged language, and it bespeaks Jake's peace, at last. Rather curiously—and again distorting the text—Williams writes: "And in the second swimming scene at San Sebastian, the last mountain configuration—a green hill with a castle closing the harbor—suggests with casual subtlety that the ultimate promise of the mountains, the ultimate romantic fulfillment, may be death itself" (61). Subtle indeed. What Jake actually sees, "*almost* closing the harbor" (238, emphasis added), is that green hill with a castle (and two churches)—Monte Urgull. What he feels, judging from the overall tone and language of this passage, has little to do with romance or death (except under the rubric of immortality), and much to do with peace, resolution, joy (or "buoyancy") and an unsinkable sense of immortality. In the language of his Church, he has the baptismal "imprint" of grace, and in the language of the novel's dramatic concerns, he has come to terms with his unhappy involvement with Brett, he is expiating the betrayal of the aficionado's code—a cleansed pilgrim, ready to take the road again. And besides, even if that harbor were closed, what's wrong with a "closed" harbor? Isn't that what a refuge, a shelter, a harbor should be? And is there any more beautiful, urbane, serene, restful—and symbolic—beach anywhere in the world than La Concha?

The second swimming scene concludes, then, as follows:

> After a while I stood up, gripped with my toes on the *edge of the raft* as it tipped with my weight, and dove cleanly and deeply, to come up through the lightening water, blew the salt water out of my head, and swam slowly and steadily in to shore. (238)

This "edge" passage requires no commentary; Jake is poised at the edge here, not tense or darkly troubled, he leaps, and holds the dive "cleanly and deeply." Feeling clean and composed, he goes back to the hotel where Brett's telegram awaits him. I have never been able to comprehend why so many commentators on the novel feel that Jake's rushing to the aid of Brett indicates that all the motion goes nowhere, that Jake is as bad off at the end as at the beginning. Because you have finally come to terms with an anguished and impossible love, as Jake has, does that mean that you discard what must be a central tenet of any code worth the name: fidelity, loyalty to friends, especially friends "in trouble"?

Jake boards the Sud Express for Madrid and takes a taxi ride which echoes the first ride examined here:

> I took a taxi and we climbed up through the gardens, by the empty palace and the unfinished church on the *edge of the cliff*, and on up until we were in the high, hot, modern town. The taxi coasted down a smooth street to the Puerta del Sol. . . . (240)

This scene is the coda, the formal culmination of the sequence of rise-edge-fall patterns which pervade the work. By this stage of the novel, such a passage takes on rich and intricate overtones. Again, there is the climb, this time, through gardens, which I would prefer not to worry with explication, though perhaps it better be said that the garden here is certainly not intended to suggest "innocence" in the usual sense (nor an imminent "fall"), although it does have something to do with knowledge and redemption, and thus with a second innocence, beyond fear and trembling. The "empty palace" evokes a general sense of the shattered post-war political order in the "hot, modern" world of the 1920s. The key element in the scene is the "unfinished church on the edge of the cliff"; this reverberates with all of the other churches in the novel, with all of the passages which show Jake at the edge. Here, perhaps, it is the Church which is at the edge, a perfect representation of what may seem to be its position in a radically secular "hot; modern" world. And, in another sense, it is Jake's Church which is on the edge, so the question becomes, in relation to the accretion of imagery—which edge? Clearly, the edge at the far side of the abyss of *nada*, where one builds after one has made the Kierkegaardian leap of faith. John Killinger, in *Hemingway and the Dead Gods: A Study in Existentialism*, seems to think that Hemingway, along with other existentialists, has proclaimed the death of God, that Hemingway agrees, for example, with Camus, "who denies the justification for Kierkegaard's leap from the crest of dread to the being of God, and claims that integrity lies in being able to remain on the dizzying crest."[14] While there may be some use in considering Hemingway under the rubric of existentialism, his kinship is certainly with the Christian existentialists, with Kierkegaard and Marcel, for example, not Camus and Sartre. There are many gods—and God—in Hemingway's work, and they are most decidedly not dead. The "unfinished church," then, is a complex metaphor which is historically and architecturally sound, since we know how long it takes to complete a church that is truly constructed, and theologically sound, too, since the Church is always "unfinished," and will remain so, we are told, until the Parousia. Finally, it is existentially sound, personally true for Jake, inasmuch as it reflects the motion and the making of the pilgrim. This scene ends, not with a precipitous descent, but with a "coast" down a "smooth street" to, of course, the Puerta del Sol—the Gate of the Sun.

Next Jake—rising again—walks up to the second floor of the Hotel Montana (in the mountains again?), enters the "disorder" of Brett's room, and they have their famous talk about her experience with Romero. Jake is perfectly composed throughout this scene, as he has not been before when alone with Brett. They go to the Palace Hotel, where they have Martinis in that ambiance of "wonderful gentility." Here they have what is surely one of the most celebrated conversations of the 20th century, and one of the least understood. Brett says:

> "You know it makes one feel rather good deciding not to be a bitch."
> "Yes."
> "It's sort of what we have instead of God."
> Some people have God," I said. "Quite a lot."
> "He never worked very well with me."
> "Should we have another Martini?" (245)

We must settle here for a look at one misreading of this passage which is, I think, emblematic of the misdirected thrust of sixty years of Hemingway criticism, i.e., the mainstream, as reflected by the appallingly inaccurate editorial commentary in the most influential anthology of American literature for the last three decades: *The American Tradition in Literature*. As an aside, as if it's a universally recognized truth, this remark is tossed off to summarize a larger statement about Hemingway's career: "Lady Brett knew the code: 'It's sort of what we have *instead* of God.'"[15] This sentence is as slippery as greased okra. The irresponsibility of the anthology remark is terrifying, if we think of the millions of students and teachers who have formed their views of American literature and Hemingway from this volume. It is irresponsible in various ways, from the insidious unacknowledged addition of emphasis to the "*instead*," to contextual distortion, to the total misrepresentation of the character of Brett, and, by extension, Jake. At best, we might say of Brett's renunciation of Pedro Romero (for that is what Hemingway's text refers to, a fact which is also distorted in their larger context) that it's sort of what she has instead of God. (We are not concerned here with the question of whether her renunciation shows moral fineness or a fear of changing her independent ways and thus, rationalization—can it not partake of both qualities?) Jake's response, which most readers and critics conveniently overlook, is that some people indeed have God—"quite a lot." And when Brett says that He hasn't worked for her, Jake—as he often does when he does not like the drift of the conversation—changes the subject. He knows there's no use saying any more about his belief to Brett, who accused him of "proselyting" for religion earlier in the book. Part of his code, too, concerning the good things, is: "You'll lose it if you talk about it" (245).

The other piece of slippery reading (or facile sophistry) reflected in the greased okra sentence cited above typifies another familiar wrenching of *The Sun Also Rises*—Brett knows the code? Brett, who from beginning to end is shown to be careless and disorderly and promiscuous, in every sense of the term? Brett, who is judged across a spectrum ranging from the smallest detail—dropping cigarette ashes on Jake's rug—to the largest symbolic form of bad behavior—discarding the bull's ear, with which she has been honored, in a hotel-room drawer with cigarette stubs? (Hemingway the astute moralist makes the point that dishonor and moral messiness begin with the smallest acts and invade the largest ceremonies by having the cigarette ashes in both scenes). This Brett—who gulps and cannot taste the fine champagne which the Count urges her to drink slowly, who cannot comprehend what he has to say about being "always in love"—she knows the code? Brett, who cannot pray, who drinks to get drunk, who prefers tight green pants to grace under pressure—she knows the code? If so, it's an odd code, and it's not Jake's, not the Count's, not Montoya's, not Hemingway's. In this acute novel of manners, Brett's behavior is mostly mannerism, when it is not blind promiscuity. One of the main thrusts of the novel is to differentiate between Jake's character and behavior and Brett's, to draw distinctions, to scrutinize and finally to discard the "one of us" rubric. The constant critical confusion over this question is probably explained very simply by the fact that it is Brett who says so-and-so is "one of us;" yet usually there is something built into the scene (see, e.g., chapter VII) which shows quite distinctly that this is not the case, i.e., that Brett, for all her facile assumption of an insider's "code" knowledge or style, is quite alone and quite without the values that sustain such characters as Jake, the Count, Montoya, Romero. All of this is not to say that she is not attractive, engaging, compelling, or that I would not buy her a drink in Paris or Pamplona: that is precisely the problem which the book presents. (But I would not take her fishing.)

If Jake's response that some people have God implies that he is one of them, as multiple passages in the novel indicate, does his "quite a lot" tell us that he has grown in grace, as a pilgrim would expect to, during the course of the novel? Yes, clearly, if we consider the facts.[16] First, we will recall that Jake has, some years before, received the "wound that made him think," as

Hemingway characterized St. Ignatius de Loyola's wound at Pamplona which
led to his conversion. (See note 1) In Paris, however, we do not see Jake in
church. He thinks of going to other pilgrimage sites in the opening pages, but
he does not go. When the pilgrimage south begins, he identifies himself as a
Catholic on the train filled with pilgrims. In Bayonne, he enters the cathedral,
says it is "nice," but apparently does not pray, probably because he is with Bill
and Robert. Arrived in Pamplona, he first sees the man about the bull-fight
tickets, and then goes to the cathedral to pray. This long prayer passage seems
to be a crux in Hemingway criticism:

> He tries to pray, but only the mockery of prayer is left to our
> day—God is so far removed from the unreasonableness of human
> events that he is become a mere abstraction. (Killinger 100)

Mockery? Abstraction? To whom? we might ask. To the critic? Certainly
not to Jake, to Hemingway, not in this text.

> The very quality of Jake's prayer in the cathedral ... points
> up the inefficacy of supernatural communication in our time.
> (Killinger 59)

One would like to know what the critic thinks prayer is. Perhaps he should
check Ignatius de Loyola, Juan de la Cruz, Theresa of Avila or any of
Hemingway's favorite saints and mystics on the nature and occasional difficulty of prayer.

> Jake and Brett attempt on different occasions to pray in the
> cathedral at Pamplona, but are unable to achieve communion, to
> establish a sense of unity with a deistic power. (Williams 57)

The critic is right about Brett, wrong about Jake. At best, he assumes a great
deal concerning Jake and prayer, without supporting evidence from the text.
Let no man pronounce on the validity of another man's communion. At
worst, he ignores contrary evidence. And what is meant by "deistic power"?
Perhaps this odd diction suggests what Hemingway meant about critics
afraid to approach God, or religion.

> The submerged God search is intimated early in the dining car:
> Jake, a nominal Catholic, cannot get a seat—i.e., he is denied
> communion—with the Catholics on pilgrimage. Later he and Brett
> try unsuccessfully to pray—Jake twice. (Williams 52)

The commentator has advanced beyond most observers of the novel in recognizing the "submerged God search." However, he fails to see that Jake, more than a nominal Catholic, is not a package-tour pilgrim on his way to Lourdes, but a pilgrim on the ancient and sacral way of Saint James. No "communion" is denied here—Jake and Bill share two bottles of wine. The critic is flat wrong, and cannot produce one shred of evidence for the assertion that Jake twice tries unsuccessfully to pray. The evidence, as we shall see, is to the contrary.

> We get the tension between an inability to believe in anything and a longing for the old certainties. Dante was able to believe that in God's will is our peace, but that was a long time ago and the Middle Ages have passed. Jake cannot let himself go to God because, in a sense, he knows too much. Jake is of his time and reflects the difficulty of accepting God in a secular age. (Shaw 48–49)

Faith is difficult in any age, but Jake, searching for "the real old stuff" (*Letters* 131) in Spain, is a pretty good medievalist and he believes in many things and has a firm hold on many "old certainties" such as the Church, the bull-fight, the values, passion, honor, morality, decorum, food, wine, for a start. Also, he probably reads Dante—as Hemingway did—with great care.

> One's net impression today is of all the fun there is to be had in getting good and lost. . . . Prayer breaks down and fails, a knowledge of traditional distinctions between good and evil is largely lost . . . and, cut off from the past chiefly by the spiritual disaster of the war, life has become mostly meaningless. (Young 59–60)

While the critic is addressing more than the specific prayer scene, the passage illustrates perfectly how incomprehension of this crucial passage and others like it can lead to the leap of meaninglessness. Cars "break down," not prayer. Jake's prayers do not "fail." Jake has, absolutely, the past in hand in the bull-fight and the Church—"intact from the old days." One's net impression is that the critic has had fun getting lost, has read another novel.

This exercise in critical counterpoint could continue indefinitely, since most commentators who have mentioned the question of religion have taken this approach: religion is defunct, the characters are lost and directionless, and Jake—or Hemingway (you can't always be sure who they're talking about)—is a radical skeptic, a nihilist, even an atheist. The iron law of Hemingway Criticism holds: decreasing accuracy (add logarithmical hysteria) in relation to increasing religious content. Even Carlos Baker, one of the few who is sound and true to the text on the question of Jake's Catholicism, inadvertently betrays the bias of the past six decades of criticism when he writes: "Without apology or explanation, Jake Barnes is a religious man" (*Artist* 89). Here, at last, is fact. But why should he apologize, pray tell? And to whom? The reader? Brett? Robert Cohn? The critics? What should he confess? (Protestants write novels to confess, Jake says: Catholics go to the confessional.) And what should he explain and who would understand it if he did? Montoya, perhaps Romero, maybe the Count, but they all know that there are certain matters of passion—such as the bull-fight and religion—that one does not expose "to people who would not understand" (131).

Since I have held forth as prosecuting attorney against the flatulence of the defunct-religion-in-the-wasteland party, I will now call the final witness, the text of *The Sun Also Rises*. In the first prayer scene mishandled by the critics Jake prays for all of his friends, prays for good bull-fights, good fishing, and a fine fiesta. These prayers are "answered," at least partially, as the text later reveals. Then his thoughts wander, and he says:

> I was a little ashamed, and regretted I was such a rotten Catholic, but realized there was nothing I could do about it, at least for a while, and maybe never, but that anyway it was a grand religion, and I only wished I felt religious and maybe I would the next time. . . . (97)

This passage is rather complex; it may require extensive theological or doctrinal annotation concerning the nature of grace and the role of the individual will in cooperating with, inviting that gift. (I cheerfully submit this matter to a higher court.) At any rate, whatever unworthiness Jake is feeling here, he is clearly not rejecting the Church, as some have argued. He is celebrating the Church. He has prayed successfully and then he has come to a conviction of his rottenness, a natural, indeed an essential condition for anyone who would believe. It is, he says, a "grand religion," and in the presence of that grandeur what can he feel but "rotten"? (Suppose he had said "I was proud I was such a great Catholic"? Would we take that straight? Would any good Catholic say that?) His fundamental stance here is: *Domine, non sum dignus*, the familiar prayer before communion ("Lord, I am not worthy . . . but only say the word and my soul shall be healed"). And as for feeling more religious the next time, this suggests the precise function of ritual, of ceremonial and sacramental forms: to carry you across the times of aridity and the vagaries of persona: circumstance, from one efficacious rite to the next, no matter how much time of dryness intervenes. (I take it as axiomatic that this is the function of all ritual, and that it informs Hemingway's life and work—which is built on ritual, on sacrament—from beginning to end. As he says, you may see many bad bull-fights before you experience the ecstasy of the real thing. You will also fish many streams before you come to the Irati, or the Big Two-Hearted River. But, in all things (and this includes wine-drinking), if you do not perform the ritual you will not come to know the ecstasy, the grace that it promises. On this subject one might well refer to most of the saints and mystics, or, for that matter, to Confucius.)

In this mood, then, Jake walks out into the "hot sun on the steps of the cathedral"; in the perfect coda to the first prayer scene, Jake says, "the forefingers and the thumb of my right hand were still damp, and I felt them dry in the sun." This is a brilliant instance of the genius of Hemingway's style. Most writers would say "he crossed himself and went outside in the sun," but Hemingway's sensuous precision makes the good reader *feel* the Sign of the Cross, physically and imagistically and durationally, as an immediately apprehended emotional and intellectual complex. The Sign is not implied or omitted, not the underside of the iceberg—it is there. For many years I have conducted a classroom exercise in which, by now, more than a thousand students have participated. I ask them to describe exactly what happens in each sentence of this prayer-scene paragraph. Less than ten percent have recognized that Jake has just made the Sign of the Cross in this sentence. This may or may not suggest the death of religion in the wasteland; more likely, it indicates the death of reading in America. (By way of contrast, some 70% of my students at the University of Paris saw exactly what Jake did and, in Peking, they at least asked about that dampness.) The Sign, of course, is "a confession of faith in Christ crucified and an invocation of His Blessing" (according to the *Catholic Encyclopedia*). If someone says this is a mere mechanical gesture on Jake's part, I will reply that it is a ritual gesture, designed to hold him steady until the next ceremony. More than that, it is a charm, a magical sign of that "tribal faith" Hemingway referred to elsewhere.

The next passage in which Jake speaks of his participation in the sacraments of the Church is at the end of Chapter XIV, as he prepares for the fiesta:

> I went to church a couple of times, once with Brett. She said she wanted to hear me go to confession, but I told her that not only was it impossible but it was not as interesting as it sounded, and, besides, it would be in a language she did not know. (150–51)

This passage has been accurately glossed by Baker. It is straightforward. Aside from what it tells us about Brett, it says most distinctly that Jake does know the language—in every sense—of the Church. The next day, before the "religious festival" of San Fermín explodes at noon, Jake goes to eleven o'clock Mass:

> Going down the streets in the morning on the way to mass in the cathedral, I heard them singing through the open doors of the shops. (152)

Now we only have to be able to count to see that Jake has been to church three times in three days. He has been confessed, absolved, and he has participated in the Mass. Since this exceeds any notion of obligatory "duty" even for a "good" Catholic, let alone a "rotten" one, it is a rather remarkable record for someone who has been repeatedly characterized as a failed Catholic, a skeptic, nihilist (etc., ad nauseam). While this essay is something of an exercise in radically revisionist literary criticism, not catechism, it may be useful or necessary to note what Jake has said and done while in church; at confession he has said "Bless me, father, for I have sinned," confessed his sins in detail, and has been counseled and absolved by the priest. At Mass, he has participated in the *Kyrie*, the *Gloria*, the *Credo*, the *Pater Noster*, the *Libera nos*, the *Agnus Dei*, the *Domine, non sum dignos* and communion. I do not wish to belabor the matter, but who would think of writing seriously about Hemingway and the bull-fight, say, without repeated presence at the ceremony, without knowledge and careful study? Yet many critics seem to think they understand the Church perfectly well without—as is quite obvious in some cases—ever having made a presence at the ceremony, without knowledge of the sacraments, without careful study. The time is just about here, I suppose, when Hemingway's texts will have to be as extensively annotated as Eliot's, if the general reader is to have any comprehension.

The next scene involving the Church occurs later during the first day of the fiesta, when Jake and Brett (with Bill, Mike and Cohn), following along in the "big religious procession," attempt to enter the chapel:

> We started inside and there was a smell of incense and people filing back into the church, but Brett was stopped just inside the door because she had no hat, so we went out again. . . . (155)

Again, the text admits one reading; Jake is not turned away, as has often been said, but he comes back outside when Brett is turned away for sartorial reasons which clearly operate thematically and symbolically here, continuing the religious contrast between Brett and Jake, and leading directly into the chanting street-dance around Brett as "image."

Finally, there is the long prayer scene near the end of the fiesta. Brett suggests they pray for Romero. Inside,

> Many people were praying. You saw them as your eyes adjusted themselves to the half-light. We knelt at one of the long wooden benches. After a little I felt Brett stiffen beside me, and saw she was looking straight ahead.
> "Come on," she whispered throatily. "Let's get out of here. Makes me damned nervous." (208)

Again, the religious contrast between Jake and Brett is clear. There is no indication of any difficulty praying, on Jake's part; it is Brett's praying which is not "much of a success," she is the one who is "damned nervous." Outside, they talk about it; Brett hopes that the wind will drop before the bull-fight and Jake, laughing, tells her she might pray. Brett says:

> "Never does me any good. I've never gotten anything I prayed for. Have you?"
> "Oh, yes."
> "Oh, rot," said Brett. "Maybe it works for some people, though. You don't look very religious, Jake."
> "I'm pretty religious."
> "Oh, rot," said Brett. "Don't start proselyting today." (209)

Again, the contrast is one point. More importantly, Jake emphatically asserts his religion; in fact, this scene indicates a progression both from the beginning of the novel (when he was not praying at all) and from the first prayer scene; from "rotten Catholic" to "pretty religious" indicates the anticipated and realized progress of the pilgrim. From the initial rather self-conscious session of prayer—through repeated prayer and confession and Mass—Jake's ritual participation has brought him to an absolute assertion of the efficacy of his prayers, his faith. A further implication, as noted above, is that he has talked about this with Brett before, since she tells him not to proselytize—to preach, to attempt to convert her—today.

Thus we are at last prepared to see exactly what Jake means when he affirms at the end that some people "have" God—he is one of them. And, in the dual sense of the phrase "quite a lot," there are many who have God and some "have" Him a great deal. (Jake's stance here is a good deal like that of Frederic Henry toward the end of *A Farewell to Arms*: "I might become very devout" (263), although Jake knows and believes a great deal more than Frederic Henry, and is far down the pilgrimage road that Henry may just be starting.) Perhaps we are ready to bulldoze into the dark pit at the edge of the cliff that crumbling wall of Hemingway criticism, sixty years in the making, which asserts one version or another of Jake's rejection of or failure at religion, one version or another of Brett as embodiment of the code as exemplified in her statement: "It's sort of what we have instead of God." If *that is* the code, then the novel is concerned to dismantle the code and to articulate a creed.

* * *

One would prefer not to bulldoze; in fact, one would prefer to say nothing and rest with Hemingway in silence, under his rubric: "Mysticism implies a mystery and there are many mysteries" (*DIA* 54). But criticism implies responsibility, textual and moral, and the need for revaluation is urgent. There are many other things that should be said about *The Sun Also Rises*, and this is a small beginning. From here, we need to see how Jake's—and Hemingway's—Catholic sensibility affects other weary shibboleths of received critical opinion; for example, the notion that there is no sense of the past in Hemingway's work. Nothing could be further from the truth. Even if it is mainly on the underside of the iceberg or buried in the allusive texture of the works, the past gnaws at the present, leans over tomorrow, throughout Hemingway's worlds, as it gnaws at, leans over Jake the pilgrim. Then there is the notion that his work lacks a sense of place. While place may not be realized as it is, say, in Faulkner or certain Southern Renascence writers, Hemingway's work is shot through with the bright particularity of place, with a sense of the numinous abiding earth, that earth which he designated the "hero" of *The Sun Also Rises*. Sometimes, as in the fishing scene on the Irati, this numinous sense of place has the quality, as Lawrence Durrell might put it, of being "tuned into" the *deus loci*. Indeed, in this mode, Hemingway is one of the great cartographers of the *deus loci*. At other times the sense of place is informed by history and by the sense of community (or communion) which is the essence of the pilgrim's way. Throughout his life and work he sought "those places where something divine still exists."[17] At all levels of Jake's world, there is a sense of life as quest and ceremony, as ritual down to the smallest details, and this life is a transaction that numinously embodies the relation of self to nature to the human community, to time, to God. There are numens—presiding divinities, creative indwelling energies—in all things, for Jake, from food and wine to pilgrimages and fiestas, to fishing and hunting, to the two primary incarnational enactments of the numinous—the bull-fight and the Church.

Some of what I have said here may seem to suggest that all we have to do is read attentively and we will get all this. Indeed, I was tempted to conclude this essay with my paraphrase of something D. H. Lawrence once said about the sun: Start with the text, and the rest will slowly, slowly happen. That is surely the place to start and finish, but what we find in the text, as Hemingway said in the *Paris Review* interview, "will be the measure" of what we "brought to the reading." Thus we must add to the familiar list of things we should bring to Hemingway, a rich sense of the Church, a deeper sense of the "sacred world of *toreo*" (as Allen Josephs recently put it), and a joyful sense of Hemingway's pilgrimage to reappropriate the "real," "old" things of what Jacques Maritain calls "the sacral age."[18] We must hear and understand with great precision what Hemingway says when he writes in *Death in the Afternoon* of the "emotional and spiritual intensity" of the bullfight, of the "faena that takes a man out of himself and makes him feel immortal while it is proceeding, that gives him an ecstasy, that is, while momentary, as profound as any religious ecstasy" (206). This sense of immortality, this ordered, formal passionate "disregard for death," Hemingway says, is accessible and some-times given in the bullring, just as it is available and availing, a gift of grace, in the more ample terrain of the Church. Thus, it is quite natural, for example, to hear Hemingway tell us that there are three acts in the fighting of each bull and the Church tell us that the dramatic structure of the Mass is a three-act sacrifice. We will have to pay attention to these congruences.

Usefully, Josephs reminds us that *toreo* is the "moral axis" of *The Sun Also Rises*. In the sense of his argument, this is absolutely correct, though the Church must also be seen as the "moral axis." Will it do to have two axes? Can we resolve the matter by saying that one is the *moral* axis, the other the *spiritual* axis? I do not think so, for in Hemingway's view both *toreo* and Church partake of both properties. We can figure the matter in another fashion: if the Church is the axis of the work, the complex motion of the world of *toreo* is the *precession*—or the axis of the precession—and the pilgrim's hunger is the torque which turns the work. Or, to move from physics to architecture, the Church is the nave, *toreo* is the transept, and at their crossing the pilgrim moves in *procession* toward the high altar. In any case, the worlds of *toreo* and the Church constitute the focus, the point of convergence of the novel's con-cern with multiple forms of grace: physical and spiritual, moral and aesthetic, sufficient and efficacious, actual and habitual, and sacramental grace. And, speaking of convergence, it is time to note that when Hemingway revised the novel, changing the name of his matador from Guerra to Romero, he was not only intensifying, as Josephs has noted, the iconographic significance of *toreo* by invoking one of the greatest matadors in history, he was simultaneously addressing the other principal motif: "*romero*," i.e., *pilgrim*.

* * *

If it is the property of a great work of literature to communicate profound feeling that is not readily understood (or in Hemingway's version to make people feel more than they understand), then perhaps it is all well and good that we have lived with this classic work, *The Sun Also Rises*, for sixty years and we are just now coming to understand it. Some of us have felt it for a long time, without knowing how to talk about it, not sure that we want to talk about it, afraid that we might lose it by talking about it. But if six decades of criticism have demonstrated anything it is that we can talk all around it, put our mouths all over it and it will still be there, shining in the sun.

On August 31, 1927, Hemingway wrote to Maxwell Perkins, asking: "Could you tell me what The Sun has done up to date?" We're still telling. That letter was written and sent from Santiago de Compostela. We will never know if Jake, the pilgrim on the great Way of Santiago, arrived all the way home. We do know where Hemingway the pilgrim was—working on his next book and studying at Santiago de Compostela—his "home office."

Notes

1. For example, in addition to Hemingway's concern with the Santiago pilgrimage documented in this paper, consider the following: Hemingway thought of giving his Nobel Prize medal to Saint Barbara, the patron saint of artillerymen and those in danger of sudden death (see the letters to Robert Brown in the collection of the Humanities Research Center of The University of Texas); Baker writes that Hemingway *seems* "to have given his medal to the Shrine of the Virgen del Cobre in Cuba" (*Letters* 865). In fact, he *did* so (see *Catholic News*, August 25, 1956), after first considering giving it to his local Virgin in Cuba, whom he thought might be better since she was from near Santiago (letter to Brown, July 1, 1956). Also, Ignatius of Loyola was an important figure in Hemingway's pantheon of Saints; among other places, he referred to Loyola in *Death in the Afternoon*, where he notes that at the siege of Pamplona Loyola received the *"wound that made him think"*—i.e., the wound that led to his conversion (274, emphasis added).

2. See, for example, Marilyn Stokstad, *Santiago de Compostela In the Age of the Great Pilgrimages* (Norman: U of Oklahoma P, 1978), or any of scores of studies of Santiago in English, Spanish and French over the past two centuries (some are listed in Stokstad's bibliography); or, for that matter, see any good traveller's guidebook, such as the Baedekers, the *Guides Bleus*, and *Guides Michelins* which Hemingway owned (see James D. Brasch and Joseph Sigman, *Hemingway's Library: A Composite Record* (New York: Garland, 1981). Concerning the Virgen del Pilar, and the naming of Hemingway's beloved boat after her, when will we stop hearing the absurd suggestions (anachronistic, too) that he named his boat—as I recently heard someone say—after Pilar of *FWBT*, since she was the "humanistic embodiment" of the Spanish earth and "the people." Pilar is, of course, Spain incarnate, i.e. the Virgen del Pilar. Baker, of course, long ago set the matter straight, partially at least. Hemingway's cruiser was named "in honor of the shrine and the *feria* at Zaragoza, and about equally for Pauline, who had chosen it as one of her secret nicknames"

(*Life* 259). This is roughly half of the story; the rest concerns the associations of Pilar with Santiago, and Santiago's *strong associations with the sea*, as in, e.g., the miraculous sea voyage which brought his body to the shores of Galicia.

3. *in their time/1920–1940*, An Exhibition at the University of Virginia Library (Bloomfield Hills, Mi.: Bruccoli Clark, 1977): item 48.

4. "Hemingway on the Road to Roncevaux: The Pilgrimage Theme in *The Sun Also Rises*," paper delivered at the VIII Congreso de la Société Rencesvals, Pamplona-Santiago de Compostela, Spain (August 1978) and published (Pamplona: Institution Principe de Viana, 1981). A related and expanded essay, "Hemingway and Faulkner on the Road to Roncevaux," appeared in Donald R. Noble, ed., *Hemingway: A Revaluation* (Troy, NY: Whitston, 1983). The reader who wishes to know more about the pilgrimage of St. James is referred to the sources in note No. 2 above. Other useful entries into the extensive material on Santiago include Georgiana Goddard King, *The Way of St. James* (New York, 1920), Walter Starkie, *The Road to Santiago: Pilgrims of St. James* (London, 1957), and Vera and Helmut Hell, *The Great Pilgrimage of the Middle Ages: The Road to St. James of Compostel* (New York, 1964).

5. At the recent Hemingway Conference in Italy, one Hemingway scholar delivered to me a cryptic message from an anonymous Hemingway scholar: "Tell Stoneback you *can* see the monastery from the road." Avoidance of an infinite series of scholarly rebuttals and clarifications may justify a detailed footnote here. Yes, it is true that from a certain place on the road you can see the monastery in clear weather. The first question is, then, where was Jake when he said he saw the monastery? Hemingway writes:

> We went through the forest and the road came out and turned along a rise of land, and out ahead of us was a rolling green plain, with dark mountains beyond it. These were wooded and there were clouds coming down from them. The green plain stretched off. It was cut by fences and the white of the road showed through the trunks of a double line of trees that crossed. the plain toward the north. As we came to the edge of the rise we saw the red roofs and white houses of Burguete ahead strung out on the plain, and away off on the shoulder of the first dark mountain was the gray metal-sheathed roof of the monastery of Roncesvalles" (108).

Anyone who knows the road to Roncesvalles (i.e., route C.C.-135) recognizes the general vantage point here: Jake's bus has already made the sharp left turn just before the Y-junction (with route 127 from Aoiz) and they are levelling down on the straight road to Burguete. Jake says that he sees Roncevaux from the "edge of the rise." Since my original assertion of an altered landscape (see essay cited in note four) was based on observations made *in situ* some fifteen years ago, permit me to quote those original journal notes: "Walked south from Burguete, past road to Garralda, to the 'edge of the rise' in the road. Could not see monastery. Only trees. Sunny weather. No clouds on mountains." On other trips I made to Roncevaux, I did not concern myself with the question because I was more interested in the pilgrimage activities I observed. Then, ten years ago, before publishing the notion about the interpolated monastery, I revisited Roncevaux, this time by car from Pamplona, and made these notes:

Could not see monastery from anywhere on road, even high up before turn. But overcast today and heavy clouds over Roncevaux. In novel it's sunny, with "clouds coming down" from mountains. Also top deck of bus. Also hard to tell, textually and topographically, exactly where Jake is when he says he sees it. *Two* rises in the road. Between Aoiz road and road to Garralda—"crossroads" of text—too low to see past trees of Burguete. Maybe see it from top, before turn, but Jake not there. Check old photographs for this, old road changes, if any, etc. Remember extensive landscape alterations in front of monastery in preparation for 1200th anniversary of The Battle. Any large trees removed?—higher than roofline—like two large pines on left front of monastery? Signs of grubbed trees. Ask monks. Maybe in 1920s monastery not visible from before turn. Did not walk beyond rise the first time—4? 5? years ago.

These faded notes formed the basis of my published observation, and together with the fact that today, *from the turn* (though not from the "edge of the rise"—one of them at least) you can see the monastery, these notes suggest the many variables which are pertinent to the visibility of the monastery. Maybe Jake did see Roncevaux, from the top deck of that bus, from the top of the turn. In any case, I would invite that anonymous Hemingway scholar to walk that road with me, text in hand, to see if we could agree about the exact location of the "edge of the rise" and if we could agree on that, and if we had clear weather with no "clouds coming down" from the mountains, we might make a small start toward determining what Jake did or did not see in 1925. The exact determination of this rather minor point—what matters, after all, is that Jake *knows* Roncevaux is there and he knows what it means—must await further historical investigation.

In the meanwhile, there are a few other matters to note in this passage. Jake says he could see the red roofs of Burguete. In fact, there are perhaps as many gray roofs as there are red roofs in Burguete, including the highest roofs and—in particular—the four-storey roof of the Hostal Burguete, where Jake and Bill stay. While I surveyed neither the good people of Burguete nor the roofing contractors of Navarra on the question of the date of those rather venerable gray roofs, it would seem that Hemingway altered a visible fact for the sake of the color in his composed landscape—to save the only gray roof for the focal point of his composition: the monastery. The next thing to note is the location of the monastery—"on the shoulder of the first dark mountain." Now for most people, I assume, the "shoulder" of a mountain suggests something "near the top" (as the OED has it). If that is so, then Roncevaux is on the ankle of the mountain and most observers would agree, I think, with Vera and Helmut Hell who write that the monastery of Roncevaux "nestles in a coomb" (165). We note, too, that after Jake's narration declares the presence of the "gray metal-sheathed roof of the monastery of Roncesvalles," this conversation follows:

> "There's Roncevaux," I said.
> "Where?"
> "Way off there where the mountain starts."
> "It's cold up here," Bill said.
> "It's high," I said. "It must be twelve hundred metres." (108).

As I read this passage, it is clear that Bill does *not* see the monastery. Maybe Jake sees it, or thinks he sees it, because he knows it's there, because he knows and loves the place from previous visits. How else would he know that the roof is "metal-sheathed"? Exceptional vision indeed, that can distinguish gray metal from gray slate or tile at a distance of five kilometers. Moreover, Jake is wrong on another score here: they are nowhere near twelve hundred metres (Burguete: 898, Roncevaux: 952). But for Jake, of course, Roncevaux is one of the "high" places, and both the monastery and the general terrain must be elevated.

Visible or non-visible from whatever point in the road, in 1925 or 1986, the monastery is the key to this emblematic passage and the thrust remains the same: everything conspires to dramatize, to foreground Roncevaux. The secondary point may or may not be that this is another instance of anachorism or interpolation, but the primary point remains that of *paysage moralisé*. Hemingway constructs a symbolic landscape and lest his readers miss—as they generally have—the main point, he has Jake identify Roncesvalles in his narrative and Roncevaux in the dialogue, thus underlining the Roland and pilgrimage associations which are the heart of the matter.

6. My essay concerned with the matter of religion in the fishing scenes, "For Bryan's Sake: The Tribute to the Great Commoner in *The Sun Also Rises*," appeared (with substantial misprints which alter the intended meaning of certain passages) in *Christianity and Literature* 32 (Winter 1983): 29–36.

7. Gerard J. Brault, "Introduction and Commentary," *The Song of Roland: An Analytical Edition* (University Park: Penn State UP, 1978): 214. For some reason that I cannot fathom, Baker rather mysteriously says of this famous horn passage in his note to the Breit letter: "How this handsome line came into EH's possession is not clear" (870). Since every French schoolboy—and some American schoolboys— knows this celebrated line (or some slight variation of it from one of the scores of editions of the *Chanson*), this strikes me as rather like asking how someone came to possess such a line as "To be, or not to be." In any case, as I first pointed out a decade ago, Hemingway knew his *Chanson*, and his imagination had long been profoundly engaged by Roland.

8. Suppose Hemingway had given his Nobel Prize Medal—the symbol of his life's work—to some symbolic repository of some radical cause, or to, say, Fidel Castro rather than the Virgen del Cobre? Surely some commentators would find this highly significant. Just so, Hemingway's actual gift of the medal to the Madonna signifies immensely, even though few seem to be aware of the fact. It was not—as I heard someone say in conversation—a joke. See note No. 2 above.

9. See letters to Brown (cf. note No. 1 above), 9/14/54 and 7/22/56.

10. Actually, there are two "old" chapels at Roncevaux. I have assumed here that Jake is standing in front of the oldest chapel, *Sancti Spiritus*, also known as "Charlemagne's Silo." He may be standing in front of the thirteenth-century Chapel of Santiago, known as the "pilgrim's church," which is the best preserved monument in Roncevaux and which looks more like a chapel than "Charlemagne's Silo," a rather odd structure which resembles a farm building. In any case, the two chapels are right next to each other; if Jake refers to one, the emphasis falls on the Roland association, if he refers to the other, the pilgrim Santiago motif is underlined. The motifs, of course, are contiguous, as are the chapels.

11. The *Liber Sancti Jacobi* is properly referred to as the *Codex Calixtinus*; the *Pilgrim's Guide* is Book 4 of the *Codex*. See Stokstad's bibliography.

12. I am told that the phrase "tenor muchas conchas" is—or was—a familiar idiom to express the possession of artfulness and reserve, qualities Jake certainly has. And for those who see sexual undercurrents in these scenes, we might note that concha—in English—is "another term for the vulva," according to the *OED* (also, a drinking vessel, a coved ceiling, an anatomical term referring to both the ear and the nose, and, of course, a shell). Also, the conch is commonly associated with the Tritons, those vague sea-figures of mythology, who are usually seen playing a conch-horn. Some of these connotations may figure in Jake's Concha sequence, but the primary resonance remains that of the pilgrim's shell—by far the best-known of the connotations, and certainly the one most appropriate to the contexts of the novel.

13. Philip Young, *Ernest Hemingway* (New York: Rinehart, 1952); 58. Young asserts that what Jake is doing is washing "away his hangovers in the ocean." But then Young thinks that this is a book about a "vacationer's Spain," all "motion which goes no place," that Jake has a minimal code ("not highly developed"), that "Lady Brett Ashley also knows the code," etc. (55, 58).

14. There is not sufficient space here to detail the ways in which Killinger mis-reads the most obvious surfaces of Hemingway's text and misses entirely the Catholic subtext. One example: he writes that Jake "prefers absinthe to communion wine" (100). It's bad enough that Killinger apparently cannot see what is plainly in the text—that Jake goes to Mass, goes to confession, etc. It is even more sadly indicative of the drift of Hemingway criticism, however, that Killinger seems to think Jake is a Methodist or some variety of Protestant who might drink "communion wine." Or is he so ill-informed concerning Catholicism that he does not know that "communion under both kinds," as the phrase is, has been forbidden in the Roman Catholic Church for well over a thousand years and that—except for a period of aberration some 800 years ago—the consecrated wine of the Mass is restricted to the celebrant? I am reminded of a graduate student who once wrote a paper in my Hemingway seminar entitled: "Hemingway and the Dead Critics"; and that reminds me that I am grateful to all of those students who—expressing their puzzlement and outrage over the years at the strange inaccuracies and befuddlements of much that has been written about Hemingway and his texts—have helped me to see what *is* there.

15. George Perkins, Sculley Bradley, Richmond Croom Beatty, and E. Hudson Long, eds., *The American Tradition in Literature.* Sixth Edition (New York: Random, 1985): 1267. This remark has stayed through all the editions of the volume. One can almost hear it being made on the 6 o'clock news or on a midnight talk show or some other forum of the terminally glib. Indeed, the view of the novel that it manifests was reflected in the recent catastrophic television miniseries called, for some unfathomable reason, *The Sun Also Rises.* The scholarly culpability, the inaccuracy, the sheer flatulence of the remark may be equalled only by the tyrannical pomposity of the volume's title—*the tradition* indeed? But I fear the remark does embody the dominant tradition in Hemingway criticism; thus this challenge of such an influential anthology—a deed not usually committed in literary criticism—may be attacking the problem at its source. Or is the source of this stream somewhere further back,—yes, certainly before 1956.

16. Commentary on what happens to Jake in the course of the novel divides into two major streams: those who seem to think nothing much happens to him and that he is as desperate or "hollow" or "lost" at the end as at the beginning and those who feel he has grown, changed, achieved some resolution in the course of events. Of the first bemused view, there is nothing to say. Of the second view, what has been

lacking is an understanding of the process of the resolution. Williams, for example, asserts "Jake's resurgence, transcendence, reconciliation," quite correctly, but he says that "we are not told" what causes it, and avers that "the absence of an explanation as to *how* he has done so is the most serious weakness of the book" (46). But as this essay is primarily concerned to demonstrate—through the pilgrimage motif and the Catholic subtext and text—we *are* told exactly how he has done so.

17. Hemingway's phrase, as reported by Olghina di Robilant in "Hemingway and True Grit: A Memoir," *Esquire* (March 27, 1979): 52.

18. Aden Josephs, "*Toreo*: The Moral Axis of *The Sun Also Rises*," as delivered at SAMLA, Atlanta, 1985; The Josephs article cited here is in this issue of *The Hemingway Review* in expanded form (see pp. 88–89). Jacques Maritain, *The Peasant of the Garonne* (New York: Holt, 1968): 4. In a passage describing the difficulties of Christianity for a "layman" in the "present time," Maritain recalls telling Jean Cocteau, "*We must have a tough mind and a tender heart*," for the world is filled with "dried-up hearts and flabby minds" (80). That first emphatic phrase describes Hemingway's Catholicism, I think, and his work amounts to a similar warning about "dried-up hearts and flabby minds."

WORKS CITED

Baker, Carlos. *Ernest Hemingway: A Life Story*. New York: Scribner's, 1969.

———. *Hemingway: The Writer as Artist*. Princeton: Princeton UP, 1972.

———, ed. *Ernest Hemingway: Selected Letters*. New York: Scribner's, 1981.

Brasch, James D. and Joseph Sigman. *Hemingway's Library: A Composite Record*. New York: Garland, 1981.

Brault, Gerard J. *The Song of Roland: An Analytical Edition*. University Park: Penn State UP, 1978.

di Robilant, Olghina. "Hemingway and True Grit: A Memoir." *Esquire* March 1979: 52.

in their time/1920–1940. An Exhibition at the Univ. of Virginia Library. Bloomfield Hills, Mi.: Bruccoli Clark, 1977.

Josephs, Allen. "*Toreo*: The Moral Axis of *The Sun Also Rises*." Address to South Atlantic Modern Language Assn. Atlanta, October 1985.

Madden, Daniel M. *A Religious Guide to Europe*. New York: MacMillan, 1975.

Maritain, Jacques. *The Peasant of the Garonne*. New York: Holt, 1968.

Perkins, George, Sculley Bradley, Richmond Croom Beatty, and E. Hudson Long. *The American Tradition in Literature*. 6th edition. New York: Random, 1985.

Reardon, John. "Hemingway's Esthetic and Ethical Sportsmen" *Ernest Hemingway: Five Decades of Criticism*. Ed. Linda W. Wagner. East Lansing: Michigan State UP, 1974.

Shaw, Sam. *Ernest Hemingway*. New York: Ungar, 1973.

Stokstad, Marilyn. *Santiago de Compostela In the Age of the Great Pilgrimages*. Norman: U of Oklahoma P, 1978.

Stoneback, H.R. "'For Bryan's Sake': The 'Tribute' to the Great Commoner in *The Sun Also Rises*." *Christianity and Literature* 32 (1983): 29–36.

———. "Hemingway on the Road to Roncevaux: The Pilgrimage Theme in *The Sun Also Rises*." Address to the VIII Congreso de la Société Rencesvals. Pamplona-Santiago de Compostela, Spain. August, 1978.

Williams, Wirt, *The Tragic Art of Ernest Hemingway*. Baton Rouge: Louisiana State UP, 1981.

Young, Philip. *Ernest Hemingway*. New York: Rinehart, 1952.

WOLFGANG E. H. RUDAT

Bill Gorton, Jake's Wounded Preacher: The Therapeutic Nature of Jokes

In *The Tragic Art of Ernest Hemingway*, Wirt Williams contends:

> For Gorton there seems to be no *dramatic* line at all: he does function on occasion as chorus and commentator, and sometimes perhaps as preacher, as M. L. Ross holds; ... his chief use may be simply as contrast to [those] characters who have complete personal dramas. He remains a constant, not *visibly* experiencing catastrophe or confronting the void at all and thus escaping the moral examination that accompanies both. He goes through the book unchanged—and untested.[1]

In the final chapter of my study, I will demonstrate not only that Bill Gorton has a very important function in the novel, but, eventually and more specifically, that his importance resides in *quite* visibly experiencing catastrophe and confronting the void—that in fact he is morally tested if not more thoroughly then at least more frequently than any of the other characters. Let us take a closer look at Jake's Eden, the fishing expedition at Burguete, where Bill is a central character. While, as Waldhorn notes, "Jake seems to find that Eden without Eve is not only possible but preferable,"[2] even during the paradisiacal fishing vacation he is not spared the topic of Brett. After

From *A Rotten Way to Be Wounded: The Tragicomedy of* The Sun Also Rises, pp. 153–76, 209–14. Copyright © 1990 by Peter Lang Publishing.

utilizing their blessings—gesturing "with the drumstick in one hand and the bottle of wine in the other," Bill had called upon Jake: "Let us rejoice in our blessings. Let us utilize the fowls of the air. Let us utilize the product of the vine" (p. 122)—Jake and Bill are ready for a nap. Jake asks his friend:

> "You asleep?"
> "No," Bill said. "I was thinking."
> I shut my eyes. It felt good lying on the ground.
> "Say," Bill said, "what about this Brett business?"
> "What about it?"
> "Were you ever in love with her?"
> "Sure."
> "For how long?"
> "Off and on for a hell of a long time."
> "Oh hell!" Bill said. "I'm sorry, fella."
> "It's all right," I said. "I don't give a damn any more."
> "Really?"
> "Really. Only I'd a hell of a lot rather not talk about it."
> "You aren't sore I asked you?"
> "Why the hell should I be?"
> "I'm going to sleep," Bill said. He put a newspaper over his face.
> "Listen, Jake," he said, "are you really a Catholic?"
> "Technically."
> "What does that mean?"
> "I don't know."
> "All right, I'll go to sleep now," he said. "Don't keep me awake by talking so much."
> I went to sleep, too. (pp. 123–124)

In a sense this is the kind of event which in Pamplona Brett will ask Jake to let her witness: Confession. Jake will intimate to her that there would be no point in going to Confession with him because she would not be able to understand the language of the Christian religion. By contrast, Bill is allowed to witness Jake's going to Confession—in fact Bill is acting as brother-confessor—because Bill does understand that language. Bill shows that he understands the language when he simply accepts Jake's answers. When Jake answers with "I don't know" Bill's question of what being a Catholic "Technically" means, Bill merely replies, "All right, I'll go to sleep now." Bill is saying that he recognizes that he has trespassed a little and will not push any farther. Bill is practicing what he had preached a few minutes earlier: "Let us not pry into the holy mysteries of the hencoop with simian fingers. Let us accept on faith" (p. 122). Having made a reference to the creationism-versus-evolution-ism controversy, Bill does not wish to pry with "simian fingers" into what it means to be technically a Catholic.

Yet not only does Bill accept Jake's answer, but he is also reassuring Jake that Jake need not be defensive about having given that answer when he jokingly says, "Don't keep me awake by talking so much." Bill, of course, had initiated the conversation and had done a good deal of the talking himself: in the spirit of the seriocomic man—a spirit which is exemplified *truly* by the Count and *parodically* by the would-be Falstaff Mike Campbell, who is inca-pable of mastering reality—Bill had conducted a quasi-religious ceremony in celebration of the "blessings."[3] And Bill succeeds in reassuring Jake, for Jake too goes to sleep—something he had rarely been able to do after thinking about Brett. After confessing to the seriocomic man and confessing in what Bill had called "God's first temples," "the great out-of-doors" (p. 122), Jake is able, as he had not been in the cathedral, to be a "good Catholic" by forgetting his self, i.e., by ceasing to be self-conscious about his physical and his spiritual wound.

It should be noted that Bill asks Jake whether he *had* ever been in love with Brett: a question about his *present* feelings might put him on the defen-sive. Jake's answer that he had been in love with Brett "Off and on for a *hell* of a long time" (italics added) convinces Bill that Jake is still emotionally involved, and hurt by it; in order to elicit a significant response, Bill expresses a little more sympathy than is really called for: "Oh hell! . . . I'm sorry, fella" expresses a degree of sympathy that makes Jake look so pitiful that he will be forced to reject it if he has any will to live left. Jake is heading toward possible recovery when he says that "It's all right" and that he doesn't "give a damn any more."

To reinforce Jake's will to become healthy, Bill asks, "Really?" Jake's answer, "Really. Only I'd a hell of a lot rather not talk about it," tells Bill that Jake's road to recovery may be an arduous one. Therefore easing up on Jake, Bill not only honors Jake's wish not to talk about Brett but, to mol-lify him, also inquires whether he was sore about having been asked about Brett. Jake's reply, "Why the hell should I be?", satisfies Bill for the time being, but the many *hells* and *damns* in Jake's replies, i.e., religion-related swear-words, suggest to Bill that Jake's problems with Brett may be tied up with religious problems, and he proceeds to ask him about his religion. Bill, the seriocomic brother-confessor, convinces Jake that it is all right not to tell anybody—since it is nobody else's business—whether (to express it in Jake's own terms) he is a good or a rotten Catholic. By doing this, Bill has brought Jake to the point where, on the morning after Brett's first night with Romero, Jake will be able to *laughingly* suggest to Brett that she try prayer to calm the wind and, perhaps even unselfconsciously, affirm that he himself has had prayers answered.

Jake will not, however, be able to deal with Brett's "You don't look very religious" assault, simply because the road to recovery from his problems with Brett is more difficult than a homecoming to the "grand religion": whereas all the latter cure takes is faith, i.e., "Catholic" passiveness, the cure of "this Brett *business*" (italics added: Hemingway's use of that word may well be more than just a colloquialism, namely, a pointer to Protestant pragmatism) requires something that is more anthropocentric, more typically 'Protestant,' namely, action—the militant act of killing his love for the woman. But then, the author, a Protestant converted to Catholicism, is ingeniously conflating the two religions—or perhaps more precisely, showing their potential basic unity—when he presents Jake's 'Protestant' solution as executed in a Catholic fashion: as an act of exorcism. At that point Jake shows that he is indeed a Catholic "Technically"—i.e., as Stoneback puts it, "a pilgrim seeking a deeper participation in grace through the careful practice of ritual and discipline"[4]—something he had been reluctant to admit in his confession to Bill.

Bill serves as a foil for Brett in Jake's life, a positive foil because unlike women, who from Jake's sarcastic perspective make "such swell friends" and sooner or later will present their bills (p. 148), Bill is a genuine friend. As an unselfish friend Bill Gorton never presents Jake with a bill. In fact, Bill's desire to be an unselfishly helpful friend to Jake accounts for some of the seemingly strange things that transpire between the two of them. Hinkle makes the following observation:

> The narrator, Jake Barnes, is not the only one in the book who is alive to puns. On the evening Bill Gorton arrives in Paris Jake asks him:
>   "What'll we do to-night?"
>   "Doesn't make any difference. Only let's not get daunted. Suppose they got any hard-boiled eggs here?" (73)
> "Hard-boiled" eggs to guard against becoming daunted.
> The meaning of "hard-boiled" we already know from Jake:
>   It is awfully easy to be hard-boiled about everything in the daytime, but at night it is another thing.[5]

Hinkle is making an excellent point without saying it in so many words. Transcending mere punning, Bill's pun on *not daunted* and *hard-boiled* on p. 73 is thematically important only if in his response to Jake's "What'll we do to-night?" Bill is addressing the problem which Jake communicated to the reader on p. 34, i.e., if Bill is aware of what Jake finds difficult to cope with at night even though it may be easy to deal with during the day. Bill's pun shows us how intimately he can communicate with and how clearly he understands Jake. If in discussing with Bill his night-time problem Jake has actually used the word "hard-boiled," then Bill is being an excellent psychotherapist when he employs that word as a trigger word to subliminally reinforce the positive suggestion that he is trying to implant in Jake's mind, i.e., not to get daunted. If Jake has *not* used the word "hard-boiled" to Bill, then in Bill's use of the word Hemingway is symbolizing the depth of Bill's insights into Jake's psyche—and the word is the author's way of expressing verbally the existence of a non-verbal type of communication between Bill and Jake.

Only someone with an intuitive understanding of psychology and intimate knowledge of another person would dare to crack jokes about that person's sexual handicap, as Bill does on the morning before he and Jake go out fishing. Jake is mistaken when he is "afraid" that Bill thought he had hurt him with the crack about being impotent: Jake is being needlessly "daunted." Bill's idea is to make Jake "undaunted," or to use a modern term, to desensitize Jake. Bill had "stopped" because he had already made his point: referring to Henry James' supposed impotence, Bill had suggested that Jake should work his handicap up into a mystery.

After lunch Bill continues the therapy and in fact brings full circle the wheel which had been set in motion in Paris by their "What'll we do to-night?"—"Doesn't make any difference. Only let's not get daunted. Suppose they got any hard-boiled eggs here?" exchange:

> We unwrapped the little parcels of lunch.
> "Chicken." [Jake said.]
> "There's hard-boiled eggs."
> "Find any salt?"
> "First the egg," said Bill. "Then the chicken. Even Bryan could see that."
> "He's dead. I read it in the paper yesterday."
> "No. Not really?"
> "Yes. Bryan's dead."
> Bill laid down the egg he was peeling.
> "Gentlemen," he said, and unwrapped a drumstick from a piece of newspaper. "I reverse the order. For Bryan's sake. As a tribute to the Great Commoner. First the chicken; then the egg." (p. 121)

As noted, Baskett observes that Bill "insistently concerns himself with what might be called—'The Education of Jacob Barnes'."[6] Since the lunch parcels have been opened and their contents seen, there is no need for Bill to state that there are hard-boiled eggs—unless he wishes to make a point. That point is not only funny but also downright ingenious. In order to be able to continue the comments on Jake's situation, Bill deliberately and perversely in a well-intentioned way chooses to take Jake's "Chicken" as a reference to young women—it is thematically significant that Jake's sexual drama in the novel begins when, shortly before his reunion with Brett, he picks up the *poule* (literally *chicken*) Georgette—which gives Bill an opportunity to remind Jake that he must become "hard-boiled" about, or desensitized to, women.

Thus, when Jake asks about salt, he may be showing the naivete of having taken Bill's "There's hardboiled eggs" literally—or he may have understood Bill's reference to desensitization, in which case Jake's question, "Find any salt?", would in turn be asking Bill whether the latter had any salt to rub into Jake's wound: having caught Bill's deliberate perversion of his exclamation "Chicken" into a reference to the opposite sex, Jake would be asking for salt for the *chicken*, i.e., he would be inquiring about salt that could be rubbed into the wound which the opposite sex does not allow to heal. Refusing to let Jake off the hook in any case, Bill applies what today we would call reality therapy: when Bill says, "First the egg . . . then the chicken," he is telling Jake that he has to become hard-boiled before he can deal with women.

However, Bill's mocking reference to Bryan brings the joke therapy to a pause, for Bryan could *not* "see that": Bryan could not see the point Bill is making because Bryan had just died. So, having made his point, Bill "reverse[s] the order" in a jesting tribute to the prosecutor in the Scopes trial (the language is intended to sound legal): according to creationism, the species, in this case the chicken, of course comes first. Bill's reversal of the order leads to a culinary gloss on Genesis, which is started by Jake:

> "Wonder what day God created the chicken?"
> "Oh," said Bill, sucking the drumstick, "how should we know? We should not question. Our stay on earth is not for long. Let us rejoice and believe and give thanks."
> "*Eat an egg.*" (pp. 121–22, italics added)

This is a variation on the earlier exchange, "What'll we do tonight?"— "Doesn't matter. Only let's not get daunted. *Suppose they got any hard-boiled eggs here?*" (p. 73, italics added). Whereas in the exchange on p. 73 Bill had suggested that Jake become hard-boiled, he is now suggesting that Jake rejoice, give thanks, but above all have faith. Jake is indicating that he now is aware of what Bill has been doing when he says, "Eat an egg." Jake is not only acknowledging that he needs to have faith *and* become hard-boiled, but he is also acknowledging that first he has to become hard-boiled, i.e., that Bill's "First the egg . . . Then the chicken" advice was right, and Jake is therefore reversing Bill's reversal.

Their dialogue is followed by Bill's 'sermon,' given in the spirit of the Preacher of Ecclesiastes, about "utilizing" the good things of the earth, the "fowls of the air" and the "product of the vine;" he advises Jake to accept on faith rather than "pry into the holy mysteries of the hencoop with simian fingers." Although Bill pokes fun at the zealous opponents of evolutionism, he is pointing to what he considers the salutary aspects of the teachings of the Bible. Bill, the seriocomic man, while he satirizes the zealous proponents of creationism, is distilling from their dogmatic positions the *underlying principle*, faith, and recommending it to Jake as a cure. As Stoneback notes, in his article entitled "'For Bryan's Sake': The Tribute to the Great Commoner in Hemingway's *The Sun Also Rises*,"

> The very center of the [Burguete] chapter, the pivot on which the humor as well as the serious thematic concerns turns, is the three-page sequence in which William Jennings Bryan is the subject. The thrust of this rich sequence has entirely escaped the notice of commentators on the novel, for it has generally been read as a throwaway passage, a humorous aside or digression; and if the role of Bryan in all this has been noticed, the perfunctory assumption has been made that he is here the target of Hemingway's mockery. It is necessary, however, to take another look, for this is the center of the novel in more ways than one.[7]

I agree with Stoneback that "what most readers of the novel have failed to notice is that there is very little actual fishing in this purported fishing chapter," or rather that very little fishing is actually *described*, and with Stoneback's characterization of the novel as "scrupulously orchestrated in terms of a pilgrimage undertaken by Jake Barnes in order to grow in grace."[8] And I agree with Stoneback's observation, made in his article, "From the rue Saint-Jacques to the Pass of Roland to the 'Unfinished Church on the Edge of the Cliff'," that "none of [the Hemingway criticism] deals precisely with Jake's Catholic sensibility, with the moral and spiritual anguish and joy of the pilgrim," and I agree with Stoneback's interpretation that the fishing trip symbolizes an "Ichthus-quest."[9] But I would add that, within what Stoneback calls the novel's "Catholic subtext," Hemingway has Bill recommend faith as a cure which has to be used *in conjunction with desensitization*.

In fact, Bill is applying a combination of both cures when, after lunch, he first asks Jake about "this Brett business" and immediately thereafter about being a Catholic. The chronology of the application seems to suggest that Bill feels that Jake *will* have to desensitize himself to Brett first before he can be whatever constitutes a good Catholic, i.e., Bill agrees with Jake's reinstatement of the egg–chicken order: the chicken, which in the context of the creationism-versus-evolutionism argument represents faith, comes after the egg.

It is in order to help Jake become hard-boiled that Bill introduces a particular woman into Eden by mentioning "this Brett business." Bill is now able to do so because, when Bill responded to Jake's observation, "Chicken," by pointing out that "There's hard-boiled eggs," thus transforming Jake's observation into the exclamation "Woman," Bill had in the manner of a reality therapist already forced Jake to acknowledge that, while he is able to run away from an ephemeral kind of "chicken," from the *poules* roaming the streets and cafes in Paris, he cannot simply run away from the problems he has with the opposite sex—so that Jake's question, "Wonder what day God created the chicken?", means as well "Wonder what day God created the woman?" The question of *when* God created the woman shows that Jake no longer laments but, instead, accepts the creation of the opposite sex.

Hemingway carefully prepares the stage for the psychological treatment which Bill will administer to Jake during the Burguete episode. Jake, Bill, and Cohn are waiting for Brett and Mike to arrive in Pamplona. With "an air of superior knowledge that irritate[s] both [Jake and Bill]" (p. 95), Cohn accepts Bill's bet over whether Brett and Mike would arrive on the announced date. Cohn wins the bet, and Cohn and Bill go out drinking together until two o'clock in the morning. The next morning Jake finds Bill in his room shaving:

> "*Oh, yes, he told me all about it last night,*" Bill said. "He's a great little confider. He said he had a date with Brett at San Sebastian."
>
> "The lying bastard!"
>
> "Oh, no," said Bill. "Don't get sore. Don't get sore at this stage of the trip. How did you ever happen to know this fellow anyway?"
>
> "Don't rub it in."
>
> Bill looked around, half-shaved, and then went on talking into the mirror while he lathered his face.
>
> "Didn't you send him with a letter to me in New York last winter? Thank God, I'm a traveling man.

Haven't you got some more Jewish friends you could bring along?" He rubbed his chin with his thumb, looked at it, and then started scraping again. (p. 101, italics added)

Hinkle observes: "It would be easy to read right over that passage without realizing that Jake has made a small joke with 'Don't rub it in' and that Bill, by interrupting his lathering and turning around, acknowledges that he understands it."[10]

I suggest that the "Don't rub it in" joke actually is thematically important. The surface meaning of the joke as consciously intended by Jake is that he does not want Bill to rub in the fact that Jake has Cohn for a friend. But that there is also a subsurface meaning is suggested by the portion I italicized. The *it* that Cohn had told Mike "all about" the night before refers to some question or remark of Jake's. Let us therefore examine the preceding lines. Cohn is explaining to Jake why Brett and Mike have not arrived yet:

"I'm afraid they expected to meet me at San Sebastian, and that's why they stopped over."
"What makes you think that?"
"Will, I wrote suggesting it to Brett."
"Why in hell didn't you stay there and meet them, then?" I started to say, but I stopped. *I thought that idea would come to him by itself, but I do not believe it ever did.*
He was being confidential now and it was giving him pleasure to be able to talk with the understanding that I knew there was something between him and Brett.
"Well, Bill and I will go up right after lunch," I said.
"I wish I could go. We've been looking forward to this fishing all winter." He was being sentimental about it. "But I ought to stay. I really ought. As soon as they come I'll bring them right up." (pp. 100–101, italics added)

The idea that he should have stayed in San Sebastian may indeed never have occurred to Cohn, but the idea that he could go back to San Sebastian must have, the night before the morning on which Jake started to give him another idea but then stopped. Jake, then, has been outmaneuvered by Cohn, and his exclamation, "That lying bastard," indicates how angry Jake is at having been bested by him. The exclamation is unfair because, while Cohn's statements that he ought to stay in Pamplona and that he would bring Brett and Mike to Burguete as soon as they had arrived could be construed as withholding information—information, however, which Cohn was under no obligation to reveal—they do not really constitute lying. Nor does Jake have a right to call Cohn a liar for saying that he had a date with Brett at San Sebastian: Jake cannot *know* whether Cohn had advised Brett that he would meet her in San Sebastian.

What, then, does Bill's "Oh, yes" refer to? It must be a response to a remark in which Jake mentioned something not only about Cohn but also about Brett: note that Bill immediately calls Cohn a "great little confider." While on the surface of the joke Jake intends the "Don't rub it in" as a reference to Cohn, Bill, the natural psychologist, senses that there is an unconscious message in Jake's request, i.e., that the *it* in Jake's request concerns Brett more than it does Cohn. Bill decides to comply with Jake's conscious request and not the unconscious message and, instead of talking about Brett, talks about Cohn and "more Jewish friends" for a while—but only for a while: Bill says, "Don't get sore *at this stage* of the trip" (italics added), implying that there may be reasons to get sore later when certain things may indeed have to be rubbed in. By interrupting his lathering and turning around Bill acknowledges that he understands the "Don't rub it in" joke as it had been consciously intended by Jake, but when he rubs his chin with his thumb he is indicating that his compliance with Jake's conscious request has ended.

After the smokescreen about Cohn and other Jews has cleared, Bill takes the bull by the horns. When Jake asks if Cohn had been "very bad" the night before, Bill replies:

> "Awful. What's all this about him and Brett, anyway? Did she ever have anything to do with him?"
>
> He raised his chin up and pulled it from side to side.
>
> "Sure. She went down to San Sebastian with him."
>
> "What a damn-fool thing to do. Why did she do that?"
>
> "She wanted to get out of town and she can't go anywhere alone. She said she thought it would be good for him."
>
> "What bloody-fool things people do. Why didn't she go off with some of her own people? Or you?"—he slurred that over—"or me? Why not me?" He looked at his face carefully in the glass, put a big dab of lather on each cheek-bone. "It's an honest face. It's a face any woman would be safe with."
>
> "She'd never seen it."
>
> "She should have. All women should see it. It's a face that ought to be thrown on every screen in the country. Every woman ought to be given a copy of this face as she leaves the altar. Mothers should tell their daughters—about this face. My son"—he

pointed the razor at me—"go west with this face and grow up with the country."

He ducked down to the bowl, rinsed his face with cold water, put on some alcohol, and then looked at himself carefully in the glass, pulling down his long upper lip.

"My God!" he said, "isn't it an awful face?" (p. 102)

When Bill slurs over the "Or you" he is actually drawing attention to it; he is indicating that he *knows* this is painful to Jake—or in other words, he is rubbing in what he will later call "this Brett business," his subsequent "or me. Why not me?" in front of the mirror notwithstanding. In fact, the long talk about his face that follows is part of the reality therapy which Bill is already administering to Jake and will continue to administer during their trip. When Bill says, "My God! . . . isn't it an awful face?", he means it: Bill's face, with its long upper lip, is ugly.

This is suggested by several facts. First, Jake does not even respond to Bill's apparently rhetorical question about his face: Jake knows Bill well enough to know that there would be no point in trying to argue away what Bill considers a problem. Second, at a time when the average American male in Bill's age group was or at least had been married, Bill apparently has never been married. Third, in a "little treatise on promiscuity including a Few Jokes" Bill seems to be unique in that he is never mentioned as being sexually involved, although during their first meeting Brett makes a definite play for him. Hemingway presents Bill's carefully viewing his face in the mirror and calling it "awful" as a foil for Jake's French-mirror scene: Bill quite literally faces his problem head-on and accepts it, and he is trying to teach Jake to do the same with his problem.[11]

But Bill's ugly face is not his biggest problem, as can be seen in what I consider one of the subtlest jokes in *The Sun Also Rises*, and possibly the most surprising joke in Hemingway's treatise on promiscuity. Significantly, this joke first appears in the free-associating context in which Hemingway alludes to the scene in Sterne's novel that tells us exactly what Jake's problem is. For a proper understanding of the context I requote that passage in its entirety (Bill speaking):

" . . . You spend all your time talking, not working. You are an expatriate, see? You hang around cafes."

"It sounds like a swell life," I said. "When do I work?"

"You don't work. One group claims women support you. Another group claims that you're impotent."

"No," I said. "I just had an accident."

"Never mention that," Bill said. "That's the sort of thing that can't be spoken of. That's what you ought to work up into a mystery. Like Henry's bicycle."

He had been going splendidly, but he stopped. I was afraid he thought he had hurt me with that crack about being impotent. I wanted to start him again.

"It wasn't a bicycle," I said. "He was riding horseback."

"I heard it was a tricycle."

"Well," I said. "A plane is a sort of tricycle. The joystick works the same way."

"But *you* don't pedal it."

"No," I said, "I guess *you* don't pedal it."

"Let's lay off that," Bill said. (pp. 115–16)

In his chapter, "*The Sun Also Rises*—But No Bells Ring," commenting on the seeming nonexistence of a sex life for Bill, Stallman has suggested that Bill's remark about the joystick should be read as "But *you* don't pedal it" (i.e., as Bill claiming that Jake has no sex life) and Jake's rejoinder as a joke which is being tossed back to the joker: "No ... I guess *you* don't pedal it."[12] Yet Stallman catches only the tip of the iceberg making up this double-talk joke: "To pedal it is approved by the prescribed code, but Bill takes no pride in that code." Heeding Hinkle's advice that occasionally a passage needs to be read aloud, I will go beyond Stallman and suggest that we read the exchange as follows and make Jake an even more convincing winner in the joking contest:

"But *you* don't PEDDLE it." [Bill said]

"No," I said, "I guess *you* don't PEDDLE it."

If Bill were simply insinuating, "But *you* don't PEDAL it," this would not be a free-associating joke. For whereas today's tricycles have handlebars just as bicycles do, some of the earlier ones were not pedaled but indeed had a joystick of sorts, i.e., one stick rising straight up with the rider pumping backward and forward to propel the tricycle, whose front wheel he steered with his feet.[13] The free-associating joke is that Bill is returning to the question of how Jake makes a living—Bill has just said that Jake does *not* work but instead hangs around cafes—and deliberately, and perversely in a good-natured way, misunderstands Jake's preceding statement to mean that "the joystick works the same way" as, i.e., that pumping one's "joystick" back and forth to make a living is as effective as, working at an ordinary job because there are enough women in Parisian cafes who are willing to support an expatriate gigolo. And Bill playfully replies to Jake that the latter's joystick must *not* be working as he does not peddle his sexual services—but, instead, works as a newspaper correspondent—i.e., Bill is suggesting that Jake must indeed be impotent. In other words, Bill is doing exactly what Jake, according to his communication to the reader, had wanted him to do: "I was afraid he thought he had hurt me with that crack about being impotent. *I wanted him to start again*" (italics added).

Bill is trying to evoke a healthy reaction from Jake, to make Jake feel better, by enabling him to talk about his problem, even jokingly, and even retort that Bill has a similar problem. And Bill is indicating that he has received that response when he says, "Let's lay off that."[14] Bill has got from Jake, who knows Bill as well as Bill knows Jake, the hoped-for answer, healthy and spirited, that Bill does not make a living out of that which Jake lacks and therefore cannot peddle but which Bill would seem able to offer for sale or rent—because Bill himself suffers from that which he had jokingly attributed to Jake: Bill does not make a living out of pumping his joystick because he is impotent.

Bill's impotence is in the under-water portion of Hemingway's iceberg, but the author gives us another hint. Perhaps thematically significantly for the narrative movements within the novel, Bill's impotence is suggested first in the womanless Eden of Burguete and then, a little more directly, in what is probably the most hellish moment in the hell of Pamplona, the brawl in the Cafe Suizo: Hemingway may actually be insinuating Bill's condition through a palimpsestic interaction between the two contexts. Edna, vaguely designated as "a friend of Bill's from Biarritz" (p. 180), and seemingly a marginal character in the novel, makes several odd remarks about Bill in his absence while Jake is trying to recover from having been knocked out by Cohn:

> "I say, you were cold," Mike said.
> "Where the hell were you?"
> "Oh, I was around."
> "You didn't want to mix in it?"
> "He knocked Mike down, too," Edna said.
> "He didn't knock me out," *Mike said. "I just lay there."*
> "Does this happen every night at your fiestas?" Edna asked. "Wasn't that Mr. Cohn?"
>
> . . . . .
>
> "It was quite a thing to watch," Edna said. "He must be a boxer."
> "He is."
> "I wish Bill had been here," Edna said. "I'd like to have seen Bill knocked down, too. I've always wanted to see Bill knocked down. He's so big." (p. 191, italics added)

A brawl in a cafe, of course, is not Edna's idea of a fiesta. However, her question as to whether this happens every night at their fiestas does not really address the brawl itself; instead, her question is an unconscious reaction to Mike's immediately preceding statement, "He didn't knock me out . . . I just lay there." Hemingway is having Edna treat us to a Shandean free-associating joke.

When Edna points out that Mike had, like Jake, been knocked down, she is defending Mike against Jake's imputation of cowardice. Mike, however, nonchalantly admits his cowardice, saying that he "just lay there"—an unmanly failure to act. This triggers in Edna the process of free association. Mike's admission causes Edna to unconsciously reveal in her question, "Does this happen every night at your fiestas?", that a "just [lying] there" has happened before in their fiesta: once is happenstance, but twice is worth inquiring about. And her subsequent statement that she would like to see Bill knocked down associates Bill with the earlier unmanly failure to act which is implicit in her question; she wants a public demonstration of—and, equally, punishment for—the impotence of this man who is "so big" but "just lay[s] there."[15]

In the cafe-brawl scene, then, Hemingway presents Edna as, indirectly, in a free-associating fantasy, doing to Bill during his absence something comparable to what in their final cab ride together Brett will consciously do to Jake: since, like Jake but unlike the Mike who had displayed unmanly behavior, Bill *cannot* make his deportment more 'manly,' Edna too is a *vagina dentata* of sorts (and it might be well to note that Gajdusek has pointed out that not only "Brett" but also "*Ed*na" is a masculine name[16]). Thus Pamplona may be a hell for Bill no less than it is for the narrator himself, which would tie in ironically with Bill's attempt to teach Jake to accept himself—*ironically* because Bill is not even present during this lesson he is giving Jake at the Cafe Suizo.

It is quite natural that Edna should associate her potential sex partner Bill with the Mike who was knocked down and just lay there, for Mike had earlier addressed her as a sex object, and he had unabashedly done so in the presence of Bill:

> "You're an extraordinarily beautiful girl." Mike turned to Bill's friend. "When did you come here?"
> "Come off it, Michael."
> "I say she is a lovely girl. Where have I been? Where have I been looking all this while? You're a lovely thing. *Have* we met? Come along with me and Bill . . ." (p. 180)

Edna had interpreted Mike's words as an attempt to compete with Bill for her affections: it is probably Brett, an expert on such competition between males over sex objects—Mike is addressing Edna much as he had addressed Brett: "You're a lovely thing"—who tells Mike to "Come off it." But then, since Hemingway does not identify the speaker of the "Come off it, Michael" and the dialogue on this page has been and will continue to be (until the next-to-last line of the page) between Mike and Bill, the speaker could well be Bill himself, whose defensiveness—or admirably loyal protectiveness toward Edna—could reasonably manifest itself in the use of the formal "Michael"; Mike's "Come along with me *and Bill*" would then be appeasing Bill's objection. If this ambiguity is intended by the author, we would have the irony of a gelding trying to keep possession of a mare. At any rate, now at the Cafe Suizo, Edna's would-be conqueror Mike not only has lost his own fiancée to another man, to Romero—Mike has just told Cohn, "Brett's gone off with the bull-fighter chap. They're on their honeymoon" and Cohn has just called Jake a "damned pimp"—but her would-be conqueror has also been defeated in a fistfight started on account of his fiancée, a fistfight in which he had behaved in a rather cowardly, i.e., unmanly, fashion.

Edna's 'manly' hero in this context is Cohn, who, perhaps for the first time in the novel, is being accorded respect when Edna refers to him as "Mr. Cohn." Unlike the other two men, one present and the other absent, both of whom "just lay there," Cohn had shown his manliness, or at least his capacity for passion, by getting involved in a fight because of his feelings for a woman. When Edna says, "It was quite a thing to watch," Hemingway is having her echo the enthusiastic statements which Brett had made about Romero's performance in the bullring. And Edna is certainly stepping into the 'corner' of the former Princeton boxing champion, whose feats the narrator had in the opening lines made fun of, when she declares that she would, like to have seen Bill knocked down by Cohn, too.

Bill Gorton, too, has been wounded in a rotten way, not only once but actually twice. First he was wounded by Mother Nature when she gave him an "awful face." Later he received a wound of sorts in his genitals. Bill, too, received his sexual wound as the result of a war, ironically not in the Great War as Jake did but, instead, in the battle between the sexes: when Bill says to Jake that he has a face that "any woman could feel safe with"—we remember Brett's early comment that in the company of homosexuals "one can drink in such safety" (p. 22)—he is reminding Jake that his face has caused him so many rejections from, and so much humiliation by, the opposite sex that he has been traumatized into impotence.

Hemingway does give us a cue as to the cause of Bill's impotence, but we discover the cue only if we reread the novel after we have deduced that Bill is impotent. Significantly, Hemingway gives us the cue a few lines before the "What'll we do to-night?"—"Doesn't make any difference. *Only let's not get daunted.* Suppose they got any hard-boiled eggs here?" exchange in Paris (p. 73, italics added), where Bill begins "The Education of Jacob Barnes":

> "Certainly like to drink," Bill said. "You ought to try it some times, Jake."
> "You're about a hundred and forty-four ahead of me."
> "Ought not to daunt you. Never be daunted. Secret of my success. Never been daunted *in public.*"
> "Where were you drinking?"
> "Stopped at the Crillon. George made me a couple of Jack Roses. Know the secret of his success? Never been daunted."
> "You'll be daunted after about three more pernods."
> "Not in public. If I begin to feel daunted I'll go off by myself. I'm like a cat that way."
> "When did you see Harvey Stone?"
> "At the Crillon. Harvey was just a little daunted. Hadn't eaten for three days . . ."
> "What'll we do to-night?"
> "Doesn't make any difference. Only let's not get daunted. Suppose they got any hard-boiled eggs here? . . ." (p. 73, italics added)

When, in a context where within the space of less than one page Hemingway uses the words *daunt* or *daunted* nine times, he has Bill emphasize that he has never been daunted *in public,* the author is telling us, and Bill is reminding Jake, that Bill has been daunted *in private,* i.e., that in certain situations when Bill was seeking intimacy he has been "daunted" into impotence, possibly because of his self-consciousness about his looks. In the sense that Bill has been put down by the cutting ridicule of females and/or by the fear of such treatment, then, he too is the victim of the destructive power, real or imagined, which the female has over the male. In other words, Bill had been a victim long before Edna unwittingly cut him down in Pamplona. This further illustrates the idea that, even when not directly touched by the instruments of killing as is Jake's case, after the Great War romantic love is in a diseased state.[17]

As Lewis notes in the study in which he observes that *The Sun Also Rises* presents romantic love as sick, here the only love which is still healthy is agape, brotherly love. Lewis adduces Bill Gorton as the prime example of agape;[18] I would suggest that Bill practices agape mainly because he is "sick" when it comes to romantic love. It is especially in his attempt to help Jake come to terms with his handicap that Bill shows his brotherly love. In the "joystick" dialogue Bill does not *have* to risk either hurting Jake or being mis-understood by him. That Bill *is* misunderstood is indicated by the narrator's comment, "I was afraid he thought he had hurt me with that crack about being impotent": at this point, i.e., before Bill has made his intentions clear by escalating the joke to "But *you* don't PEDDLE it," Jake fails to understand that Bill is conversationally playing on Jake's handicap in order to bring him to treat it as a joke, a joke between men, and not only in a cynical, defeatist manner as he does when he is with Brett, to whom Jake says that his injury is "supposed to be funny." Jake had likewise failed to understand why Bill had slurred over the "Or you?" and immediately added the "or me. Why not me?" First of all, Bill had been trying to cause Jake to feel pain in broad daylight over the problem which, according to the narrator himself, while it is difficult to cope with at night, is "awfully easy to be hard-boiled about . . . in the day-time" (p. 34). In addition, Bill had been trying to remind Jake not only that both of them had similar problems but that he, Bill, had to 'face' his problem not just at night but also during the day—and that in fact he was reminded of his own night-time problem every morning when he was shaving.

Unlike Jake, whose injury normally is not visible, Bill also has a prob-lem that he cannot simply "work up into a mystery": even if his face does not appear "on every screen in the country," it is always visible and thus it is an open wound insofar as it is constantly exposed to possible repulsion and ridicule. Thus, although Bill's sexual 'wound' is psychologically based and therefore, at least theoretically, curable, Bill is probably wounded in a more "rotten way" than Jake but is nevertheless undaunted—which, he says, is the secret of his success—and therefore a good tutor for Hemingway's narrator. Bill's point, then, is not that "Every woman ought to be given a copy of this face as she leaves the altar": what Bill is driving home to his friend is that it is *Jake*, destined never to leave the altar, who needs Bill's picture—lest he suffer a relapse into the spiritual illness of self-pity. And when by forcing Jake to "rub . . . in" Bill's own problem ("No . . . I guess *you* don't PEDDLE it") Bill shows his acceptance of his own problem, i.e., when Bill shows that he is "hard-boiled" himself, he is performing the most important part of the psychotherapy which he administers to Jake. In fact, if Jake were carrying on him a picture of Bill's face, it would be like having a pill handy: in a sense, the "I just lay there" episode provides Jake with a picture of Bill—and not just a portrait but a full-length shot.

Bill's mode of psychotherapy is mostly based on jokes, but in order for it to be effective, the patient himself has to practice the joking modality; as I have shown, it is through a joke that Hemingway's narrator eventually exorcizes the source of his self-consciousness about his sexuality and about his religiosity. Yet I have also suggested that some of the jokes are defensive reactions on the part of the author; concluding my study of the tragicomedy ambiguously entitled *The Sun Also Rises*, I now would like to submit that Hemingway's creation of a foil for his physically crippled narrator, his creation of Bill Gorton, who is impotent from psychological causes but successful as a writer, was a special abreaction on the part of the author, hidden in the under-water portion of the iceberg.

It was the abreaction of a man who, in his mid-twenties, was beginning to blossom as a writer but was obsessed by fears of what might still happen to him—happen to him as a result of what had been a traumatic experience during his very young adulthood. As Benson notes in *Hemingway: The Writer's Art of Self-Defense*:

> We are familiar enough in a general way with Freud's discussion of the relation between wit and the unconscious to recognize as a truism the idea that what we joke about most often is what we really take most seriously. We also recognize as true the premise that for a male in our society laughter is a much more acceptable expression of emotion than tears. In his clinically orientated discussion *Beyond Laughter*, Martin Grotjahn states that "laughter is based on previously mastered anxiety" and that it "helps us to repeat the victory and in doing so to *overcome residual anxiety which is not quite assimilated*." ... Perhaps, since his humor is so often obsessively motivated, Hemingway's idea of what is funny is often too "dark" to be widely appealing. Jake Barnes' condition is on the one hand "tragic," but at the same time, particularly in connection with a [sexually eager woman], a condition that can be very funny. But perhaps it is the kind of joke that only a soldier with a soldier's anxieties can really laugh at. There is evidence that Hemingway's own wound involved a temporary cessation of his ability to have sex ... The resulting anxiety, along with the male role anxiety from his childhood, leads to a complex literary response in *The Sun Also Rises* which mixes both mockery and sadness. If the reader insists on tears alone, it is because he prefers sadness. (italics in the Grotjahn quotation are mine)[19]

I would suggest that especially the jokes involving Bill Gorton's psychologically based impotence[20] were an attempt on the author's part to overcome residual anxiety which had not quite been assimilated. In his interview with George Plimpton, before almost indignantly emphasizing that Jake's wound was physical and *not psychological*, Hemingway, when asked about the effects the traumatic shock may have had on his writing, would pointedly say that sometimes wounds give confidence, i.e., make one "un-daunted"—but *only sometimes*. While the sun, the subject in the final title of Hemingway's cock-and-bull story, *always* rises, something else may not, at least not always—for "Chaps never know anything, do they?"[21]

NOTES

1. Williams, p. 48. A small portion of this chapter first appeared in an article, "He 'Just Lay There': Bill Gorton as Wounded Preacher in *The Sun Also Rises*," *Wascana Review*, 23 (1988), 22–30.

2. Waldhorn, p. 107.

3. By "quasi-religious ceremony" I do not mean parody. I disagree with Reynolds' following observation on the Burguete episode, especially in light of the parallels which in the parenthesis he draws to Brett: "[Jake] and Bill drink their bottles of wine in a parody of religious celebration (just as Brett in her garlic necklace down cellar in Pamplona becomes a pagan alternative to true religious worship)" (*Twenties*, p. 66).

4. Stoneback, "Road to Roncevaux," p. 145.

5. Hinkle, p. 4.

6. It might also be pertinent to quote in full Balassi's observation concerning the Burguete episode: "Together, [Jake and Bill] show how to live the good life that the Count and Jake had talked about . . . *Bill is such an important character* that Hemingway twice tried to make him the first-person narrator, once in the Ledoux–Kid Francis fight, which is described in the manuscript, and *later at Burguete*" (p. 70, italics mine).

7. Stoneback, "'For Bryan's Sake'," p. 29.

8. Stoneback, "'For Bryan's Sake'," p. 29.

9. "From the rue Saint-Jacques," pp. 4 and 8, respectively. Stoneback notes:

> Even Carlos Baker, one of the few who is sound and true to the text on the question of Jake's Catholicism, inadvertently betrays the bias of the past six decades of criticism when he writes: "Without apology or explanation, Jake Barnes is a religious man" . . . But why should he apologize, pray tell? And to whom? The reader? Brett? Robert Cohn? *The critics*? (p. 24, italics mine)

Stoneback believes that Hemingway eventually chose the name Romero because *romero* means *pilgrim* (p. 28).

10. Hinkle, p. 36.

11. Cf. p. 176:
> "He looks like Villalta," Romero said, looking at Bill. "Rafael, doesn't he look like Villalta?"
> "I can't see it," the critic said.
> "Really," Romero *said in Spanish*. "He looks a lot like Villalta."
(italics added).

Why would Hemingway emphasize the fact that Romero makes his comparison of Bill's appearance to Villalta's in Spanish? The idea is that Romero does not want to be understood by Bill—because the historical Nicanor Villalta was spectacularly ugly, as Hemingway would on numerous occasions elaborate in *Death in the Afternoon*. Hemingway admired Villalta for coming to terms with his problem and becoming a brilliant bullfighter, and he expressed his admiration by naming his son John Hadley Nicanor. And the primary model for Bill, who has a "long upper lip," Don Stewart, had an abnormally long neck and a long upper lip, which not only earned him the nickname "Duck Lip" but also made him timid, especially with girls. (For the biographical information in this footnote I am indebted to Professor Hinkle, who kindly provided me with a copy of his Madrid Conference paper, "What's Wrong with Bill Gorton in *The Sun Also Rises*?", and gave me permission to cite material from it).

12. Stallman, p. 175.

13. For the point about earlier tricycles having had a joystick of sorts rather than handlebars and pedals, I am indebted to Professor Hinkle.

14. Bill's "Let's lay off that" indicates that Bill feels he has made his point and thinks it is time to talk about other things. In his 'Education of Jacob Barnes,' "this Brett business" and religion are his next targets.

15. After pointing out that "The Spanish word 'huevos' is literally translated 'eggs' but also carries a vulgar meaning of 'cojones' or their equivalents," Linebarger, "Eggs as Huevos in *The Sun Also Rises*," *Fitzgerald/Hemingway Annual* 1970, 237–38, observes that on the last day of the festival Jake, Bill, and Belmonte eat eggs together and comments:

> All three of these men need to eat eggs, symbolically to replace their own 'huevos': Jake lost his during the war; Belmonte, during the afternoon's bullfights, demonstrates his lack of masculinity (pp. 222–223); and Bill Gorton, although not noticeably unmasculine, still is the only major male character (except of course for Jake) who does not manage to end up in bed with Brett Ashley. Since the Circean Lady Brett delights in symbolically castrating her lovers, it may be that she is not attracted to Bill because of an inherent lack of maleness in him that she senses. Some such indication of lack of symbolic *cojones* may be inferred from the fishing scene, when [during their chicken–egg argument] Jake tells Bill "Eat an egg."

I disagree with Linebarger's interpretation that Brett is not sexually interested in Bill, but I find the comment on Jake's "Eat an egg" thought-provoking; in a Biblically cloaked discussion of women, Jake is simply repeating (on p. 122) what he had said on p. 116: "No . . . I guess *you* don't PEDDLE it." In fact, if Jake knows that in some countries (e.g., in Germany and Scandinavia) eggs are believed to increase the male's potency, he is telling Bill what he should do to be able to enjoy the "chicken." I first made the preceding points about Bill being impotent in the *Wascana Review* article listed in n. 1 above, where I elaborate on associations radiating from the "you don't pedal it" joke, in the process disposing of the not infrequently heard interpretation that Bill is homosexual.

16. Gajdusek, p. 29.

17. In his presentation of Bill Gorton as impotent, Hemingway may actually be reshaping a real-life event involving an impotent man named Bill, although the primary model was the humorist Don Stewart (cf. n. 11 above). Meyers reports:

Hemingway's oldest friend, Bill Smith, who had recently recovered from a nervous breakdown, . . . announced his arrival in Paris in April 1925. Hemingway later explained Bill [Smith's] problems in a letter to Buck Lanham [in 1948]: After serving in Marine Aviation during the Great War, Bill fell in love with a girl. She was married, and he had no sexual experience. He naturally became very excited and was impotent during their first time in bed. Instead of performing a small kindness, the girl gave him the works, ruined him and sent him into manic depression. When he came out of the hospital, Hemingway invited him to Europe and tried to help him. (pp. 154–55)

If the Bill Smith who presumably "just lay there" was indeed in Hemingway's mind, then the author has reversed the roles: the Hemingway wishing to help the manic-depressive Bill Smith becomes the sexually incapacitated and depressive Jake, whereas Bill Smith is conflated with the humorist Don Stewart into the humorous Bill Gorton. However, in 1950, when asked about his models for the novel, Hemingway told Hotchner: "Bill Smith, who was an awfully good guy I used to fish with, was pretty much Bill Gorton" (Hotchner, p. 48). Bill Smith *is* in the novel if we can trust Hemingway's statement to Frances' model, Kitty. Baker, *Life Story*, p. 154, writes about a walk Hemingway and Kitty took in September of 1925, where the author gestured toward Bill Smith as well as Harold Loeb, announcing that he would include them in his novel and tear them apart. Did Hemingway tear Bill Smith apart by reproducing his sexual disability in the narrator's best friend, in a man "so big"—i.e., a man of Hemingway's own physical stature? If that is the case, it could be an abreaction of impotency fears on the part of the author. See the concluding paragraph and the final footnote of this study.

18. Lewis, p. 28.

19. Benson, pp. 56–57. I substituted the bracketed phrase ["sexually eager woman"] for Benson's "nymphomaniac" because, as I have discussed, that term seems unwarranted.

20. I discuss several jokes involving Bill's impotence in the sixth *Alchemy* chapter, relating some of them to what, in the long passage I quoted, Benson calls "the male role of anxiety from [Hemingway's] childhood."

21. It is ironic that shortly after the composition of his novel Hemingway was unable to get an erection—for *psychological* reasons. It happened during his honeymoon with Pauline in Grau-de-Roi. Meyers reports:

In Grau, he experienced the first of several periods of impotence, which were usually associated with new wives. In this case, as Hemingway realized, the reasons were more psychological than physical. He still felt guilty about betraying Hadley and feared that he was now trapped in another marriage: "Don't know if it was autosuggestion from *The Sun Also Rises* or maybe reaction to having just divorced Hadley, but . . . I couldn't make love. Had had very good bed with Pauline during all the time we were having our affair, and after Hadley left me, but after our marriage, suddenly I could no more make love than Jake Barnes." (pp. 194–95)

Considering that Jake's handicap was physical rather than psychological, it is interesting to note not only that Hemingway should compare himself to Jake but also that he should speak of autosuggestion from a novel which he had written "from a personal experience in that when [he] had been wounded at one time there had been an infection from pieces of wool driven into the scrotum [because of which he] wondered what a man's life would have been like after that if his penis had been lost and his testicles and spermatic cord remained intact . . . [so he] tried to find out what his problem would be when he was in love with someone who was in love with him and there was nothing they could do about it" (cf. Chapter I, n. 4). That Hemingway would even *think*, however jokingly, of autosuggestion from a story which he himself had created in response to his war injury invites the suspicion that his impotency with Pauline was a result of the trauma—and that once the trauma had affected him with a new wife it would repeat itself with other new wives, almost in a self-fulfilling prophecy. In a sense, as a result of the occurrence of impotency after the composition of *The Sun Also Rises* Hemingway unconsciously came to identify himself with the character he had created. He became a Jake whose prayer was miraculously answered, for when nothing worked Pauline, "a very religious Catholic," asked him to pray:

> There was a small church two blocks from us and I went there and said a short prayer. Then I went back to our room. Pauline was in bed, waiting. I undressed and got in bed and we made love like we invented it. We never had any trouble again. That's when I became a Catholic. (Hotchner, p. 51)

"Chaps never know anything, do they?"

PAUL CIVELLO

The Sun Also Rises: *Learning to Live in a Naturalistic World*

Even though *The Sun Also Rises* is an earlier novel than *A Farewell to Arms*, its protagonist finds himself in the same predicament at the beginning of that novel as Frederic Henry does at the end of the later work. Like Frederic Henry after the death of Catherine, Jake Barnes must find a way to live in a world in which there are no absolutes, must create a personal order that is neither based on an abstraction nor belied by experience. To this end, he learns to create a personal order within natural, temporal cycles—a means by which he can "live in it," as he says—rather than an order "above" and "beyond" those cycles as we saw in the case of Frederic and Catherine. Jake's personal order is thus grounded in his experience with the natural world. By asserting his consciousness in the face of natural forces, Jake gives meaning and justification to his existence. It is a "modern" response that, unlike Frederic and Catherine's, proves efficacious in reconciling the self to a naturalistic world.

As in *A Farewell to Arms*, Christianity has become obsolete in the postwar world of *The Sun Also Rises*. It no longer "works," no longer provides a moral and spiritual order in which the self can feel "at home." And although Jake, like Frederic Henry, yearns nostalgically for that absolute Christian order, for the comfort and solace that it had formerly provided, he nevertheless finds himself banished from it by his own modern sensi-

From *American Literary Naturalism and Its Twentieth-Century Transformations: Frank Norris, Ernest Hemingway, Don DeLillo*, pp. 92–111, 179–80. Copyright © 1994 by the University of Georgia Press.

65

bility. Jake is a Catholic, but, he laments, a "rotten Catholic."[1] Again, the word "rotten," just as it is used in reference to the priest's experience in the war in *A Farewell to Arms*, here too suggests decay and dissolution; in the case of Jake's Catholicism, it connotes the demise of faith through Jake's experiences in a naturalistic world that moves ineluctably toward the ultimate rot and decay of death. Catholicism for Jake, whether he is willing to admit it to himself or not, has become an empty abstraction that no longer accords with his own experience in the world. He tries to pray in the cathedral in Pamplona, yet his prayers remain distinctly earthbound: he prays for good bullfights, for good fishing, even for that root of all evil, money. To paraphrase Emerson, Jake's "praying" is more akin to begging, for there is no spiritual vision informing his prayers. He begins to sense this, for after a long passage in which he describes himself as praying, he switches to describing himself as "thinking of myself as praying" (97). Prayer itself has become alien to Jake's experience; he is reduced to vague nostalgia: "I only wished I felt religious" (97).

The fiesta of San Fermin also illustrates the demise of Christianity and Christian order. Jake tells us that "San Fermin is also a religious festival" (153), but this casual, offhand remark—made after describing the peasants drinking in the wine-shops and "shifting" their values for the fiesta—is indicative of the place to which Christianity has been relegated in the festival: to a nominal or, at best, ancillary role. It may "also" be a religious festival, but it is primarily a pagan ritual devoid of any Christian spirituality. The Dionysian continually overshadows the Christian in Pamplona: drunken revelers obscure the religious procession as it makes its way through the streets; *riau-riau* dancers and various grotesques—"great giants, cigar-store Indians, thirty feet high, Moors, a King and Queen" (155)—enclose the procession, dwarfing and parodying the religious icon of San Fermin; and after the procession disappears into a church, the revelers discover a new icon to worship—Brett Ashley, who, ironically, had just been denied entrance to the church for not wearing a hat. Brett, who, as we shall see in a moment, is a "natural" woman—that is, a woman whose unrestrained sexuality is emblematic of natural, biological forces—is transformed into a pagan ordering principle: she becomes "an image to dance around" (155). Even Jake and Bill Gorton are swept into the dance, the entire scene suggesting the moral inversion—the overturning of absolute values—that characterizes the fiesta. Shortly thereafter, the Christian aspect of the fiesta fades entirely; when the religious procession passes outside the wine-shop where the revelers are drinking, one of them responds to Mike Campbell's question—"Isn't that the procession?"—with "Nada. . . . It's nothing" (158). Indeed, for all the significance with which it now imbues the fiesta, Christianity itself has dwindled to nothing.

Yet this scene also points toward an alternative to the Christian moral and spiritual order—namely, a secular order imposed by the human consciousness in which natural force is celebrated and camaraderie, particularly male camaraderie, is exalted. Values may be overturned during the fiesta, but new values are established. And these new values are shown to be "truer" to one's experience in the world, generated as they are by that experience rather than by an antiquated creed. The wine-shop takes on connotations of a "new" church; in a parallel image, Jake describes it as a dark place just as he had earlier described the cathedral, yet a celebratory rather than solemn dark place in which people sing rather than pray. Brett replaces the Virgin as the central icon, her sexuality neither a sin nor a source of discord and strife but a source of order and power. She represents the natural life force, a pagan goddess of nature in stark contrast to the "unnatural" image of immaculate motherhood embodied in the Virgin. Money, something Jake had earlier prayed for in the cathedral and that, since the start of the fiesta, has lost its "definite value in hours worked and bushels of grain sold" (152), needs no value here; it is not really necessary, for it is subsumed to the value of human companionship.[2] When Jake tries to pay for his wine, someone puts his money back in his pocket. Jake then passes around his wine-bag, and in a type of secular communion, everyone drinks from it. And finally, in contrast to the Catholics on the train to Bayonne who preempt the dining car and thereby deny food to the other passengers, the peasants in the wine-shop show a true spirit of brotherhood by sharing their food with the expatriates. Jake tells a peasant who hands him a fork, "I don't want to eat up your meal," to which the peasant replies, "Eat, . . . What do you think it's here for?" (157).

We see a similar instance of male camaraderie in the fishing scene at Burguete, and once again such an elemental celebration of life is put forth as a replacement to the obsolete Christian order.[3] Jake and Bill parody organized religion while eating and drinking beside the Irati River:

> "Let us rejoice in our blessings. Let us utilize the fowls of the air. Let us utilize the product of the vine. Will you utilize a little, brother?"
> "After you, brother." (122)

Yet their parody is certainly truer to the original acts of the Apostles than, say, the acts of the Catholics on the train to Bayonne. Again, it is performed in a true spirit of brotherhood, and it envelopes nature in its celebration. "Let no man be ashamed to kneel here in the great out-of-doors," Bill says. "Remember the woods were God's first temples" (122). Later, Jake and Bill, with the Englishman Harris, go through the monastery of Roncesvalles.

The contrast between the monastery and "God's first temples" is made patent when Bill asks Harris, "It [the monastery] isn't the same as fishing, though, is it?" and Harris responds, "I say not" (128). They then "utilize" a nearby pub, the pub like the wine-shop a place of secular celebration. Again, money has no value: Harris will not let the others pay for the wine, and the innkeeper will not even take Harris's money. (Before going fishing for the first time, Bill had asked Jake jokingly, but significantly, if when he was digging for worms he was really "burying" his money, indicating its valuelessness in the country.) In the face of an indifferent universe, Jake, Bill, and Harris assert their common humanity that gives their existence in that universe genuine value. Harris even tells the other two that they "don't know how much it *means*" (129, my emphasis) to him to have had their companionship. His gift to them when they depart—trout flies he himself has tied—is a gift from one human to another two whose worth transcends monetary value.

Even Jake and Brett find a peace and a genuine companionship in a bar that they are denied in a church. Their experience in the cathedral in Pamplona, an experience in which their praying "had not been much of a success," ends with Brett saying, "Let's get out of here. Makes me damned nervous" (208). Yet, at the end of the novel, they come to a quiet understanding in the bar of the Palace Hotel in Madrid. It is a "clean, well-lighted place," a humanly ordered oasis that confronts and withholds the summer heat just outside the window. Like the café in "A Clean, Well-Lighted Place," this bar of "wonderful gentility" (244) enables Jake and Brett to uphold their dignity and, in doing so, acts as a stave against the impinging forces of the world outside.

This becomes a recurring theme in Hemingway's work: the need for the individual to maintain his dignity and integrity in the face of powerful forces. He must create his own order—his own meaning and justification for existence—that preserves his dignity and integrity *within* a world of material force. This order may be metaphorically described as a clean, well-lighted place, as an island in the stream, as a trout holding himself steady in the current with wavering fins, or as a work of art that endures through changing literary fashions, but it always suggests stability within change. And it is this stability within change that Jake must learn to provide for himself in the course of the novel.

As in *A Farewell to Arms*, the universe in *The Sun Also Rises* is depicted as one of constant flux. With the collapse of the Christian conception of an ordered universe, natural processes are no longer conceived as moving toward a teleological goal; rather, they become indifferent material forces operating in repetitive cycles. We remember that the central metaphor in *A Farewell to*

Arms was of a car stuck in the mud, its wheels spinning but going nowhere, leaving humanity trapped. We see similar metaphors in *The Sun Also Rises*. The epigraph from Ecclesiastes introduces us to such a world: it describes a universe of cyclical process—ironically, a universe that in the context of the novel is devoid of a transcendent principle which could give that material process meaning. The earth, the "hero" of the novel as Hemingway explained in a letter to Maxwell Perkins, can do no more than "abideth forever."[4] To abideth, to endure with patience and fortitude, maintaining stability within change, is all that the individual can do if he too is to become a "hero." The heroic self, in other words, must imbue the inherently meaningless, cyclical universe with meaning through his stoic endurance of its often destructive processes.

Death, of course, is the ultimate destruction, and as we saw in *A Farewell to Arms*, the dust that powders the leaves of the trees connotes its natural occurrence. Similarly, the revolving wheels of the car that takes Jake and Bill from Pamplona to Burguete churn up dust—"dust rose under the wheels" (105)—the image again suggesting natural, cyclical process leading ineluctably toward death. Dust, in fact, is everywhere in Spain, an elemental land more closely tied to the earth in Hemingway's imagination than France. It is a "white dusty road into Spain" (93), "dust powdering the trees" (104). The porter in the hotel in Pamplona brushes the dust off Jake's shoulders and collar, making a point that he could tell Jake was traveling in a motor car—that vehicle of aimless, circuitous movement in the novel—"from the way the dust was" (96). And after driving from Spain to Bayonne after the fiesta, Jake significantly rubs his fishing rod-case through the dust that covers the car, telling us that "it seemed the last thing that connected me with Spain and the fiesta" (232). Indeed, as we shall see, sexuality (intimated here by Jake's phallic rod-case) and the fiesta are both closely linked to cyclical natural processes of which death, of course, is a part and in which Jake must learn to live.

The structure of the novel also suggests a universe of cyclical process devoid of any meaning other than that which the self may give it. As Richard Lehan has pointed out, the action of the novel begins and ends with Jake and Brett in a taxi, first in Paris and then in Madrid.[5] Their movement through these two cities is also circular and aimless: "tell him [the taxi driver] to drive *around*" (24, my emphasis), Brett tells Jake in Paris. And, of course, Jake and the expatriates move aimlessly from place to place and back in the course of the novel; Jake even sleeps alone in the same room in Bayonne at the end of the novel as he did with Cohn and Bill toward the beginning.

In an echo of the epigraph from Ecclesiastes, Jake tells us early in the novel that "I had the feeling of going through something that has all happened before. . . . I had the feeling as in a nightmare of it all being something repeated, something I had been through and that now I must go through again" (64). He is referring to his futile relationship with Brett, who has just told him "I'm so miserable" (a sentiment she will repeat throughout the novel). The futility of their relationship is of course due to Jake's inability to consummate it; as in *A Farewell to Arms*, sexuality is depicted as the motive force behind natural process. "It always gets to be" *that* (i.e., sex), Jake tells Brett (26); it always comes back *around* to it.

As suggested earlier, Brett is the "natural" woman in the novel, the woman who "can't help" (183) her sexual promiscuity.[6] "It's the way I'm made" (55), she tells Jake. She often refers to herself as a "bitch," a term that connects her to natural animal sexuality and that is in stark contrast to the unnatural "stuffed dogs" to which Bill refers at one point. Just as Frederic Henry's sexuality had trapped him within the "whirling" rooms of the brothels—that is, within the whirling cycle of natural process—so too does Brett's sexuality trap her "biologically," pushing her from man to man in an aimless circuit. She is the woman who never finishes sentences, according to Count Mippipopolous, nor does she finish anything else. She is constantly *in the process*; even her oft-repeated expression "rot" suggests a connection with natural process and its ineluctable progression toward decay.

As a pagan ritual, the fiesta is also closely connected to nature and natural process.[7] It is an annual occurrence, a festival that recurs with the seasons. Like the "nightmare" of Jake and Brett's repetitive relationship, it too is, in Bill's words, a "wonderful nightmare" (222). And just as in natural process, there are no values inherent in the fiesta other than those human beings give it. We immediately see that the fiesta requires a "shifting in values" (152), and that any preconceived or established values—"definite value" (152)—are overturned. Monetary value is shown to lie outside of "hours worked" and "bushels of grain sold" (152)—that is, outside *things*. Again, value or "meaning" is not intrinsic. It is imposed from without by humans: the prices of food, drink, and lodging are doubled for the fiesta. For some, even human life is devalued; there seems to be no great concern for the man killed during the running of the bulls. When Jake tells Bill of the death, Bill says indifferently, "Was there?" (204). Only a waiter—a man who seems to have a rigid set of values, values most likely derived from the established Christian belief in the sanctity of human life—is shocked. He sees no sense in a death "all for sport. All for pleasure" (197). And the value Pedro Romero places in killing the bull who had killed the man, and in giving its ear as a gift to Brett, is lost on Brett. She leaves the ear in the back of a drawer, along with several cigarette butts, at the Hotel Montoya.

In *A Farewell to Arms* Hemingway connects sexuality, war, and the "whirling" life of the city through the symbol of the rain: all are facets of natural force. The fiesta too, in addition to being repetitive, intrinsically value-less, and "whirling," is connected to those forces beyond one's control by its association in Jake's mind with the war. At a dinner during the fiesta with the expatriates shortly after some verbal fisticuffs between Mike and Cohn, Jake makes an explicit comparison:

> It was like certain dinners I remember from the war. There was much wine, an ignored tension, and a feeling of things coming that you could not prevent happening. Under the wine I lost the disgusted feeling and was happy. It seemed they were all such nice people. (146)

As in the war, Jake realizes that there are violent forces operating which he cannot forestall, only endure. There are other connections, too. Jake tells us that when the fiesta began, it "exploded." "There is," he says, "no other way to describe it" (152). He then compares the explosion of the rocket that signals the start of the fiesta to a "shrapnel burst" (153). Later, in describing the disastrous fireworks performance of Don Manuel Orquito, the "fireworks king," we sense a subtle, subconscious recognition of his wartime experience. Don Manuel sends up "fire balloons" as a military band plays; yet the fireworks, like the war itself, spin out of control, falling into the crowd and exploding. In what must be an allusion to Jake's particular wound, the fireworks, we are told, "charged and chased, sputtering and cracking, *between the legs* of the people" (179, my emphasis).

This sense of forces out of control, of process in repetitious cycles, is reproduced in another image that is also found in *A Farewell to Arms*. We remember Frederic Henry's experience in the "whirling" rooms of the brothels, his libidinal drives connecting him to nature's wheel. In *The Sun Also Rises*, just before the start of the fiesta, Jake experiences the same drunken sensation of a room going "round and round" (147). Later, toward the end of the fiesta, Jake must look at "some fixed point" (223) to make the room stop whirling. As does Frederic in the brothels, Jake in this instance finds only a blank wall on which to improvise a "fixed point." Outside, the fiesta too continues "going on," but, Jake remarks significantly, "it did not mean anything" (224).

It is in the midst of this whirling world that Jake must find some form of stability. And his ability to do so, an ability he develops as he goes through experience in the course of the novel, is a marked departure from the fate of characters in most works of nineteenth-century literary naturalism. Vandover, we remember, is crushed beneath the "iron wheels" of nature, his attempts at avoiding such a fate little more than "instinctual" reactions to circumstance. He never gains an awareness of his predicament great enough to enable him to create an order to fill the void left by the collapse of former ordering principles. In *The Octopus*, a much different naturalistic novel than *Vandover*, the source of order is ultimately discovered within nature itself, although this discovery does little to prevent the death and destruction produced by the Railroad. In Hemingway's work, we see a naturalistic world much like that found in *Vandover* (yet cyclical, rather than linear), a world in which there is no meaning immanent in natural process. Yet experience is not lost on the Hemingway protagonist; he gains an awareness as he goes through it, and it is this experience, in the form of consciousness, that he asserts in response to meaningless natural force. He can, in other words, create his own order, his own meaning, yet one that must be grounded in his experience—a fact that separates Jake Barnes from Frederic Henry. After all, it is only at the end of *A Farewell to Arms* that Frederic realizes that an abstract order—that is, any order not grounded in one's experience with the natural world—is doomed to failure. Jake, on the other hand, develops this awareness throughout *The Sun Also Rises*. He gradually moves away from Robert Cohn's form of sentimentality and romanticism and toward the personal and aesthetic order embodied by Pedro Romero, ultimately using the latter as a model on which to base his own personal order.

Robert Cohn is a character whose conception of the world has been formed by books, particularly romances.[8] It is thus a conception divorced from his own experience, a conception that implies there is an order external to the self, and it has the effect of preventing him from ever learning directly from life. He insists that life conform to his unrealistic conception. One of the first things we learn about Cohn is that "he read too much" (3). And the one book we learn that he has read, and that Jake claims was a major influence on him, is W. H. Hudson's *The Purple Land*. As its title might suggest, *The Purple Land* is a romance, accurately described by Jake as a book that "recounts splendid imaginary amorous adventures of a perfect English gentleman in an intensely romantic land" (9). Cohn obviously conceives of himself as such a perfect gentleman and believes that life holds out the possibility of such amorous adventures. He even goes to the absurd length of asking Jake to travel with him to South America, the setting of *The Purple Land*. When Jake tells him, "You can see all the South Americans you want in Paris," Cohn replies, "They're not the real South Americans" (9). Cohn is clearly confused about the nature of reality.

His view of women and love is likewise derived from romances. Cohn has an idealized view of love, one that never conforms to his own relationships. He had thought that it would be too cruel to leave his first wife, and then she subsequently leaves him. He is "sure" that he loves Frances, his current girlfriend, yet she treats him like something less than a lover. He is then sure that he loves Brett—or as he pompously tells Jake, "I shouldn't wonder if I were in love with her" (38)—even though he has only just met her and really knows nothing about her. Jake, undercutting Cohn's romanticism, tells us that "I am sure he had never been in love in his life" (8).

It is Cohn's idealistic view of Brett that is the most absurd. He conceives of her as one of the "ladies" in a romance, and of their brief and meaningless affair as an "amorous adventure" of the ages. His first address to Brett at the Bal Musette could be a line of dialog right out of *The Purple Land*: "Will you dance with me, Lady Brett?" (23). He later comments to Jake about Brett's qualities of "fineness" and "breeding"—qualities we see Brett distinctly lacks—and refuses to believe the "facts" Jake tells him about Brett and her life, preferring his own idealized conception of her. He even becomes ludicrously offended by Jake's knowledge: "I didn't ask you to insult her" (39), he says.

Cohn never does see that Brett is nothing like a lady in a romance. And Jake's descriptions of Cohn's behavior after his affair with Brett ridicule Cohn's romantic delusions. Jake mocks Cohn's "affair with a lady of title" (178), laughs at Cohn's readiness "to do battle for his lady love" (178) with Mike. Cohn remains with Brett in Pamplona, Jake tells us, because Cohn believes "love would conquer all" (199). Bill, too, laughs at Cohn's misguided chivalry in beating up Romero and in wanting to take Brett away with him "to make an honest woman out of her" (201). As if it were right out of a romance, Bill comments, "Damned touching scene" (201).

The direct experience of life, apart from books, escapes Cohn. He misses those moments of genuine value such as the fishing in Burguete and the revelry in the wine-shop. His delusions regarding Brett and their relationship keep him from the former, and he passes out during the latter. He even fails to appreciate the beauty of the Spanish land—a beauty both Jake and Bill acknowledge—falling asleep in the car on the road to Pamplona.

Yet Jake has much in common with Cohn, especially at the beginning of the novel. Both are outsiders: Cohn is a Jew among Gentiles, and Jake is a de-phallused man in a world that exalts virile manhood. Even Jake's name—a contraction of Jacob—connects him with the Jewish Cohn. There are other subtle connections deliberately placed throughout the novel. Cohn saves Jake a place on the bus to Burguete; Jake too falls asleep during the fiesta when everyone else continues to carouse; Jake falls asleep on Cohn's bed and wears his jacket. But, of course, the central connection between the two, the connection that all the others reinforce, is their shared romantic idealism.[9] Jake, too, reads too much, and his reading colors his apprehension of experience. He dislikes riding down the Boulevard Raspail in Paris because, he supposes, "I had read something about it once" (42). He goes on to say that "that was the way Cohn was about all of Paris" (42). Jake, like Cohn, also reads romances, as we see him do alongside the Irati River. Jake takes a break from fishing by reading a book by A. E. W. Mason containing a love story as ludicrous as those in *The Purple Land*. And Jake's relationship with Brett, at least until the end of the novel, is marked by sentimentality. He too idealizes her, crying over her even though he comes to realize that she is not worth the emotion. He also futilely follows her around as does Cohn.

Such romantic idealization threatens to destroy Jake emotionally, as it certainly does destroy Cohn. The imposition of a preconceived order on experience is doomed to failure in an implacable world of force, just as Frederic Henry's idealization of love is doomed in *A Farewell to Arms*. Jake must learn to move away from such romantic notions if he is to become "hard-boiled" (34). (Note how the term "hard-boiled" connotes arrested natural process, the creating of stability within flux.) Jake gradually abandons the belief in and the search for absolutes and settles for an approach to life that can give it a personal meaning—a genuine meaning because it is one derived from experience in the world. He succinctly sums up his slowly acquired philosophy when he says, "I did not care what it was all about. All I wanted to know was how to live in it" (148).

As do other protagonists in Hemingway's work, Jake learns to acquire a philosophy of life by observing and emulating another character who lives by it. Such a mentor for Frederic Henry in *A Farewell to Arms* is Count Greffi. In *The Sun Also Rises*, Jake learns from two mentors: Count Mippipopolous and Pedro Romero. The Count is a man who has "been around very much" (59); he has lived in the whirling world and, like Jake, has been wounded by his experience in it. His wound, or more precisely, the confrontation with death that it evinces, has made him appreciate life. As he says, "it is because I have lived very much that now I can enjoy everything so well" (60). He knows how to "get his money's worth out of life," a metaphor that Jake will reiterate when he meditates on learning "to live in it." The Count has already learned to live in it. He has gotten to "know the values" (60), values that are not decreed and absolute but that are self-discovered, grounded in his experience. He is not interested in titles—unlike Brett, who, in her own words, has had "hell's own amount of credit" (57) on hers—for he sees no intrinsic value in them. (Note the play on "credit.") They have no value unless the titled person's life and character give them value, something we see little of among the titled characters in the novel. Avoiding socially decreed values, the Count prefers the quiet of a restaurant in the Bois (another clean, well-lighted place) in order to drink and socialize with Jake and Brett to the smoke and noise of Zelli's in Montmartre, a place much like the city cafés Frederic Henry visits in *A Farewell to Arms*. The Count also embraces those values we have already examined: camaraderie and the celebration of life.

The Count, however, leads a retired life, a life Jake's financial situation, at least, prevents him from emulating. He finds a model for the active life, though, in Pedro Romero. Romero's bullfight becomes a visual metaphor for the way to "live in it": the self alone, confronting natural force with courage, grace, and dignity. The bull, of course, is the natural force, its blackness suggestive of the darkness of death it embodies. The bullfighter, like everyone, is up against that force, up against death, and the way in which he conducts himself in the face of it is all that gives the experience meaning. Natural force, then, becomes something more than the destructive process it had been, for example, in *Vandover*, it becomes a necessary component in one's self-definition, a necessary condition for imbuing life with meaning. It becomes, in other words, a means of transcending its own meaninglessness.

Yet, again, it is the individual himself who must effect that transcendence, who must create meaning through the integrity of his actions. In an era of decadent bullfighting, Romero has, in Jake's words, "the old thing" (168). His courage is evident to all but the Biarritz crowd. He does not needlessly wind the bull during his cape-work; he works closely to the bull and its horns; he does not counterfeit the danger and the emotion it produces; he doesn't quail when confronted with a difficult near-sighted bull. Romero's courage is contrasted with that of the aging Belmonte, a matador who once possessed courage but who has, with age and pain, lost it. Belmonte now handpicks his bulls, choosing small bulls with small horns in order to lessen the danger to himself. As a result, bullfighting—and, it is implied, life itself—no longer holds any meaning for him. "Things were not the same" for Belmonte, Jake tells us, "and now life only came in flashes" (215). Even these flashes, these moments of his former greatness in the bullring, "were not of value because he had discounted them in advance" (215) by choosing bulls for safety. Again, we note the recurrent monetary metaphor, here again indicating that meaning, that "value," is not something intrinsic in things but something one bestows on them, something one creates for oneself.

In addition to courage, Romero demonstrates grace in the bullring. Everything he does is "straight and pure and natural in line" (167). There are no brusque movements, no contortions. He maintains "his purity of line through the maximum of exposure" (168), a quality that has become popularly known as "grace under pressure." In the face of brute force, Romero remains in control. Nor does he kill like the "butcher-boys" Hemingway describes in *Death in the Afternoon*, those practitioners of decadent bull-fighting, but rather "like a priest at benediction"—that is, with a grace that confers dignity on the bull as well as on himself.[10]

Dignity, of course, is that other all-important element that the bull-fighter must preserve. The decadent bullfighters have no dignity. By choosing the bulls for safety, by counterfeiting the danger, by using tricks rather than skill, by turning the aesthetic performance of the bullfight into a tawdry spectacle, they rob themselves, the bull, and the audience of the dignity that can give meaning to both life and death. Romero, however, does none of those things. His bullfight is an aesthetic performance that does not pander to the cheapest emotions of the audience. He ignores the Biarritz crowd, the English philistine tourists who know nothing about bullfighting but pretend to. Rather, Romero does it "all for himself inside" (216), and in that way he does it for Brett and for those in the audience who can appreciate the well-executed *corrida*. But, Jake emphasizes, he does not do it for others "at any loss to himself" (216). Bullfighting is Romero's craft, his *metier*, and it is an intensely personal *metier*. Regardless of its vicarious effect on the audience, bullfighting is above all else Romero's means of creating an order for himself, a means of defining himself and maintaining his human dignity in a naturalistic world that *by nature* undermines it. When bullfighting, Romero is always alone. Even in preparation for the bullfight at the Hotel Montoya, Romero is "altogether by himself" and "far away and dignified" (163). The electric light that illuminates him and sets him off from the surrounding darkness—an image recapitulated in "A Clean, Well-Lighted Place"—suggests a personal illumination, a man-made order that holds off the impinging void.

It is important to note that outside the ordered medium of the bullfight, Romero is as flawed as any man and as susceptible to the whirling world.[11] This is Montoya's fear: that the young matador will fall among those who do not know what he is "worth" and who do not know what he "means" (172), particularly among women such as Brett. Indeed, Brett—the embodiment of sexuality and therefore of natural, biological force—pulls Romero into this whirling world, and it almost destroys him. Cohn's physical assault, brought about by sexual jealousy and romantic delusions, epitomizes the chaotic, orderless world outside the bullring. It is only through a return to the bullring, a return to his personal order, that Romero can "wipe out" Cohn. The bullfight, in other words, acts as a form of redemption: a personal redemption, man redeeming himself. With each well-executed *faena*, Romero purges the loss of dignity he suffered at the hands of Cohn. With each pass of the bull, he "wiped that out a little cleaner" (219).

As mentioned, Jake gradually moves away from Cohn's disastrous romanticism and toward the personal order embodied by Romero. The big break with Cohn comes when Jake panders Brett to Romero. Several critics have commented that by this act Jake gives the woman he loves but can never possess to the man whom he would like to be; but he also makes a break with the false chivalric code that, up to this point, he has shared with Cohn. It is a conscious break: "It was understood all right" (187), Jake says of the act. Shortly after this, Cohn knocks Jake out, and significantly enough, when Jake regains consciousness, "everything looked new and changed" (192). Cohn's punch brings about an epiphany. "It was all different," he says. "It was all new" (192).

Of course, just as Whitman's protégé cannot travel his own road by traveling that of his mentor, neither can Jake create his own personal order by imitating Romero. Rather obviously, Jake can never be a bullfighter, nor does he aspire to be one. He must create an order that is unique to his own personality, talent, and experience—one that nevertheless confronts the world with the same courage, grace, and dignity with which Romero confronts the bull. It is only in this way that he can bring meaning and stability to life. Yet, through parallel imagery—a device Hemingway employs quite often in his work, such as in the connections he draws between Jake and Cohn—Hemingway links Jake and Romero quite closely. After the conclusion of the fiesta, Jake travels to San Sebastian. Significantly enough, he travels alone, the first time he does so in the novel. Moreover, unlike when he would be alone in his apartment in Paris, Jake never dwells on or even thinks about Brett, their relationship, or his wound. Instead, he carefully and deliberately goes through a private ritual that prevents him from thinking about those things and that recalls Romero's private ritual before the bullfight. He pays close attention to each detail, each seemingly insignificant act:

> After lunch I went up to my room, read a while, and went to sleep. When I woke it was half past four. I found my swimming-suit, wrapped it with a comb in a towel, and went down-stairs and walked up the street to the Concha. The tide was about half-way out. The beach was smooth and firm, and the sand yellow. I went into a bathing-cabin, undressed, put on my suit, and walked across the smooth sand to the sea. The sand was warm under bare feet. (234)

Jake awakes in the late afternoon, the time of the bullfights in Spain (cf., the title of Hemingway's book on the bullfight, *Death in the Afternoon*). The bay of San Sebastian—the Concha, or "scallop-shell"—is a nearly enclosed, circular bay here reminiscent of the bullring. And the beach with its smooth and yellow sand likewise recalls the sand of the bullring, which Jake had earlier described as "smooth-rolled and yellow" (211). Jake then ventures out into the sea; again, the self alone confronting nature. He is attentive to the aesthetics of his dives, diving "cleanly and deeply" (238), just as Romero plays and kills the bull.

The parallel imagery here is neither gratuitous nor overwrought; not only does it connect Jake to Romero, but it also shows Jake emulating the implicit philosophy of Romero's art—that is, ordering his life through the deliberateness, gracefulness, and dignity of his actions. Jake has learned to "live in it." He can now bear the solitude; in fact, he even enjoys it, for. it keeps him safely ensconced within his own stoic order, holding off the whirling world outside. "I was through with fiestas for a while" (232), he says. He now finds company in a bottle of wine, the slow and deliberate enjoyment of it providing an island of repose amid the flux, in sharp contrast to the unbridled drinking during the fiesta. In addition, when he rejects the liqueur a waiter recommends to him—"the veritable flowers of the Pyrenees," the waiter had called it (233)—he is rejecting any preconceived or ordained "truth" in favor of his own experience of it. The waiter may call it what he will, but to Jake, who tastes it, it "looked like hair oil and smelled like Italian *strega*" (233). We even see that his attitude toward Brett and their relationship has fundamentally changed; even though he travels to Madrid after she wires him, he does so—as he had said of Pedro Romero's performance—without "any loss to himself" (216). He does not become maudlin, does not succumb to the sentimentality that would trap him once again in a repetitive cycle. Rather, he evinces a new awareness, stoically resisting Brett's own sentimentality. Regardless of the "damned good time together" they could have had if Jake had not been wounded, he was wounded. His famous closing retort to Brett—"Isn't it pretty to think so?"—shows that he has come to terms with his experience, that he realizes it is that reality which he must "live in," and not any romantic or idealized falsification of reality.

There is still, however, another dimension to *The Sun Also Rises*: the metafictional dimension. In addition to learning from Romero an approach to or a stance in life—a "code," as it has been called—Jake learns an aesthetic, one that also acts as a stave against implacable process. Several critics have pointed out the parallels between Jake's description of Romero's technique in the bullring and Hemingway's own literary style; Hemingway would draw those parallels between bullfighting and writing more explicitly in *Death in the Afternoon*, and in other works he would use hunting (cf., *Green Hills of Africa*) and fishing (cf., *The Old Man and the Sea*) as metaphors for, among other things, his own aesthetic. Certainly Hemingway's clean, stripped-down style possesses an affinity with Romero's smooth, controlled bullfight in which there are no brusque movements, no contortions. Hemingway argued in *Death in the Afternoon* that a writer should write clearly, that he should not mystify merely "to avoid a straight statement,"[12] thereby hiding incompetence, just as a bullfighter should not contort himself "to give a faked look of danger" (168). Such tricks, both in writing and in bullfighting, inevitably "turned bad and gave an unpleasant feeling" (168) and, in writing, prevented the work from achieving immortality. In addition, to Hemingway, the writer, like Romero, was a man alone, working "all for himself inside," finding in his *metier* a means of ordering experience and using that order to hold off external forces. In the *Paris Review*, Hemingway told George Plimpton that the most difficult part of life to get through was the time between when he quit writing for the day and when he resumed writing the following morning.[13] Moreover, like Romero who works close to the bull's horns, the writer to Hemingway must work close to experience, must write about those things that he has experienced and therefore knows. The problem with Mencken, as Harvey Stone tells Jake, is that "he's written about all the things he knows, and now he's on all the things he doesn't know" (43).

The well-executed bullfight, like the well-wrought work of literature, also succeeds in achieving an aesthetic union between the self and the natural force that opposes it. Such a union involves a fundamental transformation, the creation of a new, distinctly human order and human meaning. During Romero's cape-work, Jake describes Romero and the bull as "*one* sharply etched mass" (217, my emphasis); when Romero kills the first bull, Jake says "for an instant he and the bull were one" (218), and when he kills the second bull, Jake reiterates, "he became one with the bull" (220). It is a transcendental moment; no longer opposites, the self and nature are one, the experience producing in the audience that sense of timelessness and immortality always associated with the transcendental—that is, a sense of arrested process (cf., "*for an instant* he and the bull were *one*"). Throughout *Death in the Afternoon*, Hemingway discusses the feeling of immortality produced by the well-executed bullfight; at one point he says:

> Now the essence of the greatest emotional appeal of bullfighting is the feeling of immortality that the bullfighter feels in the middle of a great *faena* and that he gives to the spectators. He is performing a work of art and he is playing with death, bringing it closer, closer, closer, to himself, a death that you know is in the horns because you have the canvas-covered bodies of the horses on the sand to prove it. He gives the feeling of his immortality, and, as you watch it, it becomes yours. Then when it belongs to both of you, he proves it with the sword.[14]

This "feeling of immortality" is also produced by the great writer. Like the bullfighter, the writer fundamentally transforms experience through the aesthetic act, imbuing it with order and meaning. If executed well enough, the work of art—the union of consciousness and experience—becomes the experience itself. In this way, it achieves immortality, the experience remaining valid for any reader at any time. It is this to which Hemingway refers when, in the *Paris Review*, he claimed, "I have tried to eliminate everything unnecessary to conveying experience to the reader so that after he or she has read something it will become a part of his or her experience and seem actually to have happened."[15]

In *The Sun Also Rises*, we see an example of this phenomenon when Jake reads Turgenev's *A Sportsman's Sketches* while drunk in his hotel room in Pamplona. He says,

> I turned on the light again and read. I read the Turgenieff. I knew that now, reading it in the oversensitized state of my mind after much too much brandy, I would remember it somewhere, and afterward it would seem as though it had really happened to me. I would always have it. (149)

Significantly enough, reading Turgenev stops the room from whirling, it is that metaphorical "fixed point" which arrests cyclical process. Turgenev, an influence Hemingway frequently acknowledged, has succeeded through art in transmuting his own experience into Jake's. He has created, in other words, a timeless experience. The work of art thus acts as a stave against process, serves as an island of stability within cyclical change. Art becomes a sanctuary, a man-made sanctuary, what Wayne C. Booth has called the "clean, well-lighted place of art."[16]

The Sun Also Rises, then, can be read as Jake's *Künstlerroman*. As the first-person narrator, Jake is of course the implied author of the novel; and by the end of the action of the novel, Jake has undergone those experiences and learned those things that make him able to write it. He moves away from the false aesthetics of Cohn—who is also a writer, though the writer of "a very poor novel" (6)—and toward the aesthetics evinced by Romero. He moves, in other words, away from romances and toward a literature that, rather than presuming an order in the world, creates that order and gives it meaning. In effect, Jake in *The Sun Also Rises* "re-writes" romances such as Hudson's *The Purple Land*, substituting a lyrical ordering of experience—that "clean, well-lighted place of art"—in place of a prefabricated and obsolete literary mode.[17]

Jake can never be the hero of a romance; he can never be like the narrator of *The Purple Land* because he is of course incapable of any "amorous adventures." He must, therefore, find a new definition of manhood—one that we have seen involves maintaining one's courage, grace, and dignity in the face of powerful forces. He must create an order that enables him to preserve those human qualities, an order that is true to his experience *in* the world. The self-created order of art, then, must also be true to his experience; it must not be an aesthetic Procrustean bed, a literary mode that experience is forced to fit. Rather, experience must shape the mode.

Jake's narrative, therefore, while it certainly maintains the external trappings of Hudson's romantic travelogue, is a very different travelogue, even in regard to its lyricism. Jake's descriptions of place—of the Spanish countryside, the fiesta, the streets of Paris—are lyrical compositions that go beyond description as mere recording, and become description as conscious aesthetic creation. Landscape becomes mindscape, revealing not just external features but the consciousness observing them. Jake's description, for example, of the café where he had left Brett with Romero, reveals not just the external "facts" but Jake's reaction to those facts:

> When I came back and looked in the café, twenty minutes later, Brett and Pedro Romero were gone. The coffee-glasses and our three empty cognac-glasses were on the table. A waiter came with a cloth and picked up the glasses and mopped off the table. (187)

Again, Jake reveals more than the external scene; he reveals his own disgust at the tawdriness of his actions and the profound emptiness he feels on account of them. Like the aesthetic union Romero achieves between himself and the bull, Jake here, as he does throughout the narrative, forges a union between his consciousness and the external world. We see the scene, but more important, we see a consciousness ordering that scene, a consciousness creating its own aesthetic "clean, well-lighted place."

Hemingway, in granting the human consciousness the power to order experience—in effect, to *create* order and meaning—moves away from nineteenth-century literary naturalism in which consciousness had little or no power to shape its world. While still existing in a largely naturalistic world— that is, a world of material force devoid of a moral and spiritual order—the Hemingway hero is nevertheless able to maintain his human dignity and integrity in the face of it by creating his own personal order.

Yet, as we have seen, any such order must be grounded in experience; it cannot be based on an abstraction, on an order decreed by authority, whether that authority be religious or aesthetic. Hemingway's "modernist" apotheosis of consciousness, however, would not make the transition into the postmodern world; for, . . . in that world consciousness is no longer conceived of as an autonomous entity, but as itself absorbed into a greater system or "field" from which it cannot extricate itself.

NOTES

1. Hemingway, *The Sun Also Rises*, 97. Subsequent references to this edition are provided within the text.

2. For a thorough discussion of the economic/financial metaphor that runs throughout the novel, see Scott Donaldson, "Hemingway's Morality of Compensation," *American Literature* 43.3 (November 1971): 399–420.

3. Mark Spilka has noted that in this scene fishing is "given an edge over religion." See Mark Spilka, "The Death of Love in *The Sun Also Rises*," in *Modern Critical Interpretations: Hemingway's "The Sun Also Rises*," ed. Harold Bloom (New York: Chelsea House Publishers, 1987), 31.

4. Ernest Hemingway, *Ernest Hemingway: Selected Letters, 1917–1961*, ed. Carlos Baker (New York: Scribners, 1981), 229.

5. Richard Lehan, *A Dangerous Crossing: French Literary Existentialism and the Modern American Novel* (Carbondale: Southern Illinois University Press, 1973), 47.

6. For a different view of Brett and her behavior, see Wendy Martin, "Brett Ashley as New Woman in *The Sun Also Rises*," in *New Essays on "The Sun Also Rises*," ed. Linda Wagner-Martin (Cambridge: Cambridge University Press, 1987), 65–82. Martin examines Brett in a social and cultural, rather than naturalistic, context, making the case for her as a "self-reliant modern woman" (71).

7. Allen Josephs, in *"Toreo*: The Moral Axis of *The Sun Also Rises*," *Hemingway Review* 6.1 (Fall 1986): 88–99, argues that the fiesta embodies a primitive spiritualism that is closely connected to natural process.

8. Mark Spilka calls Cohn "the last chivalric hero, the last defender of an outworn faith [romance], and his function is to illustrate its present folly—to show us, through the absurdity of his behavior, that romantic love is dead, that one of the great guiding codes of the past no longer operates." See Spilka, "Death of Love," 27.

9. Mark Spilka was the first to note this connection; he refers to Jake as "a restrained romantic, a man who carries himself well in the face of love's impossibilities, but who seems to share with Cohn a common (if hidden) weakness." See Spilka, "Death of Love," 28.

10. Hemingway, *Death in the Afternoon*, 259. For discussions of the spiritual aspect of bullfighting—its connection to pagan and Christian ritual—see Josephs, *"Toreo"*; Stoneback, "From the rue Saint Jacques," 2–29; Peter L. Hays, "Hunting Ritual in *The Sun Also Rises*," *Hemingway Review* 8.2 (Spring 1989): 46–48.

11. Allen Josephs makes this important distinction between the bullfighter and the bullfight, Romero and his *metier*. "It is *toreo* itself, the *art of toreo* [as opposed to Romero himself], that is at the core of *The Sun Also Rises*." See Josephs, *"Toreo*," 92.

12. Hemingway, *Death in the Afternoon*, 54.

13. Hemingway, "The Art of Fiction XXI," 66.

14. Hemingway, *Death in the Afternoon*, 213.

15. Hemingway, "Art of Fiction," 84.

16. Wayne C. Booth, *The Rhetoric of Fiction* (Chicago: University of Chicago Press, 1961), 299.

17. Carlos Baker quotes Maxwell Perkins on *The Sun Also Rises* and its satire of romantic novels. Perkins called *The Sun Also Rises* "a healthy book, with marked satirical implications upon novels which are not—sentimentalized, subjective novels, marked by sloppy hazy thought." See Baker, *Writer as Artist*, 86.

JAMES NAGEL

Narrational Values and Robert Cohn
in The Sun Also Rises

*T*he Sun Also Rises is a first-person, retrospective novel told by Jake Barnes
shortly after the conclusion of the festival of San Fermin in Pamplona. As
such it has an inherent temporal duality (the time of the action rendered
from the time of the telling) and a corresponding thematic doubling, for
things have a different significance in each of the time schemes. Jake is not
the same person after the fiesta as before, and his assessments of himself and
his friends have altered, in varying degrees, as have the values he places on
even common events and observations. Indeed, Jake, one of the most vulnerable figures in American literature, has lost much that is important to him
during his holiday in Spain, and his recounting of it seems motivated by a
need to come to terms with his altered circumstances, with his diminution
of self-esteem, and with his sense of guilt. As he reflects at one point, the
world can be a good place, but "all I wanted to know was how to live in it.
Maybe if you found out how to live in it you learned from that what it was
all about."[1] Telling the novel is part of the process of learning how to live in
the special circumstances of his world.

Jake has much to deal with. What he reveals about himself, largely
through indirection, is that he was a pilot in Italy during World War I when
he was wounded and sent to the Ospedale Maggiore in Milan, where he fell
in love with Brett Ashley, a British V. A. D. After he learned that he was

From *Hemingway: Up in Michigan Perspectives*, edited by Frederic J. Svoboda and Joseph J.
Waldmeir, pp. 129–36. Copyright © 1995 by Michigan State University Press.

impotent, they separated, only to meet again in England, where their relationship deepened. In material Ernest Hemingway cut from the galleys, Jake explained further that he left London in 1916 and went home to America to work on a newspaper in New York. In due course he started the Continental Press Association with a friend and moved to Paris in 1920 to head the European office of the firm.[2] Although Jake is silent on these details in the published version, that would still seem to be his position when he sees Brett in Paris in 1925.

In the nine years between London and Paris, Jake has struggled to live with his condition, finding meaning in work (he is one of the few characters in the novel who takes work seriously), in friendships, and in sports, where his interests lie in boxing, bicycle racing, fishing, and, especially, bullfighting, for which his sensitivity and perception make him not only an expert observer but an aficionado, part of Montoya's sacred group of insiders. He loves Paris, enjoys his profession, makes friends easily, and knows how to value the simple things in life, the avenues and restaurants and historic monuments near his apartment. It has not been easy for him, however: he has dealt not only with his physical wound but with its implications for his life as well, the loss of romance and family. It is not for nothing that he notices and records, without special emphasis, the intimacy of young lovers walking with their arms about each other on the streets of Paris (77), or on the raft in San Sebastian (234), or the husband and wife and young son on the train to Bayonne (85). As Robert E. Meyerson has pointed out, Jake's restraint and humane nobility have given his situation special qualities: "Where the others are pathetic . . . Jake is tragic; where the others have lost their nerve, Jake has lost his manhood."[3]

Everywhere around him there are reminders of what he and Brett can never have. As Jake says in the first draft of the manuscript, where Hemingway's tendency was to make explicit much that is only implied in the novel, "there was a time once when I had loved her so much that it seemed there was nothing else. There could never be anything else."[4] But Jake has made a life for himself, and he explains that although "such a passion and longing could exist in me for Brett Ashley that I would sometimes feel that it would tear me to pieces and yet in the intervals when I was not seeing Brett, and they were the greater part of the time, I lived a very happy life."[5] The novel he tells is about how all of that changed, how after seeing Brett in Paris he regressed to depression and insomnia, to fits of crying and self-pity, to the turmoil of attempting to establish some emotional stability again.

That all of these events have happened before Jake tells the first page of the novel has important implications for the meaning of what is told, for he does not tell everything and, after the passage of time, either cannot remember or is unsure of certain details.[6] What he includes would seem to be events that mean something special to Jake at the time of the telling, even if they seemed unimportant at the time of the action. That he has established an orderly and comforting routine of work and pleasure in the opening scenes has a special poignancy after the turmoil to come, for example, as does all of the anticipatory pleasure of the fiesta in Pamplona. By the time he tells the novel, Jake is all too painfully aware that everything went wrong in Spain, and that he will never fully recover from it. An informed reading of the novel requires the recognition that there is an irony from the narrative perspective that is not inherent in the active past.

All of this is especially true of the portrait of Robert Cohn, a figure who has given rise to a great deal of scholarly speculation, as though Hemingway used this novel simply to savage some of his friends, most commonly Harold Loeb, who was a Jewish friend from Princeton,[7] or, most recently, and less plausibly, Gertrude Stein, a mentor he needed to reject.[8] However. Robert Cohn is a figure in a novel with only a speculative reference to actual persons. What is important about him is his relationship with Brett and his role in the destruction of Jake's therapeutic construct. In this regard, there is a clear distinction between the kinetic and narrational values in the novel.

At the time of the initial action of the novel, it is clear that Robert Cohn and Jake Barnes are quite good friends, unencumbered by what some readers have come to regard as Jake's anti-Semitism.[9] Robert calls him his best friend (39), and Jake asserts, more than once, that he likes Robert (7). There is a good deal about him to interest Jake, for he is good at things Jake admires: he was a boxing champion at Princeton; he is a good tennis player, and an even better sport when he loses; and he keeps himself fit. In his relationships with men, he shows admirable restraint in responding to taunts and insults, for he is clearly the best fighter in his circle of friends. With women, Robert is sincere and considerate, failing with Brett primarily in his assumption that because she was willing to spend a holiday with him, there must be some special emotional bond between them.[10] He is naive, but never vicious: to him, Brett at first appears "fine and straight," when in reality she has been, to some extent, "coarsened and twisted by life and war."[11] Jake has yet to attempt his first novel at a time when Robert has actually published a good one and is working on his second, although suffering from writer's block. Indeed, he resembles Jake in many respects, not the least of which is that he can be a genuinely nice guy and is capable of deep affection, as is soon revealed by his obsessive love for Brett. The friendship between Jake and Robert is implicit from the beginning, when Robert drops by Jake's office unannounced to go to lunch, and later naps in Jake's office, implying that they are so close he feels free to do so. Jake also reports that Robert was a husband and father who left the States for expatriation and a writer's life in Paris.

The central dilemma that critics have not confronted is why, in the context of an established friendship between the two men, Jake presents such a devastating portrait of Robert, making him the most negative character in the novel, more pathetic, hopeless, obtuse, and impossible than any other member of the lost generation. Anti-Semitism does not present a viable explanation, in that Robert was just as Jewish in Paris before the fiesta as he is in Pamplona during the bullfights: Jake does not suddenly discover Robert's ethnicity and turn against him. Nor are Robert's personality traits indicative of any specific ethnic group. A more plausible answer is that, in his relationship with Brett, Robert has hurt Jake deeply, in the most vulnerable part of himself, and at the time Jake tells the novel he is deeply bitter. The devastating portrait of Robert Cohn in Paris, in effect, derives as much from the retrospective imposition of Jake's feelings after the fiesta as it does from the events themselves. When Jake reflects that "somehow I feel I have not shown Robert Cohn clearly," it is evident that he is speaking retrospectively after the events in Pamplona, when objectivity and accuracy would not be his primary obsessions. Many of Jake's negative observations about Robert are petty, as in the suggestion that he did not think much about his clothing, that his tennis went all to pieces when he fell in love with Brett, that in social situations his conversation was unremarkable (45). From another perspective, these traits might even be seen as admirable. Indeed, if Robert were truly an ass of the first water from the very beginning, Jake and his friends would never have permitted him to come along.

If, at the time of the telling, Jake is disgusted by Robert, he is also, clearly, disappointed in Brett and not at all pleased with himself. Indeed, as negative as the comments about Robert are, Cohn has not transgressed as grievously as has Jake, violating fundamental, sacred principles that define him as a person. At the center of it all is Brett. Even the structure of Jake's narrative stresses his vulnerability: during his first encounter with Brett at the *bal musette* Jake handles his emotions well until he goes home to his apartment on the Boulevard St. Michel and discovers the wedding announcement from the mysterious Kirby family. The document triggers his first psychotic episode, as his mind races ("to hell with Brett. To hell with you, Lady Ashley" [30]) and he cannot sleep. He dwells on his wound ("of all the ways to be wounded. I suppose it was funny"), even though he has had nearly a decade to reconcile himself to the fact of his condition. When he thinks back to meeting Brett in Milan and seeing her again in England, he loses control and begins to cry. This is not macho posing that Jake would be proud of at the time he recounts it, but it is part of the reality he must learn to face. He pulls himself together, but when Brett drops by his flat he has a bad time again. As he reflects: "It is awfully easy to be hard-boiled about everything in the daytime, but at night it is another thing" (34). His problems surface again after Brett and the count visit him, but his deepest despair does not begin until he learns that Robert had an affair with Brett on their trip to San Sebastian. When Brett asks if Robert is going to Pamplona with the group, Jake answers:

> "Yes. Why?"
> "Who did you think I went down to San Sebastian with?"
> "Congratulations," I said. (83)

Jake's question seems to imply that at that moment, before he knows about the affair, Jake can think of no reason why Robert should not be included in the trip. Once he knows the truth about them, this revelation shatters Jake's defenses against the world, and in response he destroys nearly everything that has meaning for him.

Jake's explanations of all of this were more direct in the first draft of the novel than in the published version: "When she went off with Cohn it hurt me badly again. As badly as in the worst days."[12] Jake's preoccupations are not with striking out at Robert, for he never harms Robert physically in Pamplona, but with introspection: "I was through with hurting myself. Somewhere I must have registered it all though because of the way I hated Cohn now."[13] His hatred seems to derive not simply from Robert's sexual liaison with Brett, for Jake does not hate Michael, who has an ongoing relationship with Brett, nor the Count, who propositions her, nor Pedro, who runs off with her. The problem is that, as Jake progressively discovers, Robert acts outside of the codes of behavior that give Jake's life an ethical foundation. Jake did not fully realize this at the time of the initial action, when Cohn's transgressions seemed harmlessly "frank and simple" (4); he is all too aware of it by the time he narrates his story.

Jake derives meaning from simple friendships and proper conduct, from his work, his city, his principled life. As Jake comes to realize, Robert violates all of it, and he has no instinct for the values that guide Jake and his friends. He is, from the very beginning, an outsider, the only central character in the novel who was unscathed by the war, who retains his idealism and illusions, and who seems utterly incapable of recognizing tragedy.[14] He hates Paris, neglects his writing, intrudes on the activities of others. Just when it is most called for, as in the abuse Frances gives him in Jake's presence,[15] he has no substance, and he takes what no one with self-respect should ever permit; to compound the issue he attempts to pay off his ethical obligations to Frances with money.[16] He sleeps through the Spanish countryside that fascinates Jake and Bill, and his only concern in viewing his first bullfight is that he not be bored. He assumes a superior air in knowing the schedule of Brett and

Mike, and he irritates Jake immensely with excessive barbering, as though Brett will be attracted to him based on his appearance.[17] When she shows no romantic interest in him in Spain, he pursues her relentlessly, and when even that fails he resorts to violence, although it should be remembered that the only account of the fight between Robert and Pedro Romero comes to Jake through Mike Campbell, hardly an objective reporter of the incident.[18]

Robert's ultimate impact on Brett is even more devastating, as Jake is acutely aware, for their brief affair has changed her. This is more subtle in the novel than in the manuscripts, where Jake makes the point directly: "She had never been that way before. She was ashamed, that was it. She had never been ashamed before. It made her vulgar where before she had simply gone by her own rules."[19] Beyond what it does to Brett, it also destroys something precious in Jake, his unconditional love for Brett. In going off with Robert, he explains, "she had wanted to kill off something that was in her and the killing had gotten out of her control. Well she had killed it off in me. That was a good thing. I did not want to be in love with any woman. I did not want to have any grand passion that I could never do anything about. I was glad it was gone. The hell I was."[20] Even though it is clear that Jake continues to love Brett, something valuable has been destroyed.

It is Robert's incessant pursuit of Brett that inspires Jake to introduce her to Pedro, a step that causes additional damage: it violates Jake's sacred code of bullfighting, and it costs him his long-standing friendship with the revered Montoya; it puts Brett through a destructive and disorienting relationship in which she discovers that Pedro is ashamed of her iconoclasm.

It destroys Robert in his fight with Romero, against whom his boxing prowess is not effective and not appropriate; and it costs Jake yet again, for he abandons his palliative sojourn in San Sebastian to go to Madrid to assist Brett. Jake says: "Send a girl off with one man. Introduce her to another to go off with him. Now go and bring her back. And sign the wire with love. That was it all right" (239). In the manuscript, he has an even more difficult time: "I had certainly acted like anything but a man. . . . Well I could not apply the rules to myself. I was not a man anyway. Oh stop that stuff. There was not going to be any of that stuff."[21] Jake's emotions are more submerged in the published version—but it is still clear that seeing Brett again may well engender yet another bad time for Jake.

Indeed, the narrative stance of the, novel suggests that *The Sun Also Rises* is Jake's attempt at cathartic synthesis, his effort to face the painful realities of his condition and construct the best life he can for himself. It is an exercise in self-definition, and he does not portray himself to advantage nor spare his own feelings. What he reveals is that he has corrupted his most sacred values, violated the codes that gave his life structure, and compromised his relationship with the one person he truly loved. He tells of his episodes of psychological instability and leaves little reason to expect that he will ever be entirely healthy. He can never go back to the Hotel Montoya and the cult of aficionados he so treasured, and he will have to live with what has happened to Pedro Romero. Far from showing himself as a man who is strong despite his wound, he portrays himself as a passive figure, a spectator who is not an active suitor for Brett, a rotten dancer who does not box or race a bicycle or wade the Irati to fish for trout or run with the bulls, who is knocked out by Robert and rendered helpless, weeping in the night, when he attempts to face his condition. As Michael Reynolds has said, "Jake Barnes is no tough guy."[22] As negative as he has been in his portrait of Robert Cohn, he is even harder, in retrospect, on himself. Yet, in the rendition of the harsh reality of it all, he exhibits his one act of extreme bravery, for his story is essentially a confession[23] and a confrontation, and whatever cathartic virtues are inherent in relating this painful narrative will help form the basis for the rest of his life.

Notes

1. Ernest Hemingway, *The Sun Also Rises* (New York: Scribner's, 1926), 148. All quotations are from this edition.

2. The most readily available record of Hemingway's excisions from galley proof is Frederic Joseph Svoboda's excellent study *Hemingway and The Sun Also Rises: The Crafting of a Style* (Lawrence: University Press of Kansas, 1983). The passage regarding Jake's move to Paris is on page 134.

3. See Robert E. Meyerson, "Why Robert Cohn?: An Analysis of Hemingway's *The Sun Also Rises*," *Liberal and Fine Arts Review* 2, no. 1 (1982): 65.

4. My quotations from the first draft of the novel are from *Ernest Hemingway, The Sun Also Rises: A Facsimile Edition*, ed. Matthew J. Bruccoli, 2 parts (Detroit: Omnigraphics, 1990). This quotation is on page 398. Since the pagination is consecutive throughout the two volumes, I will give only page numbers for citations.

5. *Facsimile Edition*, 617–18.

6. For Jake's lapses of memory, see pages 90–91.

7. Harold Loeb has given his version of the events portrayed in *The Sun Also Rises* in "Hemingway's Bitterness," *Connecticut Review* 1 (October 1967): 7–24. A consideration of his perspective is essential to an understanding of the biographical background of the novel.

8. See Linda Wagner-Martin, "Racial and Sexual Coding in Hemingway's *The Sun Also Rises*," *Hemingway Review* 10, no. 2 (1991): 39–41.

9. Michael J. Hoffman argues that it is precisely Robert's Jewishness, particularly his intellectualism and need to verbalize his feelings, that make him out of place in the undemonstrative and disillusioned social circle of the lost generation. See "From Cohn to Herzog," *Yale Review* 58 (Spring 1969): 342–58.

10. I am indebted here to Arthur L. Scott, "In Defense of Robert Cohn," *College English* 18 (March 1957): 310.

11. S. A. Cowan, "Robert Cohn, the Fool of Ecclesiastes in *The Sun Also Rises*," *Dalhousie Review* 63 (Spring 1983): 103.

12. *Facsimile Edition*, 402.

13. Ibid.

14. See Meyerson, "Why Robert Cohn?" 66.

15. One of the best scenes in the novel is the conversation among Jake and Robert and Frances Clyne in which she punishes Cohn verbally for his treatment of her. Her comments are so vicious that Jake comments, in retrospect, "I do not know how people could say such terrible things to Robert Cohn. There are people to whom you could not say insulting things. They give you a feeling that the world would be destroyed, would actually be destroyed before your eyes, if you said certain things. But here was Cohn taking it all" (49). A more positive reading of the scene would give Robert some credit for his gentlemanly restraint.

16. See Michael S. Reynolds, *The Sun Also Rises: A Novel of the Twenties* (Boston: Twayne, 1988), 53. Reynolds' study is a valuable introduction to the novel.

17. Robert McIlvaine, in "Robert Cohn and *The Purple Land*," *Notes on Modern American Literature* 5, no. 2 (1981): Item 8, suggests that Robert is basing his actions on Richard Lamb, the protagonist of W. H. Hudson's *The Purple Land*, who is a noble and courageous fighter among men and irresistible to women.

18. Scott makes this point on page 312.

19. *Facsimile Edition*, 397–98.

20. Ibid.

21. Ibid., 590.

22. Reynolds, *The Sun Also Rises*, 52. Reynolds also offers an excellent discussion of Jake's role as an anti-hero.

23. For alternative approaches to the meaning of Jake's confession, see Svoboda, *Hemingway and The Sun Also Rises*, 102, and Reynolds, *The Sun Also Rises*, 29.

RON BERMAN

Protestant, Catholic, Jew:
The Sun Also Rises

Throughout the early and mid-1920s, Eliot would react to Unitarian liberalism; Hemingway would satirize the values of provincial Congregationalism; and Fitzgerald would secularize the themes of both Protestant and Catholic idealism. All would in the course of their work deal—badly, and in such a way as to compromise the value of that work—with Jews. In Hemingway, the three religions would be connected.

Two conflicts between Catholic and Protestant affected Hemingway in 1925 and 1926—one was the culmination of a public debate on the uses of history and the idea of progress, the other an *affaire* which became charged with literary meanings. Both are important in *The Sun Also Rises.* The "deeply ingrained Catholicism" of Pauline Pfeiffer is said by Michael Reynolds to have "controlled her life" (*Paris Years* 318). She brought to her relationship with Hemingway a good deal of moral anxiety, causing him to take seriously doctrine, especially of sin, and observance, especially of prayer. He became a convert. As Reynolds sees it, Pauline's ideas were catalytic:

Pauline was a devout Catholic, and Ernest's profession of faith seemed too convenient. But ... [not even] doubters thought of Hemingway as a Protestant, and he, himself, never looked back on his Congregational training which he associated with Oak Park

From *The Hemingway Review* 18, no.1 (Fall 1998): 33–48. Copyright © 1998 by the Ernest Hemingway Foundation.

hypocrisy, his father's unbearable piety and his mother's church politics of who would rule the choir loft. In Italy during his first war, he experienced a country where religion was woven into every facet of the culture.... Before Hemingway was involved with Pauline, the ritual, ceremony and mystery of the Catholic Church were a strong attraction for a man who needed all three. As became more obvious later in his life, Hemingway was deeply drawn to all things medieval, which is to say all things ancient and Catholic. Pauline Pfeiffer's presence in his life probably accelerated his profession of faith. (*Paris Years* 346)

Elsewhere Reynolds notes the specific values of prayer and charity in *The Sun Also Rises*, and the large number of incidents in the novel that have to do with religion (*SAR: A Novel of the Twenties* 25–26). The exceptionally detailed study of Hemingway's Catholicism by H.R. Stoneback describes the period 1917–1925 this way: "bitter rejection of Protestantism and discovery of Catholicism, an awakening to an aesthetic sense centered on ritual and ceremony ... deepening engagement with the sacramental sense of experience" (Stoneback 117). But, while criticism has often noted Catholic ritual and observance, it has tended to ignore ideas and ideology. As in any Hemingway work, the text of *The Sun Also Rises* deals with and argues ideas.

There are formal oppositions in *The Sun Also Rises* between Paris and Pamplona, between Jew and Gentile, between medieval and modern and, most important, between the values located by Hemingway in Catholicism and those connected with the idea of progress. The last of these pairings had from 1920 to 1926 become part of a public debate. A book owned by Hemingway (Reynolds, *Inventory* 199), *The Outline of History* by H.G. Wells, was at first a success, on the best seller list for both 1921 and 1922. Albeit no longer read, the book had an impact on the century's mind. *The Outline of History* was a review of the many failures of civilization—but also an argument for a new "world order" and "universal law" (Wells 1096). It was necessarily dismissive of the past, especially of its baggage of religion and tradition. Wells's concern was the shaping of a more rational future—his conclusion describes "The Next Stage of History" and how to get there. From the viewpoint of scientific socialism it was easy to see that "great rearrangements are necessary" because the world as historically constituted was deeply unsatisfactory (946). These rearrangements had to do with abandoning supposedly primitive forms of human behavior and the institutions guilty of fostering them. For example, "that mere witless killing which is called sport to-day would inevitably give place in a better educated world community to a modification of the primitive instincts that find expression in this way" (1099). This might well have been of interest to those adversarial presences the "Old Lady" in *Death in the Afternoon* and Robert Cohn in *The Sun Also Rises*. But the *Outline* is full of challenges to a mind like Hemingway's—it discounts heroism; presumes unearned moral equality; discards the traditional, historical, and primitive; and argues, tenuously, for secular salvation.

Except for discussion of the Crusades, it is difficult to find much about the medieval period in Wells's *Outline*. The period was imaginatively important to Eliot, Fitzgerald, Hemingway, and Pound, but signified to Wells only the recalcitrance of the mind. Like most on the left, he preferred the Renaissance for its utility as a social metaphor. Wells had no feel for medieval art, whereas Hemingway, understanding its relationship to modernism, wrote in 1925, "As for Yeats he and Ezra and Anonymous are my favourite poets." Hemingway cited at length what he took to be a definitive form of poetry, the medieval ballad (*SL* 187, 189). *The Sun Also Rises* is impacted with medieval images, allusions, echoes—and convictions. In a central way it retells the story of Eloisa and Abelard, and we are supposed to know what the Song of Roland was about. The enormous aggregate of the novel's medievalism, its sense of the sheer historical mass still imaginatively alive is itself a response to the Wellsian frame of mind. With his *Outline*, Wells had provided a text like an overgrown *Dial* or *New Republic* to despise (*SL* 165).

But Hemingway and those others who objected to the limits of "progress" had other texts to consult. Wells had for several years been satirized as efficiently by Hilaire Belloc as Fenimore Cooper and Mary Baker Eddy had been by Mark Twain. By 1926, the year Belloc published *A Companion to Mr. Wells's Outline of History*, Wells had been discredited from a specifically Catholic point of view. *The Sun Also Rises*, a novel about Catholicism and the authority of medieval ideas appearing in 1926, might well carry a double weight.

In reviewing Wells, Belloc had both a historical and a doctrinal point of view. The *Outline* suffered because of its ignorance of medieval institutions—but it suffered even more from viewing the period as a hiccup before modernity. The *Outline* was fixated on a Victorian prejudice: "there runs through the whole . . . the nineteenth-century idea of 'progress.' It is taken for granted, in all its crudity, all its tautology, all its unproved and untrue postulates, and all its flagrant contrast with reality" (Belloc 179). The idea of progress was more useful, even more noble than Belloc imagined. But it had become exaggerated and politicized. Reinhold Niebuhr's great synthesis *The Nature and Destiny of Man* observed that the idea of progress had provoked a demonstrably false certainty on the part of the Enlightenment, "that reason will generate individual virtue" and destroy "superstitions." And Victorianism, even when most scientifically disposed, believed with false optimism that "the most tragic conflicts of history" could be resolved into "harmony and progress" (*Nature and Destiny of Man* 2:164–65).

The point of Belloc (and, in a far more sophisticated way, of Hemingway) was that Wells misunderstood both religion and nature. It was idly utopian to think of change at will, of escaping the fixed boundaries of the self. Mankind is not "a mere phase in process of passing, but a fixed type with a known nature" (Belloc 228). That is an idea central to Hemingway, and he took pride in its deployment. In *The Sun Also Rises* the idea underpins character:

> Probably I never would have had any trouble if I hadn't run into Brett when they shipped me to England. I suppose she only wanted what she couldn't have. Well, *people were that way*. To hell with people. The Catholic Church had an awfully good way of handling all that. (*SAR* 31; emphasis added)

The passage resonates to Belloc, who argued against Wells that "the Catholic Church . . . lives its whole life by consulting and realizing the common man" (188). And the passage implies much about Robert Cohn and others who think, read, edit, write—and are ignorant of and hostile to preexistent truths.

Belloc was once present in the text of *The Sun Also Rises*, in the beginning section cut from the galleys on the advice of F. Scott Fitzgerald. In a long passage, Braddocks (i.e., Ford Madox Ford) thinks he sees Hilaire Belloc passing by. Fine-tuned to cultural gossip, Braddocks describes him to Jake as a man on the losing side in the wars of religion and literature. For one thing, his reactionary polemics (some violently anti-Semitic) have ensured that "not a review in England will touch him."[1] But the man he mistakes for Belloc turns out to be even more notorious, Alister Crowley. Why was Belloc invoked by the old beginning? In order to set the tone of Catholic apologetics; and even, I think, to introduce the theme of a considered, tactical anti-Semitism. Why Crowley? He was a satanic, sadistic figure involved in cult worship, *which made him Belloc's unacceptable social equivalent*. The cut passage was meant to suggest not only that Belloc has left tracks in the novel but that the dimly lit mind of Ford—the intellectual mind in general—is clueless. When the passage was cut Belloc became the man who wasn't there, but the novel retains his beliefs in an "idealized" (and excluding) "medieval Christendom" (Holmes 211).

The great point of Hemingway's two novels of the 1920s, *The Sun Also Rises* and *A Farewell to Arms*, is that they argue a particular and highly unsentimental view of human nature. Catholicism is useful in both because it provides an interpretation of human nature either consonant or productively at odds with Hemingway's, and superior to that of Wells. Catholicism is superior even in the way of ideals—as in *A Farewell to Arms*, the Abruzzi may not be a possible destination, but it is *somewhere*.

Will Herberg's book on American religion—I have borrowed its title— remarks that one of the theological problems our country has contributed to world history is the secularization of faith: "From the very beginning the American Way of Life was shaped by the contours of American Protestantism; it may, indeed, best be understood as a kind of secularized Puritanism, a Puritanism without transcendence, without sense of sin or judgment" (Herberg 94). Hemingway was well aware of this—the evidence in the mid-1920s comes from his short stories, correspondence, and his first novel. When he writes about the values of Catholicism in *The Sun Also Rises* there is a strong implication that Protestantism fails to understand the issues.[2] In this regard, the reader will benefit from looking at what might be called Bruce Bartonism—the consistent attempt in the 1920s by Protestantism to secularize the gospels. As we see in "Soldier's Home" (1924), Hemingway completely understood Bruce Barton's project of identifying "business" with "success" and both with the values of Christianity.[3] In *The Sun Also Rises*, Hemingway, developing his ideas, tackled a more complex subject, the attractions of a higher Protestant style for the urbane, educated—and unanchored—mind.

Hemingway's quarrel with America involved much more than contempt for the limits of Protestantism; it was connected also to Judaism, the last element of the American triad. Especially from 1924 to 1926, if we can judge from references in his correspondence and, of course, in his first novel, he felt impelled to attack Jews. It has become common to fumble the issue of Hemingway's anti-Semitism, and the superficiality of criticism on this subject can be judged by its willingness to abide by the false idea that the 1920s as a whole were anti-Semitic, hence that Hemingway only reflected his moment. Since the recent appearance of two important books on the subject it has become impossible to remain satisfied with the amorphous idea that, since everyone in the 1920s was anti-Semitic, so inevitably was Hemingway. The books I refer to are Bryan Cheyette's *Constructions of 'The Jew' in English Literature and Society* and, especially, *T.S. Eliot, Anti-Semitism and Literary Form* by Anthony Julius.

The Julius book does two things: it relates the writing of T.S. Eliot to the sub-literature of the time, and discriminates between kinds of anti-Semitism. By the early 1920s the doctrines of anti-Semitism had evolved considerably. There is a great range of indictments, from the relatively simple idea that Jews make money dishonestly to that hugely indefinite idea expressed around the turn of the century by J.K. Huysmanns: "'I am an anti-Semite, because I am convinced that it is the Jews who have turned France into the sad country, agitated by the lowest passions, the sad country without God, which we now see'" (quoted in Julius 93). Eliot's poetry and prose cover a certain part of the spectrum: Jews tend to be anarchic; they have philistine cultural tastes; their intelligence is tied to no particular set of values; they are gross; their own free-thinking is dangerous for Christians; they are too skeptical to be part of a culture which requires assent; most important, they subscribe to, and are wholly identified with the current practices of that liberalism which is in itself an attack on the Christian past (Julius 146–47).

Before changes in dress, language, and status allowed for assimilation, Jews had been too different to accept. In Great Britain they had been advised to come out of isolation, civilize themselves, learn English, mix with and adapt to the majority. Having successfully done so, however, they ran into another problem: they were now indistinguishable. Belloc and Chesterton wanted Jews to remain visibly separate. Michael Coren has remarked, in fact, that Chesterton became "terrified that he would encounter a Jew, and not know it" (202–03). Robert Cohn has assimilated, a special problem for Chesterton and Eliot, for Belloc and Hemingway (Cheyette 181–82). If not discernibly a political liberal, Cohn shares "false" current values of cultural enlightenment and progressivism. He is especially vulnerable to visions of personal change. This makes for a special and highly interesting correlation in Hemingway, because every now and then it is necessary for Cohn to stop being a Jew and become an imitation Protestant. He retains what makes him indefensible, but adopts what is unbelievable. That is a large issue in the text of *The Sun Also Rises*. In this novel Catholic intellectual authority is levelled against Jewish skeptical presumption in the guise of progressive Protestant style.

The Julius book outlines Eliot's argument, on display over a period of years and throughout many poems, essays, and observations: (1) a single Jew mentioned in his work stands for all Jews; (2) anti-Semitism is caused by Jews, hence has a defensive and satirical kind of virtue; (3) Jews represent disintegrative elements in western culture, and their skepticism endangers social traditions. Hemingway spends a great deal of time in *The Sun Also Rises* developing arguments which resonate to these points.

Scott Donaldson has noted that the novel "is a repository ... of ethnic and nationalistic prejudices" ("Humor in *SAR*" 30). Individual Canadians are rudely *Canadian*; Germans have their obnoxious *national* character; while to be French is naturally and nationally to grasp after money. The context sets individuals up as groups—although some, Basque and Spanish, benefit from the conjunction of individual with national character (Donaldson 30). With respect to Cohn, Michael Reynolds identifies certain "signals" obvious to "the American reader in 1926" about his group identity: because Cohn comes from a rich and old New York family he belongs also "to the Jewish establishment, which many thought to be a threat to the American way of life" ("*SAR* In Its Time" 53). And, his *individual* "dislikable characteristics" are "never" separated from his "Jewishness." In fact, when Reynolds examines the historical context, he concludes flatly that its anti-Semitism is directed not at Cohn as an individual but at "a rich New York Jew who did not know his place" (54).

Possibly the best proof is the text itself: Reynolds observes that Bill does not wonder much about the unique attractions of Robert Cohn but, instead, about why Brett does not go off "'with some of her own people.'" Mike says that Brett has gone off with men before, "'but they weren't Jews'" (quoted in Reynolds, "*SAR* In Its Time" 53–54). Hemingway knew, admired, and imitated Jews from Gertrude Stein to Bernard Berenson. Why he did so, yet wrote anti-Semitic prose and poetry, is possibly unknowable. But the text, in its uncompromising use of the plural, is not conjectural: Cohn stands for all Jews.

One of the tactics of Hemingway's narration is to offer corroborating evidence from more than one source: Jake's supporting cast agrees that Cohn is a dissonant presence both as a Jew and as a man. Early on, Bill finds him to be "superior and Jewish" a combination that is expected and irritating; later he describes Cohn's bad case of "Jewish superiority" (*SAR* 96, 162). Bill is a decent sort and tries a number of times to qualify his disapproval. But Hemingway has made him the voice of opinion: the mere intelligence of Jews, seen as ethically "detached critical intelligence" or their "unattached intelligence" is without values, hence without value (Julius 146–47). Chesterton's *Manalive* (1912) calls the Jewish refusal to honor traditions of their host society a form of "'shameless rationality'" (quoted in Cheyette 186). In the special case of Hemingway, ritual and myth were endangered by Jewish "skepticism." He had many irrationalities to protect. Like Eliot, and like Huysmanns, he is easily led to a position of purely *defensive*, virtuous anti-Semitism. When Robert Cohn is attacked in the novel it is usually from the point of view of defending manners or even morals.

In regard to Cohn, Jake alternates between hatred and *caritas*. The hatred he ascribes to jealousy. But Jake spends a good deal of time at the beginning of the novel—before anything happens—on Cohn's broken, improved nose. That may be meant to suggest another problem entirely, Jake's *agenbite of inwit*, but it's less trivial than it seems, part of what Julius calls the aesthetics of ugliness. That is a (sizeable) category of anti-Semitism offering a way of looking at characters like Eliot's Rachel and Bleistein and Hemingway's Cohn, making them emblematically ugly.[4] The technique, borrowed from cartoons and tracts, is reductive: the sordid, ugly, and comic demand no seriousness, invite little moral retaliation.

A bit later in the narrative Cohn is described as having a "hard, Jewish, stubborn streak" (*SAR* 10) and that too is contextual, derivative: Eliot describes "the hard semitic bitterness" of another Jewish novelist, Maxwell Bodenheim, as a way of implying that Bodenheim's identity makes it necessary to apply whatever norms of literary criticism might otherwise be applied to his work (Julius 145). In *The Sun Also Rises*, there is a good deal of anger about Jews writing at all, intruding into yet another sacred cultural realm. Jake is ambivalent to the point of incoherence about Cohn's talent.

The largest issue is cultural style. Mike says that Cohn has no "manners" a point echoed by Jake who says that "he's behaved very badly" and by Brett who adds that "he had a chance to behave so well" (*SAR* 181). The manners issue shows up in almost every scene: Cohn is uncompanionable, intrusive, a killjoy at the bullfight, an undesired presence in the group. He is phenomenally maladroit with women, playing bridge, talking—doing anything social. A related issue: he is a Philistine who does not understand the rules of courtly love. Manners are important as a Jewish issue in the 1920s. The problem of manners should be decoded; it is the problem of assimilation. Even where an effort is made, the Jew cannot escape his identity, cannot make the transition to civility and urbanity. He is not "one of us" (a phrase actually used in the novel, but in another context). Léon Poliakov posed a famous question that is, I think, on Hemingway's mind: "'are the Jews congenitally unsociable and rude, or are they this way as a result of having been segregated into ghettos?'" Certain Jews, self-admittedly, have "'little grace and no manners'"; they "'are not easy to live with'" (quoted in Cuddihy ix, 101). Of others, Walter Lippmann made a famous and personally unhappy observation in 1922: Jewish "'behavior in public places'" was itself a cause of anti-Semitism. It was incumbent on the Jew, as it is for Cohn in *The Sun Also Rises*, to behave well and not to be "'conspicuous'" in polite society (quoted in Cuddihy 142–43).

Towards the end, in an evocative line, Brett says about Cohn, "I hate him, too, . . ."I hate his damned suffering" (*SAR* 182). What she says is extraordinary (the unusual relationship of hatred to suffering) unless the context is figured in. She has transparently been given the language of a social code: undeserved self-pity, as Kipling would write a few years later, is a rightly-despised characteristic of the Jewish liberal mind (Julius 144–45). The point is made more than once: Cohn enjoys or practices suffering because that is a form of passive aggressiveness.

These are some of the Jewish issues.[5] There are then the Protestant issues, or ways in which Cohn merges his own identity with that to which he aspires. Texts are guides: in *The Sun Also Rises* Harvey Stone reads Mencken, is even prescient about his reputation; Jake reads Turgenieff whose style and values imply his own; but Robert Cohn, an indiscriminate man and reader, has found a different kind of guide to life:

> He had been reading W.H. Hudson. That sounds like an innocent occupation, but Cohn had read and reread "The Purple Land." "The Purple Land" is a very sinister book if read too late in life. It recounts splendid imaginary amorous adventures of a perfect English gentleman in an intensely romantic land, the scenery of which is very well described. For a man to take it at thirty-four as a guide-book to what life holds is about as safe as it would be for a man of the same age to enter Wall Street direct from a French convent, equipped with a complete set of the more practical Alger books. Cohn, I believe, took every word of "The Purple Land" as literally as though it been an R.G. Dun report. (*SAR* 9)

Alger, Hudson, and R.G. Dun outline Cohn's mind. Success, romance and rebirth, and money combine Jewish and Protestant stereotypes. The Alger books are especially useful to Hemingway because they retell a story essential to understand Cohn. We want to recall that Alger heroes, quintessentially American-Protestant, know how to box in defense of the virtues. It is a set piece in many of his stories: in *Sink Or Swim* our hero faces a bully whose "sentiment of honor was not very keen." "Flinging out blows at random" the bully is in a few moments, however, quite "prostrate" (56–58). In *Strong And Steady; Or, Paddle Your Own Canoe* the villain—particularly loathsome this time—also delivers "his blows at random" but soon lies "prostrate" on the ground. This particular fight is accompanied by a long and immensely useful apologetic in which the hero argues that knocking a man down is the only conceivable way to answer aspersions (106–8). The Alger books, with their combination of chivalry and success, may well be, as Hemingway suggests, on Robert Cohn's mind. They are a strand in the larger theme of Religion and the Rise of Capitalism (which became a famous idea and text of 1926).

But it is the Hudson book that gets top billing, a parody of New World rebirth and radical innocence. *The Purple Land* keeps on echoing in Hemingway's own text as Cohn insists on applying it to life. Most of the second chapter is about its themes: Cohn is desperate for emotional rebirth, and actually wants Jake to go with him to a (Promised) Purple Land. The issues are serious although the ideas are comical. When Cohn says that "I can't stand it to think my life is going so fast and I'm not really living it" he is at least on the verge of a spiritual insight (*SAR* 10). But Jews, evidently, do not have the Augustinian equipment to understand life. Jake does:

> "Listen, Robert, going to another country doesn't make any difference. I've tried all that. You can't get away from yourself by moving from one place to another. There's nothing to that."
>
> "But you've never been to South America."
>
> "South America hell! If you went there the way you feel now it would be exactly the same." (*SAR* 11)

Cohn hates Paris, but loves a place he has never been. The predicament was described in 1920 by George Santayana, long a critic of American Protestant optimism, who discriminated between that ridiculous idealism which was located merely "in the region of hope" and that more solidly established in the "region of perception and memory." The man who argues from hope only "idealises *a priori*, is incapable of true prophecy; when he dreams he raves, and the more he criticises the less he helps" (Santayana 109–10).

W.H. Hudson's ideas were certainly located in the region of hope. Both *The Purple Land* and *Green Mansions* seem to be on Robert Cohn's mind, and both exemplify the final attenuation of Victorian idealism. The former appeared the same year as H. Rider Haggard's *King Solomon's Mines*, and only two years before his highly accomplished *Allan Quartermain*. *The Purple Land* suffers greatly by comparison, although it deals with some of the same ideas about renewal and the romantic quest. Hemingway was, I think, trying to direct us to a central fallacy established in Hudson's opening pages: "something came to rouse me from the state I was in, during which I had been like one that has outlived his activities, and is no longer capable of a new emotion, but feeds wholly on the past. . . . I was like one who, opening his eyes from a troubled doze, unexpectedly sees the morning star in its unearthly lustre . . . the star of day and everlasting hope and of passion and strife and toil and rest and happiness" (Hudson 11–12). In the midst of this our mortal life I became lost among unfriendly nouns. Hudson represents late Victorian medievalizing, which had diminished itself into romance and become secular.

Hemingway's text states that Robert Cohn "took every word" of *The Purple Land* "literally," an allusion to more than romantic escapism (*SAR* 9). That Dantean yearning for a new life describes Cohn's uncritical mind. He may know the story literally, but I think that for Jake Barnes Cohn exemplifies it figuratively. Cohn too wants to be transformed, but the issue resolves itself into one of social identity: he wants not only to escape Paris and the civilized condition but to escape himself as he is seen by others. Cohn is a rootless Jew (it was a favorite conception of Eliot's) who imitates exhausted Protestantism which imitates a spiritual quest understandable only in terms of Catholic authenticity. Carlos Baker's great study, *Hemingway: The Writer as*

Artist, places *The Sun Also Rises* under the rubric of "The Wastelanders," but the comparison needs to be taken in some detail.

There is self-doubt in Cohn to which Jake clearly responds. But the main thing is Cohn's aspiration to the wrong model for change. In 1929, Reinhold Niebuhr reviewed the thought of the past decade about regenerating the civilized self. Critical of the Protestant moment, Niebuhr was profoundly unsympathetic to the idea, drawing upon Schweitzer and Whitehead to refute theories which had endowed moderns with *a priori* idealism. (This was to become a problem for Jews in the next decade, but in the 1920s was largely a Protestant issue). According to Niebuhr, "Albert Schweitzer interprets the whole moral bankruptcy of Western civilization as a pessimistic reaction to the extravagant optimism of its traditional religions and philosophies." Any regeneration will definitely *not* come from "the sentimentality of an unqualified optimism" (*Does Civilization Need Religion?* 192–94). An important passage about the gain and loss of ideas from medieval Christianity follows, dealing with that current Protestant optimism which in Robert Cohn so singularly qualifies his "Jewish" skepticism:

> There was something lacking in Spencerian optimism which is very vital to religion, a sense of the tragic in life and an awareness of the frustration which moral purpose and creative will must meet in nature and in man. The sentimentality of modern religion is of course older than the optimism which it derived from Spencer. Part of it derived from Rousseau and the romanticism of the eighteenth century. . . . modern churches are involved in an optimistic overestimate of the virtue of both man and nature at the very time when science tempts men to despair. . . . (*Does Civilization Need Religion?* 205–06)

Cohn does not have that "sense of the tragic in life," while Jake has in abundance "an awareness of the frustration which moral purpose and creative will must meet in nature and man." Cohn dreams of personal change (he gets that "idea out of a book" in Chapter II) while Jake understands the unyielding way we are through dogma and doctrine. The myth of personal change is bad enough, but is compounded by the issue of Jewish identity disguised by the assimilated style.

Some of Robert Cohn's problems are native, but possibly the most serious ones arise from his assimilation of and to the wrong models. He exemplifies false chivalry. When Cohn's attraction to Brett is described we see "the childish, drunken heroics of it. It was his affair with a lady of title" (*SAR* 178). And there is Cohn's romantic-medieval readiness "to do battle for his lady love" (178). The last word on this subject has, I think, been written by Mark Girouard, whose book *The Return of Camelot* exhaustively considers the ways in which late Victorianism—the source of Cohn's imagination—imitated medievalism. There was a trove to draw on of sappy posters of knights (literally) in shining armor designed to promote enlistment from the Boer War to the Great War; of doggerel and boys' stories like those that Orwell read defending virtue and Empire; and of discourse as common as that of Meyer Wolfsheim (!) praising gentlemen "of fine breeding." Hemingway knows this, and has concentrated thematically on manner, courtly love, and the derisory fate of the *vita nuova*.[6]

The important point for late Victorian medievalizing (at least in theory) was social mobility: "anyone who lived up to the standards of a gentleman automatically became one" (Girouard 263). There were infallible indicators: obeying rules and social standards; caring for self and others; and, *pace* Robert Cohn, chivalry to women. But Hemingway is attentive to distinctions. While a true British gentleman, for example, was to be known by his excellence at the "manly sports" and at social games, there is Cohn's unthinkable boasting about making a living at cards. Jewish identity and Protestant aspiration make a bad mix: the issue is that he is a fake gentleman, not, after all, that "perfect English gentleman" of W.H. Hudson's and his own imaginings.

Girouard states that upward social mobility had become an economic fact which required social authentication. In other words, before aspiring Jews could imitate Protestants, aspiring Protestants had to become gentlemen. The chivalric model became highly useful in establishing the right to social class, a way of asserting belief and substance through manner. There were two kinds of assimilation involved. The first was closer than we may think to Hemingway. It is described, memorably, by his mother:

> Stop trading on your handsome face, to fool little gullible girls, and neglecting your duties to God and your Saviour Jesus Christ. . . .
>
> This world, which is your world, is crying out for men, real men, with brawn and muscle, moral as well as physical—men whose mothers can look up to them, instead of hanging their heads in shame at having borne them. Purity of speech and life, have been taught you from earliest childhood. You are born of a race of gentlemen. . . . clean mouthed, chivalrous to all women, grateful and generous . . . See to it that you do not disgrace their memories. (quoted in Lynn 118)

The second kind of change is that of Cohn to the ascendant culture. I think that it has a good deal to do with the first, and with Grace Hall

Hemingway's particular view of it. Hemingway understands exactly which models of identity are being proposed. It suggests what someone might do to fit into a "world" of "race." Cohn becomes or tries to become what Hemingway refused to become.

The combination of chivalry, romance, and *machismo* is an upscale version of muscular Christianity. We might say that it has gone to Princeton. Cohn adds to it other culturally-acquired ideals, including those of progressive American intellectuals towards the bullfight. Here is Robert Benchley at the *corrida* in an earlier moral incarnation, at a time when he was still much under the influence of pieties: "'I left wishing I could touch a button that would topple the whole place over on top of the crowd and bury them all'" (quoted in Altman 44).

But Hemingway insists on remaking the point that the relationship of Protestant style and Jewish identity does not work: when things go bad for Cohn acting the gent, "his face had the sallow, yellow look it got when he was insulted, but somehow he seemed to be enjoying it" (*SAR* 178). This is said coldly, and in retrospect. It is a pretty bad moment, even for readers of the 1920s. We are back to Eliot and Belloc and Chesterton, but also past them, in the gutter anti-Semitism which ascribes pleasure to suffering, and the (necessary) infliction of suffering on those who deserve it. There are lines about Jews in the subliterature of anti-Semitism cited by Julius or Hannah Arendt (*The Origins of Totalitarianism*) by no means as bad. The joke for Jake and Bill, and also for Brett, is the Jewish sheep in wolf's clothing, the disguise of honor for someone incapable of understanding it.

All this is to say nothing of paganism, which may be the fourth religion in the book.[7] But it is, I think, subsumed here as in historical fact by the absorptive powers of Catholicism. Even for the three major religions there is an embarrassment of riches. Hemingway had a strategic purpose, which was to express character through belief and cultural style. But he was unable to fulfill that tactically. One of the larger problems: Robert Cohn isn't given enough of an argument to state. Most of what we know about him comes at second-hand, from others in the story. They decide for us what his character means. After the first few chapters Cohn becomes as much object as subject; and there is not much to correlate with what he is said so trivially to express. After a while we tire of hearing at second-hand that he is "nice" but "awful" (*SAR* 101). Hemingway gets lost in purposes, devoting an enormous amount of description to Cohn's relationship with women, which would seem to argue some kind of sexual motivation. Nothing is made of this, although something else is brilliantly intimated: as a novelist, writer, and universal victim of women Cohn brings out what has elsewhere been called the "impotently genteel and feminized" aspect of American character and letters (Sigg 122). He seems to represent the kind of superficial cultural literacy that Hemingway despised, to be a test case for it; a literary Macomber. But he has been made into a representative figure rather than a fully motivated personality. Ideas have been attributed to him, and in some respects he remains an idea. An interesting idea at that, and very much on the mind of Grace Hall Hemingway.

Cohn unaccountably hates Paris and "would rather have been in America," another idea he gets from books (*SAR* 5). Is he like Dorothy Parker or Robert Benchley, simply at a loss in Europe, spiritually disarmed? Parker, obtrusively both Jewish and Protestant, which turned out to be a literary convenience for Hemingway, later reacted to Spain in life as Cohn does in the novel.[8] But the issue seems more directly connected to the cultural politics of the early 1920s. There is a model for this particular situation: Santayana had written with some contempt that any thinking American leaves home and goes "to Oxford or Florence or Montmartre to save his soul" (or perhaps, more interestingly, "not to save it"). But there are, he says, those who hate Paris. The ugly American wants to return home; desperate for the comforts of what Santayana identifies as the wreckage of Protestant idealism. Americans who have been exposed to European civilization, with its harder moral edges, want necessarily to return to that infinitely jejune "belief in progress" which is the sole surviving idea of their national religion (quoted in Sigg 122). The central argument between liberal Protestantism and Spanish Catholicism was perceived some years later by Salvador de Madariaga, who wrote that Hemingway refused to be "'the Protestant ever ready to frown at Catholic superstition, the progressive commiserating on backward Spain'" (quoted in Josephs 234). In other words, Hemingway refused to be a Benchley, a Parker, a Robert Cohn, or another collateral descendant of H.G. Wells.

NOTES

1. See the reprint of the galleys in Svoboda, 136–37.

2. See the exposition of "civil religion" by Larry E. Grimes in Nagel 40–42: "When religion becomes morality, church and culture merge."

3. See especially Barton's chapter on Christ as "The Founder of Modern Business" in *The Man Nobody Knows* 159–92.

4. See Julius, 111–43; Cheyette, 62–68.

5. For an outline of anti-Semitic doctrine of the 1920s see Feldman 175–88.

6. Moreland (183–90) observes that if there is a true chivalrous hero in Hemingway's novel, it is Romero.

7. See Stanton 91–114.

8. See Meade 163f. Dorothy Parker travelled to Europe in 1926 with Hemingway and Benchley, hoping to find a new artistic and moral environment. The trip had the elements of disaster, particularly in Spain, where she found that she loathed both the culture and the *corrida*. Hemingway, in turn, became disgusted by Parker and wrote a brutal, anti-Semitic poem about her which is reprinted in Lynn 352:

The national tune of Spain was Tea for Two
you said and don't let anyone say Spain to you—
You'd seen it with the Seldes
One Jew, his wife and a consumptive
you sneered your way around
through Aragon, Castille and Andalucia.
Spaniards pinched
the Jewish cheeks of your plump ass
in holy week in Seville
forgetful of our Lord and of His passion.
Returned, your ass intact, to Paris
To write more poems for the New Yorker.

Works Cited

Alger, Horatio. *Sink or Swim*. Chicago: M.A. Donohue, n.d.

———. *Strong and Steady: Or, Paddle Your Own Canoe*. Boston: Loring, 1871.

Altman, Billy. *Laughter's Gentle Soul: The Life of Robert Benchley*. New York: W.W. Norton, 1997.

Baker, Carlos. *Hemingway: The Writer as Artist*. 4th edn. Princeton: Princeton UP, 1972.

Barton, Bruce. *The Man Nobody Knows*. Indianapolis: Bobbs-Merrill, 1929.

Belloc, Hilaire. *A Companion to Mr. Wells's Outline of History*. Rev. edn. London: Sheed and Ward, 1929.

Coren, Michael. *Gilbert: The Man Who Was G.K. Chesterton*. London: Jonathan Cape, 1989.

Cheyette, Bryan. *Constructions of 'The Jew' in English Literature and Society*. Cambridge: Cambridge UP, 1993.

Cuddihy, John Murray. *The Ordeal of Civility*. New York: Basic Books, 1974.

Donaldson, Scott. "Humor in *The Sun Also Rises*." In Wagner-Martin 19–41.

———, Ed. *The Cambridge Companion to Ernest Hemingway*. Cambridge: Cambridge UP, 1996.

Feldman, Egal. *Dual Destinies: The Jewish Encounter With Protestant America*. Urbana: Illinois UP, 1990.

Girouard, Mark. *The Return to Camelot*. New Haven: Yale UP, 1981.

Grimes, Larry E. "Hemingway's Religious Odyssey: The Oak Park Years." In Nagel 37–58.

Hemingway, Ernest. *The Sun Also Rises*. New York: Scribner's, 1926.

———. *Ernest Hemingway: Selected Letters, 1917–1961*. Ed. Carlos Baker. New York: Scribner's, 1981.

Herberg, Will. *Protestant-Catholic-Jew*. Garden City: Doubleday, 1955.

Holmes, Colin. *Anti-Semitism in British Society 1876–1939*. London: Edward Arnold, 1979.

Hudson, W.H. *The Purple Land*. 1885. London: Duckworth, 1929.

Josephs, Allen. "Hemingway's Spanish Sensibility," in Donaldson, *The Cambridge Companion to Ernest Hemingway* 221–42.

Julius, Anthony. *T.S. Eliot, Anti-Semitism, and Literary Form*. Cambridge: Cambridge UP, 1996.

Lynn, Kenneth S. *Hemingway*. New York: Simon and Schuster, 1987.

Meade, Marion. *Dorothy Parker*. New York: Viking Penguin, 1987.

Moreland, Kim. *The Medievalist Impulse in American Literature*. Charlottesville: Virginia UP, 1996.

Nagel, James. *Ernest Hemingway: The Oak Park Legacy*. Tuscaloosa: Alabama UP, 1996.

Niebuhr, Reinhold. *Does Civilization Need Religion?* New York: Macmillan, 1929.

———. *The Nature and Destiny of Man*. 2 vols. New York: Scribner's, 1949.

Reynolds, Michael. *Hemingway: The Paris Years*. Oxford: Basil Blackwell, 1989.

———. *Hemingway's Reading, 1910–1940: An Inventory*. Princeton: Princeton UP, 1981.

———. *The Sun Also Rises: A Novel of the Twenties*. Boston: Twayne, 1988.

———. "The Sun in Its Time: Recovering the Historical Context." In Wagner-Martin 43–64.

Santayana, George. *Character and Opinion in the United States*. 1920. Garden City: Doubleday, 1956.

Scafella, Frank, Ed. *Hemingway: Essays of Reassessment*. New York: Oxford UP, 1991.

Sigg, Eric. *The American T.S. Eliot*. Cambridge: Cambridge UP, 1989.

Stanton, Edward F. *Hemingway and Spain*. Seattle: Washington UP, 1989.

Stoneback, H.R. "In the Nominal Country of the Bogus: Hemingway's Catholicism and the Biographies." In Scafella 105–140.

Svoboda, Frederick Joseph. *Hemingway & The Sun Also Rises: The Crafting of a Style*. Lawrence: Kansas UP, 1983.

Wagner-Martin, Linda, Ed. *New Essays on The Sun Also Rises*. Cambridge: Cambridge UP, 1987.

Wells, H.G. *The Outline of History*. New York: Macmillan, 1921.

ADRIAN BOND

The Way It Wasn't in Hemingway's
The Sun Also Rises

Harry Levin places Hemingway in a generation of writers reacting to the disparity between the rhetoric and the actual experience of war. "Since words had become inflated and devalued," Levin writes, "Hemingway is willing to recognize no values save those which can be immediately felt and pointed out" (73). Rejecting adjective, adverb and verb, Hemingway finds the only part of speech he can trust: the concrete noun. "Hemingway puts his emphasis on nouns, because . . . they come closest to things" (79). The linguistic scepticism Levin remarks indicates a deeper inquiry into the nature of knowledge. "Things" guarantee truth claims because they open the possibility of direct verification. As contents of sensory perception—the faculties which do Levin's "feeling" and "pointing"—they are the primitives or givens of experience.

Descartes embraced radical doubt in order to find that which alone could not be disputed, but in contradiction to the Cartesian Cogito—"I think therefore I am"—Hemingway indicates that being cannot be predicated on thinking. By placing weight on sensory experience, Hemingway instead privileges body over mind, favouring largely unconscious modes of knowing over those we traditionally regard as cognitive, the play of conceptualization and rationality. Mentality, within its insistent linguisticism, is fundamentally removed from the, source of experience. In the well-worn antinomy,

From *The Journal of Narrative Technique* 28, no. 1 (Spring 1998): 56–74. Copyright © 1994 by *The Journal of Narrative Technique*.

reality becomes unreal when it enters the mind as symbolic content—when it becomes, that is, something about which we can think and speak. Thinking, in fact, is conventionally conceived as a interior monologue, but for many of Hemingway's characters it seems like a monologue delivered by someone else. Alien, extraneous, ruminative and ultimately destructive, thinking is an activity best avoided all together.[1] In its place Hemingway substitutes the testimony of simple corporeality. If the mind is inherently problematic, the body, apparently, you can trust.

The desire to tell it "the way it was" is often taken as Hemingway's artistic manifesto (Baker 26–36); central to the proposition is first-hand experience. It is not possible to trust someone else's account; you have to be there physically yourself. The body becomes integral to the truth of writing, a corroborating witness to the author's, or character's, experience. At the level of descriptive technique the body is fully evoked. It is the primary referent for knowledge. In *The Sun Also Rises* this preoccupation also shapes the narrative structure as it works its way through the issues of meaning, memory and textuality.

Corporeality creates an intimate relation between an outer world and an inner self. The body, in fact, is where the world takes place; it is that which Elaine Scarry terms "the original site of reality" (121). Following in the tradition of the British empiricists, Hemingway focuses upon pure sensation in order to convey immediate experience—the sort of "feeling," for example, which Nick Adams gets skiing in "Cross Country Snow," the thrill which "plucked Nick's mind out and left him only the wonderful, flying, dropping sensation of his body."[2] Hemingway is not the only one who turns to the body for validation and meaning; repeatedly, his characters do as well. Empirical verification seals the brotherhood of aficionados in *The Sun*; Jake remarks the "same embarrassed putting the hand on the shoulder. . . . [N]early always there was the actual touching. It seemed as though they wanted to touch you to make it certain."[3] Often characters turn the gesture inward and this physical inspection gives much of Hemingway's work the feel of a mind/body polemic. In "The Gambler, The Nun and The Radio," Frazer studies the deterioration of his own body, waiting for his nerves to give out. He is aware that his state of mental health will finally be determined by his bodily health; "'bad'" health means for him being "'out of his head'" (*CSS* 359)—an experience which, in counterpoint to Nick Adams's mindless exhilaration, might be termed with literal significance, the "ecstasy" (that "standing outside of oneself") of pain.

The Sun keeps physicality in the foreground through an inordinate attention to the daily activities of eating, bathing, shaving, hair-cutting and the like, but the body becomes most visible when it registers what Geoffrey

Galt Harpham terms "difference," the process by which corporeality is able to "rise above the threshold of awareness or communicate" (117). While Harpham accredits articulateness to disease, it is achieved equally by pain and injury, those pointed reminders that we are, after all, incarnate. Physical trauma makes the body an object of especial attention, somehow external to ourselves—like something seen in a mirror. Hemingway explores mind-body duality in this very image during his depiction of Jake's self-examination. Jake's body has already become conceptually visible because of a recent, frustrating encounter with Brett. Standing naked before the armoire mirror, Jake finds the alienated form of "himself," his body, now made literally visible, presented as an external thing. Troubled by his relationship with Brett, Jake must move from fruitless introspection to empirical inspection. It is his physical state which prevents him from following his desire (and, if there were any question about the specificity of that desire, Hemingway made it clear in an interview that Jake is not castrated, but, rather, dismembered [Plimpton 83]). The body is the place to which cognitive and affective processes must lead because it is the site of difference. Jake looks and immediately confronts the anomaly of his wound—the missing piece (30).

Amid the moral and emotional ambiguities of the novel, Jake's injury is an incontrovertible fact. Describing the metaphysics of injury in *The Body in Pain*, Scarry writes, "the visible and experienceable alteration of injury has a *compelling and vivid reality* because it resides in the human body" (121; emphasis original). Scarry's study, which documents how this reality is conferred upon disputed issues, upon ideological statements or other declarations of truth, offers insight into Jake's (and Hemingway's) reverence for the bullfighting so central to the novel's concerns, a ritualized activity underpinned by blood-letting. The truth of the art-form is incarnate, so basic as to be almost ineffable (Jake actually remarks that "There is no Spanish word for bull-fight" [173]). As an aesthetic experience, it is appreciated for the viewer by "a sudden ache inside" (220). As "something that was going on with a definite end . . ." (167), it is realized in the fact of a slain bull laying "heavy and black on the sand, his tongue out," around which, as if for closer verification, boys form a circle and dance (220).

Of course, the alteration of the matador would be equally compelling; just such an incident proved revelatory to Hemingway. In *Death in the Afternoon*, Hemingway abandons a discussion of skill and honor to determine "the thing that I had really seen" in a bull-fight in which a matador was gored. The essence of the sport he had deliberately set out to study, the truth which solves his "problem . . . of depiction," comes to him in the image of "the clean, clean, unbearably clean whiteness of the [exposed] thigh bone . . . and it was that which was important" (20).

The body is not just a recorder; it is a record, a document of experience. Whatever else may be disputed, the evidence of having been there—
Hemingway's most valued truth—cannot. The body may simply describe a
life by demonstrating the progression of time through visible aging. Jake is
fascinated by the story of the young man entombed in the glacier, dead but
unchanged—in fact, unchangeable. That body escapes time, remains integral,
while the man's bride waits for it patiently for twenty-four years, twenty-four
years in which she alone ages (120). But Hemingway realizes that experience is
rarely presented as a slow effacement. Its visitations are sudden, like the novel's
fiesta which "at noon of Sunday, the 6th of July . . . exploded" (152). If this
sounds like a war journalist's account, it should. War is an appropriate metaphor
for the way life operates generally on an individual, punctuating stupor with
moments of vivid and violent experience. Such events occur and pass away in
The Sun. The fiesta, like the "shrapnel burst" of its rockets (153), can be quickly
forgotten, the posters announcing bull-fights stripped away—Hemingway
includes just such a scene—but he draws our attention repeatedly to the records
which remain, those impressions left on the human body, such as Jake's missing
part, the count's scars, Cohn's broken nose, or Romero's battered face.

A physical semiotics begins to emerge. In a brief description, the skin
of a Basque peasant is almost literally an open book, speaking of his life and
livelihood, becoming, in fact, an artifact of that livelihood; through years of
outdoor labor it has been "tanned the color of saddle-leather" (104). Brett is
afraid of similar disclosure. While she has no trouble forgetting her sexual
dalliances, she has the repeated sense that her body might betray her. She is
always in need of a bath, as if the body like the mind must be washed clean,
turned tabula rasa. In an effort which mimics the frozen bridegroom of Jake's
story, whose material stasis encodes his failure to consummate his betrothal,
Brett attempts to falsify the document of her body.

Brett's concerns are imaginary, of course; typically the signs are real and
indelible. Near the novel's conclusion Jake sees, quite casually, two boot blacks
talking to a soldier. Jake reports, "The soldier had only one arm" (237). We
might infer the man to be uniformed, but no such description is presented.
Nor does it need to be; in the context of post-war experience, amputation
is a much simpler and more compelling signifier. The same logic leads Brett
upon examination of the count's scars to ask "'Were you in the army?'" (60),
and—in Hemingway's subversion—allows Cohn to take "a certain satisfaction" in his broken nose (3); it works for him like Stephen Crane's (ironized)
"red badge of courage," as a visible emblem of his success in surviving (civil-
ian) battle. One of the purposes war fulfils through wounding is to provide
"a record of its own activity" (Scarry 116). By referencing events in the past,
physical alteration supplies narrative.

Jake's mirror-side inspection is, therefore, simultaneously a retrospection and the metaphor of reading becomes at this point most overt. (Jake's self-examination, in fact, is followed by his reading bull-fight newspapers, as if to enforce the similarity between the two acts.) By flattening the body into the picture-plane of glass, the two-dimensional mirror becomes analogous to a written text, the pane of glass a written page. In studying his body, Jake is engaged in a reading. Faced with the problem of understanding his relationship with Brett, Jake turns, where Hemingway does, to the primary sight of reality. The body is the center of signification. It orders all his relations with women, and often with men. It is, effectively, the copy-text of his experience, recording not only a defining event in the past, but also providing a general commentary on his life since. In the body memory becomes incarnate.

Memory is a persistent concern of the novel because it isn't working properly. Some lapses are explicable; Jake reports, for instance, that Cohn "made some remark" about the Bayonne cathedral, "I forget what" (90). Although such omissions might actually undermine verisimilitude by inviting us to question the otherwise exact transcriptions of entire conversations Jake is able to provide, they do establish a credible norm of memory retention against which a systematic forgetfulness enfolds. This latter sort of memory failure is consistently the product of deliberate sabotage. The central characters—those Brett denotes by "'us'"—generally avoid remembering whenever possible. Alcohol is for them, as for Frazer in "The Gambler," an excellent "opium"; it allows you to forget yourself. As Bill advises Jake, "'Get tight. Get over your damn depression'" (223).

Opium-oblivion, however, fractures personal history in a manner suggestive of the physical injury which elsewhere actually encodes it. While Cartesianism makes mind an indivisible whole distinct from body, Hemingway likens memory to corporeality in its construction. Like body, memory is extended. Pieces of it can be broken off and lost. Reading Turgenieff's "A Sportsman's Sketches" while drunk, Jake comments "I had read it before, but it seemed quite new" (147), his forgetfulness allowing him the illusion of novelty. In this instance alcohol impedes recollection by depressing the activity of the brain. More significant, however, are those cases in which it inhibits memory formation by hindering the operations of the sensory faculties; as the common euphemism for drunkenness—"being blind"—suggests, experience is lost at the source. Accordingly, Bill can provide Jake with an itinerary of the places he has recently visited except for Vienna. Because Bill was (unintentionally) drunk in Vienna, that section of his story is largely blank. When Jake asks him where he went, Bill replies, "'Don't remember.'" Did he do anything besides writing a post-card? "'Not so sure. Possible.... Can't remember'" (70). While some details do emerge, Bill cannot provide a coherent account of Vienna because none was formed, an omission which, as we will see, has profound implications for an aesthetic based on "the way it was."

Drinking is part of a broader culture of mental absenteeism. The impromptu nightlife of the Quarter, the frenetic celebration of the fiesta, excursions into and out of vacation spots and personal relationships—transience suggests the flight from reflection, diversion from a painful rumination on self. It also, however, suggests a flight *to* something. James Farrell comments that Hemingway's characters are "constantly searching for new and fresh sensations" (56), but I think this just misses the mark. What is lacking is not panoramic width of experience, but depth. When, following his physical examination, Jake reads the same news in two bull-fight papers, the repetition, while apparently demonstrating his *aficion*, suggests he isn't getting enough out of a single reading. In another doubling, occurring at the end of the novel, two identical telegrams come from Brett, both of which are reproduced in the text, with the impact of the latter obviously emptied (238–39). Hemingway seems here to invoke for the reader the experiential deadness encountered by his characters, the déjà vu unreality of daily life figured synecdochically in the "unreal" fiesta during which "it seemed as though nothing could have any consequences" (154). Inebriation, therefore, mimics and exacerbates a more generalized desensitization. If Bill's Vienna is "'Very much like Paris at this moment'" (75), because he is drunk in both, there is also a morbid sameness about the places he can remember, the places in which he was sober, "the States," New York, Budapest, all of which he describes repeatedly and meaninglessly as "wonderful" (69–70) (the word, in fact, resurfaces in his description of the drunken fiesta as a "'wonderful nightmare'" [222]).

While there is a long tradition in psychology which equates meaningless and repetitive activity with madness, the alienation from one's self, Hemingway's depiction represents an alienation from things. His characters move across the surface of experience, never penetrating deeper. Their boredom is not whimsical but inveterate, their activity not a search for "new spectacles," as Farrell suggests (56), but more substantial experience. Seeing the bull-fight as a "'spectacle,'" or a "'wonderful show,'" as do Brett and Cohn (166), is actually a patent foil to Jake's sense of its importance as a directed activity "and less of a spectacle with unexplained horrors" (167). Despite Jake's monition that "'Nobody ever lives their life all the way up expect bull-fighters'" (10), *The Sun* characters, and Jake foremost among them, appear repeatedly to be looking for just such consummation. What is required is patient and effortful attention, one which allows slow and deeply felt involvement with the sensory present—the kind of experience which is generative rather than destructive. While Cohn speaks the traditional complaint of aging, that time is going too "'fast'" (10), and that he hasn't "'lived enough'" (47), Bill suggests a more topical privation. Remarking Mike's inability to be excited by the running of the bulls, Bill comments "'You've been in the war'" (200). The sensory deadening which follows war is for Jake particularly germane, having been imbedded in the text of his body itself. Dancing with Brett, Jake remarks "I had the feeling as in a nightmare of it all being something repeated, something I had been through and that now I must go through again" (64). Jake's most portentous moments, those with Brett, continue to replay themselves in all their nightmarish irresolution, and they continue to be new because their meaning has never been determined. They have never been concluded intellectually and emotionally, or more to the point, physically.

Physical (sensory) experience is foremost therapeutic; it is as effective as alcohol in displacing unwanted mentality. Jake frequently has trouble at night when darkness, by negating the visible world, forces introspection. He tells us that for six months he slept with the light on (148), in effect, to keep his mind off himself, and one night during the novel he ends a disturbing bedtime mediation on philosophy and ethics—"a lot of bilge"—by turning on the light and reading (149). In a formula which appears in "Ten Indians," Jake is elsewhere able, upon awakening in the night, to settle himself by finding the sound of wind blowing outside (111). Like Nick Adams who "forgot to think" about his failed romance by listening to the world outside his bedroom (*CSS* 257), Jake quite literally brings himself back to reality.

Sensory integration with an external world also allows an integration of self. By connecting lived moment to lived moment, felt experience constructs the sort of coherent memory which inebriation disassembles, and it ties that memory to real time. The central characters have actually become determined by the very past they attempt to escape. Past is the deflected center of their present, with the metaphor of loss (for which Stein is credited in the famous "Lost Generation" appellation) figuring foremost a temporal dislocation—a living outside of history. Alcohol may allow escape from thoughts on bankruptcy, failed marriages, abusive husbands, dead lovers and the like, but it actually perpetuates lostness. Stepping out of time, revellers stop living. Brett seems to acknowledge the error. Although Cohn—and the problems with her life he represents—won't disappear, she realizes she "'can't just stay tight all the time'" (184). While she had repeatedly encouraged Jake to drink up, by the novel's conclusion she is able to dissuade him, commenting, "'Don't get drunk, Jake. . . . You don't have to'" (246). After the fiesta, in fact, we find Jake deliberately sober and sensate—"It was pleasant to be drinking slowly and to be tasting the wine . . ." (232)—immersing himself in simplified experience and recording everything he can.

The methodology of patiently attending to sensory detail duplicates the activity of writing the book itself: Jake in the narrative present experiencing what Jake the self-chronicler is attempting to remember. The duality makes the novel anticipatory. As narrator, Jake is devoid of hindsight, supplies no other ordering principle than the strict chronology of events. His novel seems more like a process than a product, the writing itself a form of reading. The image of his body with its missing piece consequently becomes a metafictional referent. Jake is attempting to reassemble the discrete pieces of a puzzle, to reconstitute the text of his experience, that is, literally to "remember" himself.

Count Mippipopolous provides a test case for successful remembering. During a moment of literal revelation, the count opens his shirt and allows Jake and Brett to inspect his body. Like a text, his body narrates an event in the past. He points out two raised welts below his ribs on his front, and then, turning, presents identical scars on his back. Wounded by an arrow, his body is living proof of "the way it was." The count's subsequent story, however, diverges considerably from Jake's. The count is not dismembered by experience because he is capable of remembering on all levels. The count's scars mark the entry and exit points of an alien object which has passed "'Clean through'" and left the body integral (60). The integrity of his body matches that of his mind. Brett tells Jake that the count is one of them—that is, a heavy drinker—and yet she does note a singular difference: "'He remembers everything that's happened'" (54). This capacity makes the count distinct among the book's numerous revellers. He is capable of accounting for himself, organizing his experience in a linear form, providing a personal history. In the count's synthesizing vision, everything has "'got a place.'" The text of memory and the text of body are both integrated.

The count, more importantly, is capable of learning from experience—that is, providing a "reading," a signification. "'Because I have lived very much,'" he tells Jake, "'now I can enjoy everything.'" He has gotten "'to know the values,'" and the values are noticeably connected to body experiences. Jake says that "Food had an excellent place in the count's values. So did wine" (60–61). And so too, as the count tells Brett, does love. There is no question of what love involves for the count, and what it does not. The count is no sentimentalist. Rather, Hemingway makes him into a kind of icon of virility. When Jake and Brett leave the count at the night-club, Jake, looking back before exiting, sees that three women have appeared at the count's table (64). If there is any meaning in the count's life, it is nothing particularly cerebral. His "values" work as far as they incorporate physical experiences. His conceptual life is predicated on bodily function, and getting "'to know the values'" appears to be simply establishing an orderly allotment of sensual gratification. Meaning in the count's life is indivisible from body existence, which holds that "excellent place." The count is "'not dead at all,'" he tells Brett who finds his composure deathly (61). He is not dead mentally because he is very much body-alive.

The count's wounds are essentially different to Jake's and this is what gives Jake's story such poignancy. We find Jake through much of the novel asking Brett whether there is anything the two can do about their romance, as if he has not understood the text of his body. If we follow the textual analogy to the point at which, perhaps, it starts to lose traction, Jake's body comes closest in analogy to a text which has been edited—perhaps, bowdlerized would be the more appropriate term. The specificity of Jake's wound invokes the familiar binarism of gendered hermeneutics—his body is a "raped" text. In a particularly forthright statement of the paradigm, Catherine Dinshaw writes

> literary activity has a gendered structure, a structure that associates acts of writing and related acts of signifying—allegorizing, interpreting, glossing, translating—with the masculine and that identifies the surfaces on which these acts are performed, or from which these acts depart, or which these acts reveal—the page, the text, the literal sense, or even the hidden meaning—with the feminine. (9)

In this model acts of signifying correspond to the biological activity of heterosexual intercourse; an activity resembles rape to the degree in which signification is extratextually imposed. Into the latter category fall the "rape-acts" of textual violation such as scribal omissions or—more pointedly—deliberate fragmentation and removal of portions of text.

Whatever its value as a description of the reading act—it is remarkably sexist—the model is nonetheless consonant with Hemingway's implicit assumptions, and we will return to it at a later point. In the meantime, we might see Jake's body more simply as a text which has been violated by the signifying agency of external events. Jake's case is fascinating because his wound is such a different type of record to those in the novel which alter physiognomy—like writings on the blank page of the body—but do not delete. The bodily experience recorded in Jake's wound in part precludes future bodily experience. The dismemberment of memory, consequently, becomes more than figurative. If the text of body mirrors the text of memory, then Jake's missing piece would be analogous to a localized amnesia. Jake's injury stands for that experience which isn't recorded because it can't be recorded, the part he can never remember, sexual experience in love.

For this reason Jake can only attempt to provide complete signification where the count can fully succeed. Jake occupies the same intellectual vantage as the count, caring not what "the world" "was all about" so long as he can learn "how to live in it" (148). Like the count, Jake has a great appreciation of immediate pleasures. Brett remarks "'You like to eat, don't you?'" and Jake comments "'I like to do a lot of things.'" But when Brett asks him to elaborate, perhaps with some innuendo intended, Jake is evasive. He simply reiterates the comment (246). While Jake can know all about "the values," in one pertinent area he cannot *know* them. Among the experiences which are fundamental to the count's value system—the same experiences so central to Hemingway's work, the creaturely comforts (eating, drinking, relaxing and so forth) around which Hemingway constructs so many rituals—there is one experience completely denied Jake. He has a perception of the importance of love, but he cannot confer on that perception any primary bodily reality. Jake Barnes is Hemingway's version of a "hollow man," one deprived not of abstract spiritual truth, but of very common sensual truth.

This privation creates a structural analogy between Jake's body and his story, the novel itself. It has been argued that the novel returns to precisely the same situation—the conceptual place—at which it began, with Jake and Brett "whispering vanities like those they whispered chapters and months before" and which, through an "easy but redundant extension of the text," they could continue to whisper indefinitely (Vance 39). William Vance attributes the "futile circularity" to a largely superficial naturalistic plot structure (beneath which, however, he does find an Aristotelian unity of action [40–49]) (39). Philip Young integrates the circular form more closely with the novel's meaning ("structure as meaning, organization as content"), and makes a case for the novel's socio-historic relevance (89). But, while giving voice to a mood which in 1926 was "in the wind," Hemingway constructed his novel with an imperishable logic, one somewhat obscured by Young's allusion to a *Waste Land* theme of sterility (89, 90).

The narrative assumes the geometric structure implied by the term circular when we remark that Jake's experience remains fundamentally exteriorized; his story is circular because it revolves around a central absence. Applying the mirror's image of Jake's body, with its absence at the center, to the novel, our model of Jake's story becomes something like a ring. (Ring serves better than circle because it is exclusively defined by its circumscription of a hole). This would be the structural equivalent to the notion of a relived event, those nightmare moments with Brett that are dreamy and unreal to Jake because he senses that a waking truth remains at the inaccessible interior.

Because Hemingway made the love relationship between Jake and Brett the central concern of the novel—and not as Philip Young seems to suggests, a clumsily handled subplot (89–90)—he tends to take Jake's injury, as Jake does, seriously (31). Romantic love is a compelling subject for Hemingway's aesthetic. Since its inception in Western literature, and despite some bold transmutations it has received along the way (the attempts to conform it to social or transcendent courtship structures), romantic love has always been firmly based in erotic fact. In modern parlance, relationships become "serious" when they involve the body directly, the very reason that Cohn "'can't believe'" his affair with Brett "'didn't mean anything'" (181). Sexual experience confers a sense of importance—of reality—onto the "love" itself, that vagary of thought and emotion which Hemingway captures in the literally disembodied state of Jake's nightmare moments.

That the typical medieval appreciation of the subject was formally no different from Hemingway's is demonstrated in the *gradus amoris,* or steps of love (Friedman 166–177). This paradigm apparently enjoyed the same currency then that the sports analogy (getting to home plate, "scoring," and so forth) does today and was presumably equally attractive to the male mind in its ability to provide a neat systematization of what was involved in seducing a female. The steps of love figured courtship in terms of spatial orientation, delineating the male's physical approach as love led him progressively closer to the body itself (hers and his) and, in the final step—to the immense satisfaction of male pedantry—literally "into" the female body. The lover moved through sight, speech, touch, kiss, to sexual intercourse (*factum*)—the ultimate interior, "home plate."

If anything, erotic consummation becomes more important with Hemingway. Hemingway chooses to write about romantic love because he validates body experience above any other and he knows that among the various experiences of the body none is ranked higher in sensual fulfilment than sexual climax. Nor does any other, not even touch, involve a more immediate appreciation of one's corporal complicity—with the exception, perhaps, of death.[4] There is much watching, talking, touching and kissing between the two lovers in the novel, but these steps in love lead them only to the final point beyond which they cannot go. Hemingway makes the neat choreography a frustrating dance, with Brett "an image to dance around" (155). Hemingway's topology is insistent. Alone with Brett in a cab but having, in every sense, no where to go, Jake remarks resignedly "'Oh, tell him to drive around'" (24). With Jake's eroticism itself marginalized, the lovers plan futile escape, the most thought-out version involving the desperate simplicity of "'go[ing] off in the country for a while'" (55). But despite his own inclinations, Jake is perceptive enough to advise Cohn "'You can't get away from yourself by moving from one place to another'" (11). He speaks from experience. Reality is wherever the body is; the two are coterminous.

Unrequited love is not new to romance. What is new is the way Hemingway organizes it. Where a prudish medieval scribe would thwart love by fortifying the female in an allegorical castle (of Chastity, or the like), Hemingway simply removes the basic biological means from the male lover. And, by allowing the preceding steps, Hemingway provides the kind of sexual tension which would make the consummation something truly worth writing about. This is no small achievement in an age of liberated sexual mores. Hemingway discovered a technique capable of re-eroticizing the prosaic story of love. It is, as Jake and Brett are both aware, cruelly tantalizing, and Hemingway's intention is that the reader is as much teased by the lead-up as the lovers.

In the final, famous scene of the novel, Brett having remarked upon what a "'damn good time together'" the two would have had as physical lovers, a policeman holds up his baton, halting the taxi the lovers are riding in, and they press together accidentally (247). During this final moment of physical contact, Jake's absent member becomes intensely absent—so much so that it is tempting to retrieve it for him, finding it conveniently in the policeman's hand. This would be a clever enough symbolic transfer, although I don't believe Hemingway intended it. By the novel's conclusion, we have entered into an experience which approximates Jake's own. As readers of the novel we too, like Jake, its writer-reader, are frustrated; like him, we try to find what we know is missing. It has almost become a dismissable truism that the experience of reading in its movement to climax parallels sexual intercourse. By the end of *The Sun Also Rises* the metaphor seems all too viable. Hemingway presents a reading experience which is itself a *coitus interruptus*.

We might turn here once more to the model of gendered hermeneutics. If the role of reader is analogous to the biological role of male, and the role of narrative to that of female, we would find in the symbolic baton a kind of sexual consummation after all: the rape of the text by signifiers bringing to it their own meaning. The conflation of literary and biological gendering evident here—the signifying act is *about* sexual activity—seems unavoidable considering the number of Hemingway's male characters who are, like Jake, writers (Frances, noticeably, can't get published [47]). At times, in fact, Hemingway makes patriarchal authority explicit in the coupling of authorship with virility (Cohn wants to be in New York "when his book comes out so when a lot of little chickens like it" [48; sic]). With penis and pen yoked, the absence of the former makes the latter necessarily ineffectual. Jake is finally an impotent writer, unable to write directly about a certain experience, an important truth, because he can never experience it. Incapable of signifying, he is usurped by more potent sign-users, his readers. Emasculated on all levels, Jake produces a very "female" text, one exceptionally open to the literary rape of interpretation.

On the dramatic level the impossibility of consummation has created the love drama, its tensions, its dynamics. Structurally, Jake's body is itself an emblem for the romantic relationship which is likewise conspicuously deprived of genital centrality. The *factum* is not possible; this final interior experience is simply cut out, removed from the topology of love—a topology originally based on the physical reality of the female body. Romantic literature has traditionally been written by men and from a male perspective; accordingly, progression in the truth of love has been primarily based on the formal and physical progression into the female body as site of reality. While still working within this tradition, Hemingway does provide something of an inversion. It is the body of the male which now possesses the defining "hole," a hole that signifies not highest value but its very absence.

If the body-text relationship is to hold out, we would expect to find closer textual manifestations of such absence—something on the order of words on the page. If Hemingway's technique is to tell the story from the point of view of the body, it is only fitting that what is not experienced by the body is absent from the account—the physical body of the text. Accordingly, during a scene in a night club, we read this odd description: "'. . . . .' the drummer chanted" (64). What Jake did not hear he cannot remember, and he cannot record. A piece is lost from the continuum of sensory experience. Jake can only indicate its absence by tagging the missing monologue with a reference to the present speaker. The line of periods indicates textual fragmentation akin to dismemberment. The absence, however, is mediated by the very signs which are present in order to signify it.

Another instance of textual interruption presents a freer lacuna, and connects more closely with the novel's romantic content. Jake, feeling miserable, is alone with Brett in his apartment. Brett tells him she has sent the count for champagne. The next line in the text begins "Then, later" and relates a comment by Brett which sounds suspiciously post-coital: "'Do you feel better, darling?'" (55). Hemingway indicates that a brief moment of time is lost, and he deliberately foregrounds that absence by having Brett seem to refer to a specific action beyond our reading experience (it is, of course, possible that she has simply waited quietly for Jake to regain self-control). If Jake is tormented by the availability of Brett (actually on his bed with him), so too is the reader. This textual interruption is an infamous trouble spot to which critics bring their powers of interpretation—and interpolation. Because Jake cannot remember himself, critics amiably provide a sort of pseudo-memory, envisioning scenes of attempted sexual consummation. The most credible, advanced by Chaman Nahal and apparently endorsed by Mark Spilka, works by simply extending Brett's active role in the dialogue to the issue of sexual compromise (Nahal 44–45; Spilka 178). Given Hemingway's famous iceberg principle, such critical pimping isn't unconscionable (although it does dampen the initial effects of the text) but even the most liberal efforts of inference can't provide what Hemingway has ruled out of hand, that is, actual memberment. We can guess at what, in some loosely narrative sense, might have happened, but we know what couldn't have and nothing less than traditional consummation would have supplied for Jake the requisite experience.

Hemingway handles well the extraordinarily difficult task of signifying a nothing, producing a sign for an absence. There is no fact or *factum*. Hemingway has omitted both from the text, as from Jake's experience. He gives us neither consummation, nor body reality, but, instead, a noted lack of body reality. The "way it was," is simply "it wasn't." Jake's relationship with Brett, figured in those incomplete texts of physical body and bodily memory, is organized around a missing center—which seems the supreme statement of modernist semiology. Less is more. "Nothingness" is, in fact, the meaning of Jake's romance.

A further textual anomaly, a salient one, extends this meditation on nothingness as far as it can go. While episodic and meandering, Jake's narrative does follow a conventional linear time-line. The textual absences noted above are temporal hiatuses; they interrupt the time-line, that continuum of body experience, but they do not subvert it. During the exploding fiesta, however, something more momentous occurs. Jake, recovering from Cohn's punch, is told that a peasant named Girones has died of wounds inflicted by a bull. At this point the narrative voice alters noticeably. The vantage recedes, approaches omniscience. Jake—we presume he is still narrating—digresses on the fate of Girones' body, the funeral, the relatives, the fate of the bull. The style is even more dispassionate and matter-of-fact than usual, as if the event is deliberately being raised to the clinical truth status of a newspaper account. More importantly, however, the time frame is destroyed. The events described are those which will occur in the next few days. A passage concerning the fate of the bull's ear is distanced in time and place. Brett has wrapped it (in the near future) in a handkerchief "and left both ear and handkerchief . . . shoved back in the drawer of the bed-table that stood beside her bed in the Hotel Montoya, in Pamplona" (199). Jake is still in Pamplona, of course, and in the next passage linear time resumes complete with his smarting jaw.

Hemingway produces a sequence of body injuries, of compounded body experience that finally registers itself textually. The report of the destruction of Girones' body follows quickly after Jake has received a blow to the head from Cohn. The injuries reinforce each other, the narrative moving further into the experience of pain, ending at the last stage, with death, and with the image in the text of the generalized human body itself. Girones' wife has come to town, not exactly to be with her husband, but, rather, to be "with the body" (198).

Hemingway has a recurrent image, something that must have remained with him from his war experience. In a "A Natural History of the Dead," he describes what a dead body looks like. It is a curiously literary affair. "The surprising thing ... is the amount of paper that is scattered about the dead" (*CSS* 337). The same image from "A Way You'll Never Be" reads, "letters, letters, letters. There was always much paper about the dead ..." (*CSS* 307). The disintegration of the human body looks like the explosion of a book. It is an interesting metaphor, and serves our purpose in the degree to which Hemingway has—although I wouldn't say consciously—actualized it in the writing of *The Sun Also Rises*. Clearly, Hemingway wants to handle this apparently unremarkable detail of a peasant's death in a remarkable way. It is the body, after all, with which he began, and the reality of the human body which remains central to his writing. Accordingly, this final event of body alteration sends out a textual ripple. Death is an interference registered on the body of the text itself. Jake's linear history is disrupted, his own memory-text altered. And at the center of the disturbance is the image of the human body, violated in a way that is by now only appropriate—"with a horn through him" (198).

In this absolute test case of having been there, Hemingway provides the final proof of the primacy of bodily existence. In an echo of Jake's situation, Hemingway depicts the violent visitation of experience upon a human body which leaves a hole—and, effectively, it leaves nothing else. There is no opportunity for recovery here, as with the count; no scar tissue will mark the triumph of the body in its reintegration, in its filling in, in its remembering. There is instead a very important, interior nothing.

Death presents Hemingway's aesthetic with an impossible challenge, one he can only approach with his depiction of Jake's privation, and touch upon, in the case of Girones, through the mediation of third-person narration. If the text of self is coterminous with sensation, the cessation of the later must terminate the former. Hemingway pursues this logic in "The Undefeated" which ends, despite the aloofness of its third-person vantage, with Manuel Garcia's anaesthetization following a previous suggestion that he will not awake from the operation he is undergoing. Like sex, death is an event which brings the highest apprehension of the physical body, which involves the body itself most intimately in experience. Yet it is that one experience of the body which, being experienced, can never be remembered. It is a reality of the body which negates reality, the erasure itself of both body and memory texts.

Notes

1. Examples of thought-avoidance are numerous. Besides the characters in *The Sun Also Rises*, see also, for instance, Frazer in "The Gambler, the Nun and the Radio," Nick Adams in "A Way You'll Never Be," and Robert Jordan in *For Whom The Bell Tolls*.

2. Ernest Hemingway, *The Complete Short Stories of Ernest Hemingway*, ed. Finca Vigía (New York: Scribner's, 1987) 143. All further references will be cited in the text and keyed to the abbreviation *CSS*.

3. Ernest Hemingway, *The Sun Also Rises* (New York: Scribner's Sons, 1926) 132. All further references *will* be cited in the text. Citations will not be keyed.

4. The two, in fact, have enjoyed a long tradition of essential assimilation. Metaphors that likened sexual intercourse to dying were a common stay of Elizabethan writing. Identifying sex with death—even if it were only the "small death"—expressed, by asserting bodily truth, its consequentiality. The connection informs Montoya's belief that the artistic purity of the young, monastic (163), and quasi-virginal Romero ("'he'd only been with two women before'" [245]), could be laid waste by Brett.

Works Cited

Baker, Carlos. "The Way It Was." White 26–36.

Dinshaw, Carolyn. *Chaucer's Sexual Poetics*. Madison: U of Wisconsin P, 1989.

Farrell, James T. "*The Sun Also Rises*." White 53–57.

Friedman, Lionel J. "Gradus Amoris." *Romance Philology* 19 (1965): 166–77.

Harpham, Geoffrey Galt. *On the Grotesque: Strategies of Contradiction in Art and Literature*. Princeton: Princeton UP, 1982.

Hemingway, Ernest. *Death in the Afternoon*. New York: Scribner's Sons, 1932.

———. *The Sun Also Rises*. New York: Scribner's Sons, 1926.

———. *The Complete Short Stories of Ernest Hemingway*. Finca Vigía Edition. New York: Scribner's, 1987.

Levin, Harry. "Observations on the Style of Ernest Hemingway." *Hemingway: A Collection of Critical Essays*. Ed. Robert P. Weeks. Englewood Cliffs: Prentice-Hall, 1962. 72–85.

Nahal, Chaman. *The Narrative Pattern In Ernest Hemingway's Fiction*. Cranbury, New Jersey: Associated UP, 1971.

Plimpton, George. "The Art of Fiction, XXI: Hemingway." *Paris Review* 18 (1958): 61–88.

Scarry, Elaine. *The Body in Pain*. New York: Oxford UP, 1985.

Spilka, Mark. "Jake and Brett: Wounded Warriors." *Major Literary Characters: Brett Ashley*. Ed. Harold Bloom. New York: Chelsea, 1991. 175–83.

Vance, William L. "Implications of Form in *The Sun Also Rises*." *Ernest Hemingway's The Sun Also Rises*. Ed. Harold Bloom. New York: Chelsea, 1987. 39–49.

White, William, ed. *The Merrill Studies in* The Sun Also Rises. Columbus: Charles E. Merrill, 1969.

Young, Philip. "*The Sun Also Rises*: A Commentary." White 86–90.

DANIEL S. TRABER

Whiteness and the Rejected
Other in The Sun Also Rises

Work in the field of whiteness studies commonly treats white racial identity in terms of its constructed quality and the privileges unfairly rewarded
to white people. The prevalent critical standpoint is thus that whites work to
protect whiteness. In contrast, this essay will focus on a white literary character—authored, perhaps surprisingly, by Ernest Hemingway—who rejects
particular dominant versions of whiteness. In *The Sun Also Rises*, Jake Barnes
has often, and rightly, been treated as a conflicted protagonist attempting to
strike a balance between pre- and postwar narratives to endure a meaningless world. In this light, he can be read as a figure of hybridity who mixes
identities to avoid claiming allegiance to any one totalizing narrative. Ultimately, it is the Basque peasants, situated sufficiently outside and within
the center, to whom Hemingway has Jake turn as a viable Other to give his
world meaning. But rather than concentrate on how this Spanish Other is
represented in the novel, I wish to interrogate those forms of marginality
Jake withdraws from, specifically Jews and homosexuals.

Jake is easily read as anti-Semitic and homophobic, but by examining
how "whiteness" is used to denote a privileged economic and social class we
can move closer to a more nuanced understanding of Hemingway's intentions as subversive, though hardly without paradox. What follows is not necessarily to be taken as an apologia intent on clearing Hemingway, or Jake, of

From *Studies in American Fiction*, 28, no. 2 (Autumn 2000): 235–253. Copyright © 2000 by
Northeastern University.

123

charges of homophobia or racism; however, I do intend to complicate the way
Hemingway is today so easily written off in American literary studies—put on
exhibit as a fossilized exemplar of all that is wrong with the canon. Hemingway's evaluation and fictional treatment of forms of otherness according to
a rejected notion of centered whiteness reveals a complicated critical politics
existing simultaneously with prejudice. Jake's convoluted identity quest allows
us to see how marginality is deployed by Hemingway, and Jake's refusal of
particular othered identities exposes something other than a facile bigotry.

Michael Harper argues that Hemingway has a "preoccupation with
characters who exist on the fringes of society . . . [and] it is among the out-
cast and the despised, the incompletely or unsuccessfully 'socialized,' that an
alternative has the best chance of flourishing."[1] In the relationship Hemingway has with various marginal identities and the center this idea is both true
and untrue. As a character in transition and exploring options of subjectivity,
Jake's beliefs and practices are underpinned by politics. The anti-Semitism
voiced in the novel has always been problematic for readers, and recent critical interest in Jake's homophobia has reopened the issue of how forms of otherness—women, Jews, gays, and blacks—are approached by Hemingway. But
Robert Stephens' rationale for the plot's exclusion of certain characters calls
attention to the fact that white, Christian, heterosexual men and women are
equally guilty of breaking the Hemingway code:

> The outsiders are those like Robert Cohn, Mrs. Braddocks, Robert
> Prentiss, the artist Zizi, the bal musette homosexuals, and the
> Paris and Pamplona tourists who are unhaunted by *nada*, have no
> real cause for rebellion against their societies, and are messy and
> undisciplined as they imitate without comprehension the actions
> of the insiders.[2]

Of course, these are specific characters with specific narrative functions—to
express ideas through word and action—but it is a mistake to disregard how
some social types are given more degrading duties than others. The narrative snipes directed at those occupying certain socially marginal subject
positions exhibit a bias more attuned to a mindset of the past than any supposed freedom of progressive modern thought. To understand the criterion
Jake uses to determine the forms of marginality worth appropriating it is
necessary to analyze the groups chosen to portray the negative side of the
Lost Generation. And Cohn and the *bal musette* homosexuals are the figures
who best delineate where such boundaries get drawn.

Hemingway's ability to offer social commentary and facilitate characterization through a self-conscious manipulation of derogatory racial and ethnic

slurs—a deft maneuvering that absolutely proves he is capable of recognizing racism—is already found in the story collection *In Our Time*, published prior to *The Sun Also Rises*. An unequivocal example of this is found in the chapter 8 vignette featuring the word "wops." This piece depicts American nativism at its worst, resulting in the death of two foreigners by a policeman named Boyle who fires without warning. While his partner is worried about the possible repercussions of the act, the murderer fully understands the racial climate of the times: "They're wops, ain't they? Who the hell is going to make any trouble?"[3] It is with the heaviest of critical irony that an Irish American cop claims he "can tell wops a mile off," since the victims are actually Hungarians. Hemingway is critiquing the kind of assimilation a "Boyle" makes once he adopts the hatred toward the Other—defined as anyone different from himself—that constitutes "white" America's racial policy.

A more complex application of racial slurs occurs in "The Battler," where the African American character Bugs is referred to through a careful shuttling between the terms "negro" and "nigger." One might accuse Hemingway of essentialist racism in having Nick "know" Bugs is black by his voice and walk before he can more clearly see the man, but the significance of Nick's perceptions becomes clearer once Bugs's submissive demeanor around Ad Francis and Nick is established. "The negro" is the term most frequently used in reference to Bugs, but it is those "nigger legs" and the deferential "Mister" Bugs uses when addressing the white men that tell us more about Bugs's oppressed condition as a black man and Hemingway's possible racial politics.[4] While "negro" lacks the intentional racism of "nigger" (putting aside the issue of how scientific discourses created this racial nomenclature and conferred legitimacy upon institutionalized racism), it nonetheless remains problematic, since Hemingway has named Bugs yet continually chooses to identify him by a racial category, in effect reducing him to that category. However, race may be exactly what Hemingway hopes to emphasize, for by constantly reminding the reader of Bugs's blackness he offers a foil to Ad's psychotic behavior and the train brakeman's own violent treatment of Nick. Of course, this plot tactic opens the question of a black character once again being placed in the stereotypical role of dutiful benevolence; however, such a degree of ambiguity in Hemingway's management of otherness should forestall a too easy condemnation or apology for the way he presents such figures.[5]

In *The Sun Also Rises*, any overly generalized conclusion about Hemingway's opinion of Jews as a group proves equally difficult. In Hemingway's letters we find anti-Semitic slurs used casually, yet the correspondence also exhibits close friendships with Jews, particularly Harold Loeb (the source for Robert Cohn) and Gertrude Stein.[6] It is unwise to draw too close a connection between Hemingway's work and his life without recognizing how he manipulates the "facts," as critics like Frederic Svoboda and Michael S. Reynolds remind us.[7] Nonetheless, it is significant that Hemingway openly expresses feelings of friendship for Harold Loeb in his letters. Prior to their falling out one is struck by how insistent Hemingway is that Loeb come to visit him; he is "sad as hell," he tells Loeb, "that you're not coming [to Austria]. We'd have had such a hell of a good time."[8] In his apology to Loeb, written the night of their infamous argument in Pamplona, Hemingway is effusive in his repentance and highly self-critical: "I'm thoroly ashamed of the way I acted and the stinking, unjust uncalled for things I said."[9] Even this limited evidence suggests that Hemingway is more guilty, at least in *The Sun Also Rises*, of being angry with a particular Jew and permitting himself to take the low road of racist stereotyping to "fight" Loeb in his writing than of wielding an uncritical anti-Semitism. Yet such a biographical explanation does not fully account for how Hemingway uses the Jewish Other in his first novel.

Criticism of Robert Cohn's negative depiction as a Jewish character is hardly the result of any recent awakening in ethical consciousness, for it followed close on the heels of the novel's publication. In a December 1926 letter to Maxwell Perkins, in which Hemingway dismisses the reaction of critics to the immoral and "unattractive" characters, he is prompted to defend his portrayal of Cohn: "And why not make a Jew a bounder in literature as well as in life? Do jews always have to be so splendid in writing?"[10] This rhetorical appeal to common sense and the logic of realism has failed to convince many readers there is no ulterior motive behind a Jew being selected to play the author's primary whipping boy. And rightly so, for our ability to make sense of Cohn, as well as how otherness as a whole is articulated by Hemingway, depends on answering the question of this character's function in the novel.

Linda Wagner-Martin reads the stereotyping as Hemingway keeping to his pattern of splitting off from a mentor, in this case Gertrude Stein—a Jew whose lesbianism was hardly kept in the closet. This explanation carries weight when one recalls how Jake feminizes Cohn by accusing him of being "moulded by the two women who had trained him," suggesting that the author feared being considered solely the product of Stein's influence.[11] Wagner-Martin's idea becomes doubly significant in view of the history of Harold Loeb and Hemingway's relationship. In *The Way It Was* (1959), Loeb's memoirs of the period, he claims to have helped get *In Our Time* published by Liveright. Both Hemingway's letters and Loeb's narrative tell a story of two close friends who genuinely care for, enjoy and respect each other until their falling out over a woman. In fact, he and Hemingway shared the same opinion of the Lost Generation. Loeb criticizes Duff Twysden's fiancé, Pat Guthrie, as "typical, I suspected, of that fraction of the British upper class which chooses parasitism for a vocation."[12] This similarity of opinion, in conjunction with

Loeb's assistance with the publishers, may be why Hemingway wanted to cut himself off from his one time friend. Loeb's recollections of the time also reveal, if we are willing to take him at his word thirty years after the events, the extent to which Hemingway manipulates his characterization of Robert Cohn. There is a good deal that corresponds to Loeb's life, but the details informing Jake's rejection of Cohn do not; namely, the elite social background of the upper class that Hemingway/Jake associates Cohn with, but that Loeb presents himself as having rejected.

This authorial control over character adds credence to Josephine Knopf's reading, which locates Cohn in Jewish literary traditions as the stock type "schlemiel," a bumbling trickster who consistently fails, yet serves as a device for social criticism.[13] Knopf convincingly argues that Cohn's infractions of the expatriate code offer Hemingway an opportunity to present this Jewish character as "somewhat beyond the pale of the peculiar society in which he functioned, and somewhat superior to it," thus having the chance "either to make meaningful social commentary or to develop insights concerning the condition of man."[14] But Hemingway does not take that opening; instead, he uses Cohn as the foil to Jake (despite their being doubles as writers who have certain romantic impulses) and relies on a characterization easily read as suggesting that "the traits of meanness, corruption, and weakness are somehow closely bound up with Jewishness."[15]

Michael Reynolds appeals for a degree of clemency being granted to Hemingway on the grounds of historical context and accuracy: anti-Semitism, as well as anti-Catholicism and racism, were rampant during this period, so Hemingway is to be treated as a man shaped by his time: "To fault Hemingway for his prejudice is to read the novel anachronistically. . . . The novel's anti-Semitism tells us little about its author but a good deal about America in 1926. To forget how we were in the twenties is to read the novel out of context.[16] This evasion strikes me as too easy, as though Hemingway were incapable of changing his opinions, especially when we recall that Jake mentions how Robert became "race-conscious" at Princeton (4). The phrase implies that Hemingway, as well as his narrator, understands what it means to treat someone differently because of race or ethnicity—and, consequently, that some will consider anti-Semitic utterances in the novel to be immoral. Hence, Hemingway depicts Jake as *choosing* to express certain "racist" opinions about Robert, based on his Jewishness, that cannot simply be traced to Hemingway's socialization in a specific historical moment.[17] This is a conscious act of labeling; therefore, it behooves us to analyze why that choice is made.

To Reynolds' credit (as well as John Rouch's) he does observe the control Hemingway has over representing *Jake's* representation of Robert Cohn.[18]

But what of the authorial and narratorial control Jake is granted by Hemingway? To overlook the centrality of Jake Barnes as the narrator diminishes
our understanding of the novel's purpose: Hemingway's possible message of
hope and durability for a society so mired in meaninglessness. Jake is as guilty
as anyone of making prejudiced comments (most memorably about noses,
stubbornness, and money), but much of the overtly malicious anti-Semitism
in the novel is put in the mouths of the people whom Jake is gradually growing tired of—those he deliberately depicts himself casting aside. Mike's cruel
treatment of Cohn during the festival, by continually targeting his Jewishness, is hardly intended to win the approbation of readers. Indeed, the other
members of the group are shocked by the level of hatred Mike spews forth.
It is even explicitly condemned by Bill Gorton—"I don't like Cohn ... but
nobody has any business to talk like Mike"—who has proven himself bigoted
toward Jews and blacks (145). Yet a character like Bill proves useful for noting
how Hemingway complicates matters, since he often plays the role of comic
relief. Bill's frequent use of irony, added on top of Jake's own, causes some
of his racist comments to fall into a gray area. A prime example is when he
speaks of an African-American boxer being cheated in Vienna. Bill begins
his story by saying there is "injustice everywhere" but then uses the term "nigger" throughout; Hemingway/Jake even has Bill toss in a touch of supposed
black dialect with "musta" (71). Is this to be read as a racist blindspot or an
example of facetious (even cynical) dark humor? It is hard to tell, for although
there are several unequivocal moments when Bill speaks the language of racism with reference to Cohn, his instances of anti-conservative irony, such as
the several times he openly ridicules organized religion, work to confuse the
political identity one can attach to him; thus Hemingway/Jake disrupts the
reader's ability to make meaning or achieve sure closure.[19]

The same ambiguity can be applied to Jake's varied responses to the
Other. At the club Zelli's, after dinner with Brett and Count Mippipopolous,
Jake nonchalantly refers to the jazz musician as a "nigger drummer" who is
"all teeth and lips" (62). There are neither details nor commentary offered
to suggest a sense of irony. Nor does Jake interpret (and thus license the
reader to interpret) the drummer's behavior—including his spoken "Hahre
you?" and "Thaats good"—as the mask an African American must don to
appease the white folks who pay his salary. This representation of a black
Other (the only one Jake "himself" makes in the novel) seems an irrefutable
example of racism on Hemingway/Jake's part. Yet consider the significance of
the preceding chapter, in which lake calls attention to his authorial position
by confessing complicity in negatively representing Cohn: "Somehow I feel
I have not shown Robert Cohn clearly" and "I probably have not brought
it [Robert's cheerfulness] out" (45). Here he suggests the impossibility of

objective writing and that his statements should not be taken as unquestionable truths. No matter how stripped down the language or submerged the iceberg, authorial bias will enter the (re)presentation of characters and events. As with the treatment of Bugs in "The Battler," it would seem Hemingway is subtly undermining the very racism he has his characters display.

Hemingway ensures that any analysis of Jake is slippery because so many of his statements about Cohn are contradictory as articulations of either inclusion or exclusion. Jake says he likes Cohn (he even includes him in his prayers at the cathedral in Pamplona [97]), but will later claim to dislike him; he feels sorry for Cohn and then deliberately withholds sympathy: he feminizes Cohn as highly emotional and childish, yet has this unmasculine man physically conquer the novel's two code heroes by knocking Jake out and pummeling Pedro Romero into a bloody mess. Additionally, given Jake's Catholicism, a fact he often mentions, Jake and Cohn are both members of religious groups suffering prejudice against immigrants during the nineteenth and twentieth centuries.[20] Karen Brodkin notes that nineteenth-century "anti-Catholicism and anti-Semitism overlapped and fused with racial stigmatization of southern and eastern Europeans;" add to this the Ku Klux Klan's powerful and popular nativist voice in the 1920s against these religious Others and we have Hemingway deploying a strategically placed ambivalence which forces one to find a reason, beyond simply charging the author and/or narrator with anti-Semitism and racism, to understand why Cohn is anathema to Jake.[21]

Some reasons for Cohn being depicted so negatively are obvious: he has sex with Brett (a pleasure Jake will never be able to experience), he does not follow the code (especially the rule about emotional control in public), and as Jake's double figure he is an ever-present reminder of Jake's own proclivity for sentimental yearning. Jake has the same impossible romantic feelings for Brett, but he learns how to deal with them and continue existing without experiencing a full-fledged breakdown like Robert. Jake has achieved the kind of identity Cohn never will; he can be read as a hybrid made from equal parts of the old and new narratives who makes the leap a person like Cohn is incapable of making. Of all his offenses, the major one is still Cohn's inability to live according to the code, but this should be linked to what proves an equally important facet of Cohn's characterization: his social background.[22]

Robert is the product of one of the wealthiest and oldest Jewish families in New York. (Harold Loeb was born in 1891, related to the Guggenheims on his mother's side.) Hemingway may have come from an upper middle-class environment but that facet of Hemingway's life is never clearly ascribed to Jake. Thus it is notable that in a text so concerned with details and using words sparingly that the reader is given scenes and signifiers that emphasize

Cohn's privileged upbringing. I will point to three key moments. First, during an argument over Brett, Robert angrily stands up and demands that Jake
"take back" a disparaging but true remark he made about Brett. Jake responds
with, "Oh, cut out the prep-school stuff" (39). Second, after the fight in Pamplona (once again over Brett) in which Robert knocks Jake out, in the midst
of describing Cohn's bawling apology Jake mentions that he is wearing "a
white polo shirt [a button-down oxford], the kind he'd worn at Princeton"
(194). Third, Cohn offers a social climber's reason for being impressed by
Brett: her "breeding" and title (38).

The instances mark Robert as a well-born, well-bred and well-financed
person; he is the antithesis of the marginality found in the Basque peasants,
and that is why Jake turns away from Cohn as a source of otherness. Robert's
consciousness is shaped by his connection to the Ivy League set and connotes
a deeply-held world view rooted in the status quo that Jake finds retrograde.
Cohn's mentality and behavior—prepared to fight to protect the good name
of his "lady love" (178)—are indicative of values he has been taught in pres-
tigious schools and read in romantic novels. Jake too refers to the past to
understand his place in the world, but the ideals Cohn supports are useless to
him. Hence, the rejection of Robert Cohn supersedes merely his "race"; it is
the combination of social origin and code breaking that invalidates him.[23]

Jean-Paul Sartre's philosophy of otherness posits that forms of marginality can be used to break the binds of society, allowing one to become more
"authentic" by rejecting a society's normative values.[24] In *Anti-Semite and Jew*,
he theorizes Jewish otherness (admittedly in a romantic and often essentialist manner) as a subversive threat to white Western society's self-conception
as "civilized" and superior. Therefore, according to Sartre, non-Jews should
try to emulate the Jewish Other by placing themselves outside the center;
Jews themselves should resist the desire to assimilate into bourgeois society
or to "pass" for non-Semite. Sartre's perspective cannot be wholly attributed
to Jake, nevertheless, it does offer a perspective for understanding Jake's reaction to Cohn that allows us to go deeper than noting a callous anti-Semitism.
Like Sartre's "inauthentic Jew," Cohn has spent his life trying to shape himself according to the mainstream standards of "civility"; thus, he fails to be a
transgressive source at the level of social marginality.[25] This character offers
a way to think about whiteness as the dominant identity of the center, one
constituting a specific economic and social class based on the assumed superiority of a certain race.

The signifiers of the American upper class—boarding school, Princeton,
polo shirts—attributed to Cohn can also be read as marking a virulent form
of privileged white identity. Indeed, the details Jake gives the reader suggest
that Cohn's wealthy family—which, being one of the oldest, arrived before the

massive wave of Jewish immigration in the late nineteenth and early twentieth centuries—has trained him to desire assimilation in order to carry on the
family's mission of achieving acceptance. Cohn occupies a privileged place at
the center of marginalized peoples, all the while trying to gain access to that
more central culture of affluent whites. Jake uses a biblical allusion to describe
Cohn's reaction to Brett as akin to the Hebrews' upon entering the "promised
land," and this reference can be extended as a comment on the American-
ized version of the promised land as wealth and higher social status—the
dream Brett represents in Cohn's imagination (22). Thus Robert is depicted
by Hemingway/Jake as accepting legitimized hierarchical notions of racial
superiority and discarding the subversive potential of his own otherness.

Ron Berman comments on this situation: "Cohn too wants to be transformed, but the issue resolves itself into one of social identity: he wants not
only to escape Paris and the civilized condition but to escape himself as he
is seen by others. Cohn is a rootless Jew ... who imitates exhausted Protestantism."[26] Yet, while noting that "Cohn becomes or tries to become what
Hemingway refused to become," Berman misses a particular ramification
of this move by focusing solely on the non-Semites' reactions to Cohn as a
"false gentleman" in a defensive response to his attempted assimilation (45,
44).[27] This is surely applicable to the characters other than Jake who speak of
Brett needing to stay with her own "kind," but the novel's narrator expresses
no concern about the matter (102, 203). It is rather the problem of Cohn's
willingness to adopt that identity itself that bothers Jake. What is revealed is
not the source for his occasional expressions of anti-Semitism, but instead
Jake's repudiation of Cohn's maneuvering to affiliate himself with an elitist
Anglo-Saxonism through the likes of Brett and Mike (the holders of "true"
Anglo-Saxon "blood") that will give him further access to all the privileges
and abuses the upper class enjoy with their closed version of whiteness. This is
the identity Cohn desires; therefore, Jake chooses to dissociate himself from
Cohn in the same way he eventually dismisses Brett and Mike.

The novel's negative treatment of otherness may seem more obvious
with homosexuality, but it too has deeper ramifications as a comment on the
code and, at a further level, on race. At the Parisian *bal musette*, a group of
young gay men arrives with Brett, at which point Jake commences to objec-
tify them according to their appearance and behavior, all the while scornfully
referring to the group as "them" or "they." In their article deconstructing the
novel's code hero, Arnold and Cathy Davidson theorize Jake's negative reaction as an act of othering: "Jake may be ill-equipped to deal with Brett's
sexuality, but not from lack of desire. Lacking such desire, the gay men who
accompany Brett are thus defined as Other—not men, not Jake."[28] Jake's dislike for this group stems from their having the ability to sexually "act like

men" but choosing to conduct themselves otherwise when Jake lacks that choice. Several critics have called attention to the fact that Jake finds himself in the role of a feminized male due to his war wound; therefore, he too is a sexual Other, yet one aiming to reassure himself of his own masculinity in conventional terms.[29]

In Paris, Hemingway presents a world of inverted gender roles: boys who like boys; girls who dress like boys; boys who weep like girls and plead with their lovers; boys who must perform sex like girls because they lack a penis (which is now the sole means of truly distinguishing one from the other). I agree with Peter Messent and David Blackmore that Hemingway views these changes more as a threat than signs of a new world open to diverse, multiple forms of being.[30] Queerness threatens Jake's discourse of masculinity, reminding him how the loss of the phallus undermines that narrative, and he is not interested in adopting such a subject position. He may like Brett's short haircut, but as concerns his own sense of gender he would prefer to maintain the old values, where men are assumed to be "men." That Jake essentializes homosexuals—"They are like that"—so as to configure them as another negative example supporting his social philosophy is obvious; otherwise the reader would get a more "positive" gay character. But such an alternative never makes an entrance, and the Burguete fishing trip episode with Bill and Harris works hard to posit an idealized homosocial relationship as a counterbalance to homosexuality: men being friends with men, no strings attached.[31]

Significantly, however, Jake once again admits to breaking with postwar values of accepting difference in his refusal to condone queerness. His statement, "I know they are supposed to be amusing, and you should be tolerant" (20), carries the same implications of mentioning Cohn becoming "race-conscious" at college. Jake evaluates his own reaction as negative and unjust; he acknowledges his own failure to live up to a "modern," progressive standard (one based on the stereotype of homosexuals as "amusing"). During the fishing trip, Bill addresses the more sophisticated, lenient attitude toward diversity found in Europe and points to a growing anxiety in America. He says to Jake, "Listen. You're a hell of a guy, and I'm fonder of you than anybody on earth. I couldn't tell you that in New York. It'd mean I was a faggot" (116). In Europe, homosocial relationships are not as suspect as back home. Nevertheless, back in Paris Jake wants "to swing on one, any one, anything to shatter that superior, simpering composure" (20). He uses stereotypical signs the reader is meant to associate with queerness so as to separate these men from heterosexuals like himself. The encoded smile he shares with the policeman when Brett's crowd enters connotes his attempt to salvage a sense of stability. Jake's feelings here, on the edge of violence, can be read as symptomatic of the continued problem of prejudice in America, but additionally as an outgrowth of the challenges to provincialism made by emerging subjectivities coming out of the closet. Beyond Jake's homophobia, what else is Hemingway trying to expose through this character's voice and story? Jake's refusal to blend queer men's marginal subjectivity into his own identity is surely founded in prejudice, a closed notion of what constitutes proper masculinity, but, as with Cohn's Jewishness, it is subtly offered to the reader as something extra—a dislike for jerks.

This othering further expresses Jake's conception of the code in the novel. He overhears one of the effeminate men speak of dancing with the prostitute Georgette for a laugh: "I do declare. There is an actual harlot. I'm going to dance with her, Lett. You watch me" (20). Eventually they all take part in the joke by dancing with her, objectifying Georgette as a toy for their amusement, and this infuriates Jake. He may use Georgette to keep up masculine appearances, as the Davidsons suggest, but Jake does not treat her with outright disrespect or intentionally hire her so as to humiliate her in front of his friends (admittedly, this semblance of respect is dulled by Jake's joking about her "wonderful smile" which objectifies Georgette for the benefit of the reader [8]).[32] As a *poule*, Georgette is also a marginal social figure, an Other, but she understands the code and Jake *does* respect her for that. Certainly Jake does not want to be gay, but it is the personality of this group that is used to mark the kind of people in general he wants to separate himself from.[33] This is where Wolfgang Rudat should look to answer his question about what Jake thinks "he has that makes him superior to gays."[34] It is a matter of how he chooses to treat people that distinguishes him from the way the homosexuals are represented as acting. For even when Jake dislikes someone, and the novel is littered with people he dislikes, he is rarely shown ridiculing them publicly in the manner of Lett and his friends. Still, Hemingway/Jake's irony cuts through this moment. The smile passed between Jake and the policeman is a non-verbal example of his ability to ridicule, and on another level Jake and the homosexuals actually do behave similarly: Jake uses a version of the Other (the gay men) to make himself feel superior *morally* in the public constituted by the reader, while Lett and the boys use a different version of the Other (Georgette) to make themselves feel superior *socially* in the public realm of the club.

But what is truly curious in this scene is the way Hemingway has Jake cunningly connect the homosexuals' pompous behavior to a form of racial centeredness. Jake's description of the men when they enter the club includes a very particular detail: he calls attention to their "white hands" and "white faces" (20). The Davidsons offer an explication: "The suggestion is that the faces are pale, like the powdered faces of women; that the hands are white in contradistinction to the tanned hands of real men—the dark, leathery hands of a Basque shepherd."[35] This is compelling, but to insist that Jake's singling out of "whiteness does not mark race" is problematic because he forces the reader to "see" the whiteness of the homosexuals rather than pass over it as an invisible, assumed norm. None of Jake's friends have worker's hands, those who are not writers are ne'er-do-wells like Mike and Brett, and she is hardly a woman of the "powdered face" type. So what is the motivation for racially naming these men as white when the assumption of whiteness is adequate for the other characters?

The suggestion is that the homosexuals represent not only the kind of Other Jake repudiates, they are also the kind of white people he wishes to dissociate himself from. To name the homosexuals' race implicitly creates a hierarchy of whiteness which is composed of varying shades, so to speak, each carrying a different sense of values in Jake's mind. The homosexuals' whiteness represents that of privileged non-workers who exploit those different from themselves (here on a class level) for enjoyment. In a sense, they are not "Other" enough in that they maintain the condescending attitude of slumming tourists. They enter the environment of the *bal musette* as foreigners exploiting the exotic; indeed, this accusation is fairly applicable to all the expatriates at the club, which is usually a gathering place for the working class: "Five nights a week the working people of the Pantheon quarter danced there. One night a week it was the dancing-club" (19). The expatriates take over the club for one night rather than using it the way the workers do during the rest of the week; they impose a different meaning on it as a social space, one that cuts it off from the local culture. This symbolizes a refusal to acclimate by expatriates and tourists alike, thus conflating the two. It is symptomatic of a colonialist mentality that perpetuates a negative view of marginality to establish one group's sense of superiority over those posited as Other.

The difference between Jake and the expatriates who behave this way infuses a sense of class consciousness into his system of judging people, which can then be read back onto Jake's friends without the narrator having to directly state it. Jake's friends rise above neither their class elitism nor, by extension, their race. The *bal musette* scene quietly works to prepare the reader for judging their actions and attitudes during the Pamplona festival. They are all associated with this kind of whiteness as they exhibit the elements of "bad form" they attribute to the busloads of American and British tourists. Rather than showing respect for the culture they are in, they abuse it for their own pleasure. In one scene, a drunken Bill buys shoe-shines for Mike, having several boys working at once, because he finds it entertaining to throw money at the subaltern for a form of song and dance. Brett's own pleasure is fulfilled by "corrupting" Pedro Romero, which breaks the local cultural code of the aficionados by imposing her own values on someone who is for Brett the local Other. And, of course, Jake is eventually complicit with this process by bringing Brett and Pedro together. This colonialist type of whiteness unintentionally gets the better of Jake, and that is part of Hemingway's point. He is also commenting on the expatriates' failure to cut themselves completely off from past narratives by showing how easily one falls back into the old practices. To remedy this, one must find a way to combine the old and new in a precarious balance.

The great paradox in the novel's critique of elitism as a form of racial identity is that Hemingway accomplishes it by targeting figures from marginalized groups. The treatment of Cohn and the homosexuals points to a conscious system of exclusion, albeit one that Jake thinks is based on a higher sense of values, so his transgression is seemingly compromised. For Earl Rovit, it is Hemingway's own upper middle-class background in Oak Park that results in the author's

> casual racist, anti-immigrant, anti-Semitic, anti-urban sex chauvinism ... [and] nostalgia for preindustrialized America that was, in reality, merely a fantasy of childhood. These "new" alien Americans—immigrant, working-class, or bourgeoisie—were patently "not one of us."[36]

I have shown that Hemingway does not include Jake in that supposed "us." It should also be noted that Cohn's family would not consider itself part of those "'new' alien Americans," so Cohn's denigrated Jewishness in the novel cannot be positioned so easily as expressing anti-immigrant sentiment. Nonetheless, Rovit does offer a productive means for thinking about otherness in the novel by relating Hemingway's social training to Jake's own "way of accenting individualism [that] characteristically asserts selfhood by excluding ... [other people] rather than by absorbing creatively from others to strengthen that self."[37] This speaks to the situation with Cohn and the homosexuals, they are indeed the repugnant Other that threatens Jake's own sense of self. The problem here is that Rovit does not acknowledge how Jake is still in the process of creating that self, and that one always works from a narrative of exclusion when constituting an identity. Whether that subjectivity is based on outsider or mainstream sources, choices are made about what and how much enters the mix. He also disregards how Jake uses his experience in Spain where he does turn to a form of marginality "creatively" in order to construct his individuality.

It is the Spain chapters that offer a version of difference Jake deems worthy of integration. Cohn and the homosexuals show us people classified as Others who adopt the exclusionary practices of the center, be it respect for title and family or the arrogant mistreatment of "inferiors." This in turn emphasizes the way Jake, a figure who moves with and is accepted by the center, chooses a marginal group in Spain to develop his subjectivity, albeit a group that satisfies his desire for a modicum of traditionalism—found in a sense of order and a conventional model of masculinity. It is the conflict between staid morality and modern alienation that leads to Spain's eventual significance in the novel. Jake's need for a personal center to give him the ground from which to make moral decisions and structure his life demarcates Spanish culture as posing a better standard. The romanticized Spanish subaltern is marked as a useful source for hybridity: a form of fixity and communitarian sensibility resorting neither to the constrictive morality of the American middle class nor to the highly individualistic and hollow practices of the expatriate as romantic poseur or "authentic" libertine. Instead, Jake turns to a space he hopes will allow him to effectively interpret existence and find a way to just "live in it" (148). Ultimately, that space also fails to fulfill Jake's desires, but that remains beyond the borders of my investigation here.

NOTES

1. Michael Harper, "Men without Politics: Hemingway's Social Consciousness," *New Orleans Review* 12, no. 1 (1985), 19.

2. Robert O. Stephens, "Ernest Hemingway and the Rhetoric of Escape," in *Ernest Hemingway's The Sun Also Rises*, ed. Harold Bloom (New York: Chelsea, 1987), 53.

3. Ernest Hemingway, *In Our Time* (1925; New York: Scribner's, 1996), 79.

4. Hemingway, *In Our Time*, 57.

5. Michael Reynolds narrates how Hemingway submitted "The Battler" as a substitute story at the request of Liveright before they would publish *In Our Time*. Hemingway used "nigger"—"the word most in use by the society that raised him" and which was "true to his ear, to the sounds of the time," according to Reynolds— but the publisher changed it to "negro." See *Hemingway: The Paris Years* (New York: Norton, 1989), 279. However, that both words appear suggests that Hemingway had some final control over usage. For another discussion of Hemingway's use of African-American characters see Toni Morrison's *Playing in the Dark: Whiteness and the Literary Imagination* (Cambridge: Harvard Univ. Press, 1992), which analyzes this problem in *To Have and Have Not*.

6. For the sake of honesty, I have cataloged Hemingway's less than egalitarian moments toward groups other to his own sense of self. In his 1923–1927 correspondence in *Selected Letters: 1917–1961*, ed. Carlos Baker (New York: Scribner's, 1981) one finds: five explicit references to Jews, the first three of which can be read as directly anti-Semitic (May 2, 1924; July 19, 1924; Dec. 6, 1924; May 21, 1926; Dec. 21, 1926); one use of "coon" (April 22, 1925); and three references to "fairies," the first of which seems to carry a hint of irony (Sept. 15, 1927; Oct. 8, 1927; Dec. 13, 1927).

7. Frederic Joseph Svoboda, *Hemingway & The Sun Also Rises: The Crafting of a Style* (Lawrence: Univ. Press of Kansas, 1983) and Michael S. Reynolds, The

Sun Also Rises: *A Novel of the Twenties* (Boston: Twayne, 1988). The first person structure of the novel, along with the autobiographical roots of the events described, presents all the usual problems about where to draw the line between author and narrator. Hemingway creates Jake as both narrator and author of the text, and while that does not entirely relieve him of authorial responsibility for any racist content it certainly complicates matters. Despite Hemingway's self-promotion as a writer who does not hide behind language, he is a cagey author who consciously presents ideas in a way to forestall the reader from arriving at any "one true" interpretation. Thus I will use "Hemingway/Jake" or note the "dual" authorship in other ways when I think it necessary to mark the importance of considering both the real author and the constructed one as responsible for manipulating the novel's formal elements with a specific intention.

8. *Selected Letters*, 142.

9. *Selected Letters*, 66.

10. *Selected Letters*, 240.

11. Ernest Hemingway, *The Sun Also Rises* (New York: Scribner's, 1986), 45. Hereafter cited parenthetically.

12. Harold Loeb, *The Way It Was* (New York: Criterion, 1959), 250.

13. Josephine Z. Knopf, "Meyer Wolfsheim and Robert Cohn: A Study of a Jewish Type and Stereotype," in *Ernest Hemingway's The Sun Also Rises*, ed. Harold Bloom (New York: Chelsea, 1987), 67.

14. Knopf, 68.

15. Knopf, 70.

16. Michael S. Reynolds, "The *Sun* in Its Time: Recovering the Historical Context," in *New Essays on* The Sun Also Rises, ed. Linda Wagner-Martin (Cambridge: Cambridge Univ. Press, 1987), 54.

17. I apply scare quotes to the term racist because placing Jews within racialist categories is by no means the consensus. For some, like Janet Helms in *Black and White Racial Identity: Theory, Research, and Practice* (Westport: Greenwood, 1996), ethnicity speaks more to a group identity based on shared cultural behavior, values and beliefs, so the distinction between Semite and Jew is one between race and ethnicity. But there are those like Karen Brodkin who continue to refer to Jews as a race, although she complicates this with the term "ethnoracial" identity in *How Jews Became White Folks, and What That Says about Race in America* (New Brunswick: Rutgers Univ. Press, 1998). The trajectory of racial thinking concerning Jews has its own history. Matthew Frye Jacobson informs us that in the late nineteenth century, American political discourse often relied on a notion of whiteness but the word "did not carry the same meaning that it does in the late twentieth century: both in nineteenth-century science and in popular understanding the white community itself comprised many sharply distinguishable races. The categories 'Celt,' 'Slav,' 'Hebrew,' and 'Anglo-Saxon' represented an order of difference deeper than any current notions of 'ethnicity.'" See *Special Sorrows: The Diasporic Imagination of Irish, Polish, and Jewish Immigrants in the United States* (Cambridge: Harvard Univ. Press, 1995), 185. Within this hierarchy of the shades of pale, Jews, like so many other immigrant groups, were typically held racially as not-quite-white and thus less American. It is during the early twentieth century, with the rise of nativist attacks against "dark" immigrants integrating themselves into American life, that scientific narratives about race hold sway over more cultural-influenced arguments by attributing social and behavioral characteristics to biological and geographical/national determinants.

Sander Gilman's *The Jew's Body* (London: Routledge, 1991) discusses at length scientific theories about the superiority of the Anglo-Saxon blood of northwest Europe that differentiated between true Americans and immigrants, between the inheritors of a pure race and those "mongrelized" inferior Others weakening it. Thus Jews were not considered purely "white" during the period that Hemingway wrote *The Sun Also Rises*. According to Karen Brodkin, Jews did not "become" white in American popular consciousness until after World War Two, when larger numbers moved from ethnically distinct urban neighborhoods to suburbs where they were able to assimilate and share in the economic and social privileges accorded to "whites."

18. Michael S. Reynolds, The Sun Also Rises: *A Novel of the Twenties* (Boston: Twayne, 1988) and John S. Rouch, "Jake Barnes as Narrator," *Modern Fiction Studies* 11 (1965–66), 361–70.

19. See James Hinkle, "What's Funny in *The Sun Also Rises*." *The Hemingway Review* 4, no. 2 (1985). 31–41, for a closer study of the context and narrative function of humor in the novel.

20. The choice to make Jake a Catholic becomes all the more weighted with meaning when we recall that Hemingway had not himself converted at this time. The rituals of Catholicism, a system of order so lacking in the modern world, and the conflict arising from Jake's failure to believe in them devoutly are used symbolically in the novel. However, to overlook the equivalent prejudice expressed toward Catholics and Jews during this period will miss the subtle manner in which Hemingway complicates a reader's possible reactions to both Barnes and Cohn.

21. Brodkin, *How Jews Became White Folks*, 55. Also see Waller Benn Michaels' *Our America: Nativism, Modernism, and Pluralism* (Durham: Duke Univ. Press, 1995) for an extended study of nativism and modernist American literature. Michael's few remarks on *The Sun Also Rises* (26–29, 72–74) are concerned with the treatment of Cohn as a Jew, and I hope to problematize Michaels' reading that Cohn is a character used solely to evoke a negative, parochial response to immigrants.

22. Wolfgang E. H. Rudat, "Anti-Semitism in *The Sun Also Rises*: Traumas, Jealousies, and the Genesis of Cohn," *American Imago* 49 (1992), 263–75, mentions the economic difference between Loeb and Hemingway as a factor in Cohn's negative characterization but more as a matter of envy. Rudat focuses on how Cohn can be used to understand the issue of Jake's sexuality in the novel.

23. It may be countered that Brett and Mike are equally dependent on titles and origins in "good" families but that they do not come under the same kind of censure as Robert. This is valid to a point, for while they are lively, witty, and more adept at heavy drinking, their social credentials influence their behavior as negatively as Cohn's; indeed, more so. These characters use their names to insulate them from responsibility and repercussions; however, their class status hardly protects them from criticism in the novel. It is not Hemingway's intention that readers "like" Brett and Mike or wish to emulate their parasitic and elitist practices. Marc Baldwin states it well: "The social hierarchy, based on 'breeding' and money, does not necessarily correspond to the natural *class* exhibited by those simple people who work for a living and assume no pretentious airs of superiority." "Class Consciousness and the Ideology of Dominance in *The Sun Also Rises*," *The McNeese Review* 32 (1994), 16.

24. Jean-Paul Sartre, *Anti-Semite and Jew* (New York: Schocken, 1965). Also see Stuart Zane Charmé's *Vulgarity and Authenticity: Dimensions of Otherness in the World of Jean-Paul Sartre* (Amherst: Univ. of Massachusetts Press, 1991) for a study of this issue.

25. Sander Gilman's *The Jew's Body* documents how many Jews desired to be accepted as phenotypically and culturally white in the 1920s (179, 238).

26. Ron Berman, "Protestant, Catholic, Jew: *The Sun Also Rises*," *The Hemingway Review* 18, no. 1 (1998), 43.

27. Berman, 45 and 44.

28. Arnold E. and Cathy N. Davidson, "Decoding the Hemingway Hero in *The Sun Also Rises*," in *New Essays on* The Sun Also Rises, ed. Linda Wagner-Martin (Cambridge: Cambridge Univ. Press, 1987), 90.

29. See the Davidsons' article; Nancy R. Comley and Robert Scholes's *Hemingway's Genders: Rereading the Hemingway Text* (New Haven: Yale Univ. Press, 1994); Wolfgang Rudat's "Hemingway on Sexual Otherness: What's Really Funny in *The Sun Also Rises*," in *Hemingway Repossessed*, ed. Kenneth Rosen (Westport, CT: Greenwood, 1994), 169–79; and Peter Messent's *Ernest Hemingway* (New York: St. Martin's, 1992). All these critics also point to how Hemingway problematizes sexual pairing at the club through three groups: the heterosexual Brett enters with her gay friends; the wounded Jake arrives with the prostitute Georgette (whose very profession is the act Jake cannot perform); and the scene closes with Georgette dancing with the homosexuals as Brett and Jake leave.

30. Messent, 102, and David Blackmore, "'In New York It'd Mean I Was a . . .': Masculine Anxiety and Period Discourses of Sexuality in *The Sun Also Rises*," *The Hemingway Review* 18, no. 1 (1998), 65.

31. See Blackmore for an application of Freudian theories on latent homosexuality contemporary with the novel's publication. Blackmore offers intriguing analyses of a homoerotic subtext in the bullfighting and Burguete fishing trip episodes, but their validity depends on how much credence one is willing to grant Freud, as well as assuming Hemingway uses them *sans* parody.

32. Arnold E. and Cathy N. Davidson, "Decoding the Hemingway Hero," 91.

33. In an earlier draft of the novel, Hemingway has Jake ruminate negatively on the Parisian Left Bank homosexuals as a group, as an undifferentiated "they":

> This Paris is a very sad and dull place and it has few permanent inhabitants. It seems as though the Fairies lived there permanently but this is a mistake because they take flight like the birds and go off to Brussels or London or the Basque coast to return again even more like the birds. . . . It is interesting that they go away and quite pleasant but the pleasure is diminished by the fact that one can not count on it and many times they are gone for several days and one does not notice it and so can not enjoy it. Once I remember they were all gone to Brussels for a week and were back before I noticed they were gone away and a week's enjoyment of their absence was lost. (qtd. in Reynolds, *Hemingway: The Paris Years*, 33–34)

This is unquestionably an expression of Hemingway's (and consequently Jake's) homophobia, yet it is significant that he cut this passage out of the final draft. For whatever reason, it does not appear in the text; so we are left with the characters from the *bal musette* scene as a point of comparison to later "masculine" moments in trying to make sense of Hemingway's reasons for depicting homosexuals negatively and deciding to cast "them" as a negative form of whiteness.

34. Rudat, "Hemingway on Sexual Otherness," 74.

35. Arnold E. and Cathy N. Davidson, "Decoding the Hemingway Hero," 90.

36. Earl Rovit, "On Psychic Retrenchment in Hemingway," in *Hemingway: Essays of Reassessment*, ed. Frank Scafella (New York: Oxford Univ. Press, 1991), 187.

37. Rovit, 184.

JEFFREY A. SCHWARZ

"The Saloon Must Go, and I Will Take It with Me": American Prohibition, Nationalism, and Expatriation in The Sun Also Rises

Much scholarship on Ernest Hemingway's *The Sun Also Rises* has examined the significance of alcohol and drinking in the novel. Many critics have particularly focused on how the alcoholic tendencies of the characters seem to be a result of the dissolution and desolation of the post–World War I period. In her article "Hemingway's Drinking Fixation," Carol Gelderman notes the excessive drinking and prevalence of drinking in the novel,[1] and Matts Djos later builds on Gelderman's work in "Alcoholism in Ernest Hemingway's *The Sun Also Rises*: A Wine and Roses Perspective on the Lost Generation," arguing that "there is a considerable difference between heavy drinking and the kind of self-destructive, alcoholic drinking that we read about in the novel."[2] While most of these characters do engage in immoderate drinking throughout the novel and truly are members of this "lost generation," the American characters of Jake Barnes and Bill Gorton are affected not solely by the results of the war and the devastated Europe that surrounds them, but by the political and social climate in America as well.

In America during the 1920s, one of the most controversial topics was prohibition, which had been ratified as the Eighteenth Amendment to the U.S. Constitution and put into effect on January 17, 1920, along with the Volstead Act, which served as the prohibition enforcement law. Within *The Sun Also Rises*, Jake and Bill jokingly and satirically refer to prohibition, and

From *Studies in the Novel* 33, no. 2 (Summer 2001): 180–201. Copyright © 2001 by the University of North Texas.

yet the form of American nationalism that emerged out of and in conjunction with prohibition seems to have more profound influences on these
American characters than they openly admit. Prohibition groups such as the
Anti-Saloon League sought to create a new "Americanism" that favored the
white, Protestant, Anglo-Saxon, middle-class and excluded what they considered the unsavory immigrant element in their society. While American
expatriates certainly left America to avoid its artistically oppressive environment and to absorb the culture of Europe, I would argue that the type of
American nationalism created and spread through prohibition and by such
prohibition groups as the Anti-Saloon League became yet another oppressor
in America at this time and influenced these artists' decisions to leave America, while simultaneously influencing their behavior and attitudes while living as expatriates in Europe.

In *The Sun Also Rises*, when Jake and Bill are on their fishing trip in the
Basque village of Burguete, these two Americans engage in a satirical dialogue that alludes to American politics, and particularly prohibition. In this
scene, after Bill has just found out that Jake has brought only two bottles of
wine for their fishing lunch, Bill jokingly teases Jake: "You're in the pay of the
Anti-Saloon League."[3] Jake claims that he went to college with Wayne B.
Wheeler and tells Bill that "the saloon must go" (p. 128). Bill agrees, and says,
"The saloon must go, and I will take it with me." In the midst of this conversation, Jake and Bill mention other American political and social figures besides
Wheeler, who was the foremost leader of the Anti-Saloon League during
this period. While the significance of these allusions is lost on most modern
readers, Hemingway's readers in 1926 would have certainly understood these
allusions and known the famous and infamous American figures mentioned
in this scene. Although these individuals are merely alluded to in this banter
between Jake and Bill, the politics they are involved in at this time in American history is quite significant in the formation of the American nationalism
of this period, as well as the anti-nationalist feelings of American intellectuals
such as Bill and American expatriates such as Jake.

In addition, the setting of the Basque countryside for this discussion
and this section of the novel, which is often considered the most restorative part of the novel, seems particularly notable. During this period, the
Basques, who were caught between the countries and cultures of Spain and
France, were fighting for their independence from Spain and developing
a nationalism of their own. Jake and Bill, however, fit in with this group
of people very well, as evident from their bus ride through the mountains.
By first examining the American nationalism of this period in conjunction
with the significant allusions in Jake and Bill's satirical dialogue, by sec-
ondly examining how this nationalism influences the American characters

in the novel, and by finally analyzing the construction of the Basque people and their interaction with the Americans in the novel, I will explicate how the Basque culture of *The Sun Also Rises* actually represents a criticism of 1920s American nationalism.

I

During the fishing scene in Burguete, Jake and Bill satirize America through their allusions to five political and social figures who were consequential in the formation of American nationalism in the 1920s. The first individual mentioned by Jake and Bill is William Jennings Bryan, three-time presidential candidate, who was a leading supporter of prohibition and known for his involvement in the Scopes Monkey Trial. The historian Thomas M. Coffey describes Bryan, the Great Commoner from Nebraska, as "a devout, fundamentalist upholder of the Bible, and a fierce defender of America's rural or small-town values against the dangers of city license and sophistication."[4] Bryan's policies and platforms attempted to "purify" America, and favored the white, Protestant, rural, middle-class American. As Coffey explains, "There was danger in the cities, those bastions of cocktail-sipping intellectuals and guzzling foreigners—the Irish and their whisky, the Germans and their beer, the Italians, Jews, Greeks, French, and Spanish with their wines" (p. 10). For conservatives such as Bryan, the growing urban centers of the Northeast, especially New York, were considered the worst threats to American values, for these cities contained the largest number of working class immigrants, who were mostly Catholics and Jews.

In fact, the 1920 census indicated for the first time in America's history that America was an urban rather than a rural nation, largely in part to the influx of immigrants into these urban centers.[5] By 1920, New York City was America's largest urban center, and yet only "1 million of the city's 6 million residents were white native-born Protestants."[6] In *Terrible Honesty: Mongrel Manhattan in the 1920s,* Ann Douglas describes the social and literary culture of 1920s New York City, and particularly notes the influence that the increasing numbers of immigrants had on this urban atmosphere. Douglas explains, "conservative race ideologues of the day used the word 'mongrelization' to describe (with horror) the imminent era of miscegenation" (pp. 5–6). Americans such as Bryan thus viewed these urban centers as a threat to their rural and conservative way of life, for they believed that the mixing of various ethnic and racial groups in these cities would taint America's purity. In addition, these conservatives noticed (again, with horror) that prohibition "was a joke in most of urban America, but in New York it was an all-out full-scale farce" (p. 24). Consequently, these nationalists began to blame urban immigrants, in particular, for this violation of the prohibition law.

In his book *Our America: Nativism, Modernism, and Pluralism*, Walter Benn Michaels further explicates this ethnic and racial prejudice so present in 1920s America. Michaels uses the term "nativist modernism" to describe the prevalent 1920s nationalist attitude of Americans who made absolute distinctions between what they considered "American" and "un-American" in 1920s American culture. As Michaels explains, assimilation of immigrant groups into American society was a danger to these nationalists, for it threatened the "purity" of their Anglo-Saxon "white heritage" in America.[7] The result of this spreading nationalist attitude was increased discrimination against immigrants, as well as against all Americans not of Anglo-Saxon ethnic and racial origins.

In addition to the growing societal discrimination against immigrants in America, legal measures were taken to prevent additional immigrants from "corrupting" America during this period. The Johnson-Reed Act of 1924 severely limited the number of immigrants allowed to enter the United States; in fact, as a result of the Johnson-Reed Act, "of the 35.9 million Europeans who came to the United States between 1820 and 1975, 32 million came before 1924."[8] As Marc Dolan observes in *Modern Lives: A Cultural Rereading of "The Lost Generation,"* "In 1924, Congress passed the Johnson-Reed Act, which imposed fairly sweeping restrictions on American immigration, and almost simultaneously the mechanisms of Anglo-Saxon discrimination became both more extensive and more visible throughout American society."[9]

The mention of William Jennings Bryan in *The Sun Also Rises* is significant, for Bryan was in fact one of those Americans who made distinctions between what he considered "American" and "un-American" and desperately fought to retain what he considered a pure America. Bryan's prosecution of John Thomas Scopes in the Scopes Monkey Trial positions him—as well as the large number of Americans who condemned Darwinism and evolution—as not only a fundamentalist, but also as a bigot who was unable to accept the supposition that all humans, whether black, white, Italian, German, Anglo-Saxon, Catholic, Jew, or Protestant, evolved through a similar process and are in some way linked. During the fishing scene in *The Sun Also Rises*, Bill mimics Bryan's rhetoric from the Scopes Monkey Trial,[10] proclaiming to Jake, "Let us not doubt, brother. Let us not pry into the holy mysteries of the hencoop with simian fingers" (p. 127). In addition, "as a tribute to the Great Commoner," whose death had just been announced in the paper the day before (July 26, 1925), Bill decides that during lunch he should put the chicken first and then the egg (p. 126). While Bill's "tribute" can certainly be seen as mocking Bryan's resistance to Darwinism and evolution, it can also be examined in terms of the paradoxical Americanism that Bryan and other prohibitionists and fundamentalists supported. Through this new American nationalism, these groups were seeking to ostracize American immigrants who they believed were tainting "their America"; however, America itself was founded by immigrant groups (albeit different ethnic immigrant groups) only a few centuries prior. Hence, Bill's joke invites the question: which came first, the American or the immigrant? While Bill's chicken-egg joke mocks the creation/evolution debate, it also mocks this 1920s American nationalism.

Hemingway's satire of 1920s Americanism also appears within the satire of his contemporaneous novel *The Torrents of Spring*. Having written *The Torrents of Spring* in the fall of 1925 just after finishing his first draft of *The Sun Also Rises*, Hemingway employs the same satirical style in these two novels to parody some of the same popular political and societal issues. Most notably, Hemingway's subtitle for *The Torrents of Spring: A Romantic Novel in Honor of the Passing of a Great Race* evokes Madison Grant's widely-read, anti-immigrant book of the 1920s, *The Passing of the Great Race* (first published in 1916, with new editions appearing in 1921 and 1923).[11] Along with Lothrop Stoddard's *The Rising Tide of Color* (1920), *The Passing of a Great Race* claimed that the rapid immigration and breeding of "non-whites" (which included all ethnic and racial groups other than white Anglo-Saxons) would eventually overwhelm the "pure white world."[12] *The Torrents of Spring* satirizes this 1920s Americanism through the depiction of the Nordic character of Yogi Johnson, who since World War I had "never wanted a woman."[13] This lack of desire changes for Yogi at the end of the novel, when he sees a naked Indian squaw and departs with her into the night. The Indian squaw is not a "white" Nordic American, however, and therefore the white race is presumably doomed to extinction.[14] Through the language and plot of this story, Hemingway is clearly parodying the racist beliefs of American nationalists such as Grant and Stoddard; thus, Hemingway's mocking of this Americanism in *The Torrents of Spring* coincides with the satire of the fishing scene of *The Sun Also Rises* in which Jake and Bill mock 1920s political and social figures such as William Jennings Bryan for their American nationalist beliefs.

Historically, Bryan's rallying cry for American nationalism and prohibition did not end solely with America, however. After prohibition was legalized in the United States, Bryan made a speech that showed his desire to force this nationalism on other countries as well:

> We must turn our energies to other countries until the whole world is brought to understand that alcohol is man's greatest enemy. Thus it is a fortunate thing that the abdication of the Kaiser and the fall of arbitrary power came in the same year as does the fall of the brewery autocracy and that these two evils came down together

... Now we can go out for the evangelization of the world on the
subject of intoxicating liquor.[15]

By linking prohibition with America's victory in World War I, Bryan and
his supporters implicate America's foreign foes (particularly Germany), as
well as their American immigrants, in the "evils" of both their anti-Ameri-
can positions in the war and their alcohol consumption.

In *The Sun Also Rises*, while Jake and Bill certainly mock Bryan for these
prohibitionist and fundamentalist beliefs, they also seem to mock him for
his political hypocrisy. Bryan, who claimed the noble cause of prohibition
in speeches such as the one cited above, was secretly employed by Wheeler's
Anti-Saloon League and was paid $11,000 a year to support prohibition
and give prohibition-related speeches. In 1920, a year after he gave this prohibition speech, newspapers revealed this information about Bryan's secret
employer.[16] Thus, when Bill jokingly accuses Jake of being "in the pay of the
Anti-Saloon League" (p. 128), he is most certainly satirizing Bryan and his
Anti-Saloon League payoffs.

Also during this satirical dialogue, Bill claims he met Bryan when
Bryan, H. L. Mencken, and he "went to Holy Cross together" (p. 127). Bill
is obviously joking by implying they all went to Holy Cross, a Catholic college, but the close association of Mencken and Bryan is also ridiculous considering Mencken was a social and political critic who believed that every
reformer was "a prehensile Methodist parson, bawling for Prohibition and
its easy jobs."[17] Nevertheless, although Mencken was opposed to prohibition, he condemned the American expatriates for leaving their country. In
April of 1925 in the Paris *Tribune*, Mencken directly criticized the American
expatriates: "The emigrés who flock to Paris, seeking to escape the horrors of
the Puritan *kultur*, find only impotence and oblivion there; not one of them
has written a line worth reading."[18] Early in *The Sun Also Rises*, Jake reflects,
"Mencken hates Paris, I believe. So many young men get their likes and dislikes from Mencken" (p. 49). Jake then tells his American friend Harvey, "I
just can't read him" (p. 50). Thus, while Mencken opposes the political beliefs
of Americans such as Bryan, he still acts as a voice and presence that seeks
to conform Americans to certain opinions and to insulate them within their
own culture and country. As the character of Scripps O'Neil in Hemingway's
The Torrents of Spring considers during one of his many disconnected musings
within the novel, "Was Mencken really after him? It wasn't a pretty prospect
to face" (p. 19).

The mention of Frankie Frisch next in Jake and Bill's drunken discussion
is significant in illustrating the corruption of American society, even within
one of America's "purest" pastimes, baseball. After the joke about Bryan and

Mencken attending Holy Cross with Bill, Bill says, "Frankie Fritsch went to Fordham" (p. 127). Frankie Frisch (misspelled "Fritsch" in *The Sun Also Rises*) was a professional baseball player who graduated from Fordham University in 1919 and was a leading player in four consecutive Giants World Series pennants from 1921–1924.[19] Interestingly, Frisch is the only individual in this passage that Jake and Bill actually assign to the correct college, which is significant in light of how Frisch contrasts with the other mentioned political and social figures because of his Catholicism and non-Anglo-Saxon name. Nonetheless, Frisch also becomes implicated in the corruption of the American nation since he was suspected of being involved in a payoff to insure the Giants pennant victory in 1924.[20] For Jake and Bill, Frisch becomes a "sell-out" to American popularity. Frisch, probably the most recognized player on the New York Giants team in 1924, thus represents yet another aspect of what the expatriates viewed as America's degradation and vacuity.

Jake next joins this satirical college "name-game," claiming that he went to Loyola with Bishop Manning, who was the outspoken and well-known rector of the Anglican Trinity Parish in New York City during this period and who was both a fundamentalist and prohibitionist.[21] Like Bryan and the prohibition leaders, Manning depicts immigrants as blockades to American patriotism through his nationalist rhetoric. On May 29, 1916, in a *New York Times* article entitled "How a Nation May Lose Its Soul," Manning writes that the lack of patriotism in America "is due in part to our mixed population, including vast numbers of people who are not assimilated to our national life."[22] Jake's mentioning of Bishop Manning is particularly significant for what Bishop Manning personally represents to Jake. Manning strongly spoke out in favor of World War I and against pacifism, and claimed that "This war shows us that the religion of Jesus Christ is the one hope of the world. Christianity is the one thing that has not failed."[23] Considering the physical and emotional impotence that the war has caused Jake, and considering Jake's uncertain relationship with religion, Jake's mentioning of Bishop Manning undoubtedly contains underlying feelings of bitterness; Manning's ideology represents an American ideal of courage and Christianity that has caused Jake's post war desolation. Likewise, Jake's ironic association of Manning, an Episcopal bishop, with the Catholic college of Loyola connotes an underlying bitterness. Catholicism, the religion to which Jake is most closely linked, becomes a joke, for it is a religion very much outside of the American nationalism of Manning and the other non-Catholic, American political figures mentioned in Jake and Bill's dialogue.

The last American, though perhaps the one most entrenched within this American nationalism, mentioned in this drunken dialogue between Jake and Bill is Wayne B. Wheeler. As previously mentioned, Wheeler was the

leader of the Anti-Saloon League who pushed for the prohibition amendment to the Constitution. Wheeler's nationalism, like Bryan's, clearly condemned American immigrants, especially the Catholics and the Jews. In fact,
the Anti-Saloon League often supported the same political agendas as the
Ku Klux Klan, and due to the prohibitionist stronghold in the southern and
midwestern United States, the two groups often became conflated. Gover-
nor Al Smith of New York State, who was a Catholic, believed that at the
June 1924 New York City Democratic convention, "the Klan and the anti-
saloon forces in the convention were practically identical."[24] In addition, at
this convention, Bryan refused to denounce the Klan because of the strong
support they gave to the prohibitionist and anti-Darwinist causes.[25] Where
the Volstead Act and prohibition groups failed, the Klan often succeeded in
enforcing prohibition through their own vigilante actions.[26]

In *Strangers in the Land: Patterns of American Nativism, 1860–1925,* John
Higham analyzes the anti-immigrant sentiment of the 1920s, and particularly
its relation to the Ku Klux Klan and prohibition. Higham notes that "the ban
on alcohol hit the immigrants two ways: it increased their conspicuousness as
lawbreakers and brought down upon their heads the wrath of a 100 per cent
morality" (p. 268). The Klan believed themselves the guardians of this "100
per cent morality," and therefore prohibition "created a much more highly
charged situation, for it precipitated a head-on collision between mounting
lawlessness and a new drive for social conformity" (p. 267). Unlike the first Ku
Klux Klan of the post–Civil War era, which admitted any white man regardless of ethnic background, the Klan of the 1920s admitted only native-born
Protestant whites as members, and joined its traditional anti-Negro platform
with an anti-immigrant one (p. 288). In addition to their widespread discrimination and violence against African Americans and Jews, the Klan of
this period was particularly focused against Catholics, for, besides the alcohol
that often came along with Catholic European immigrants, the Klan feared
the threat of Papal tyranny in America. Because the Klan's fears and prejudices were similar to those of prohibitionist groups such as the Anti-Saloon
League, the two groups often rallied under the same political banners. Thus
in *The Sun Also Rises* when Jake says, "I went to Notre Dame with Wayne
B. Wheeler" (p. 128), the irony of Wheeler, the leader of the Anti-Saloon
League, going to a Catholic college is obvious.

Bill, however, objects to this irony and says, "It's a lie. I went to Austin
Business College with Wayne B. Wheeler. He was class president" (p. 128).
Austin Business College, which had just been founded in 1922, stands in stark
contrast to the Catholic colleges of Holy Cross, Fordham, Loyola, and Notre
Dame that Jake and Bill have previously associated with these American
political and social figures. By linking Wheeler with Austin Business College

and making him class president, Bill not only highlights the anti-Catholic sentiments of Wheeler, but also implies that the Anti-Saloon League is a new business that is taking over America. At this point, Jake says, "the saloon must go," and Bill responds, "You're right there, old classmate. The saloon must go, and I will take it with me." Thus, Jake's expatriation to Europe and Bill's vacationing in Europe allows each of these two Americans to free themselves, at least physically, from this new America and its spreading nationalism, and to rebel in their own way against it—by drinking.

II

In his discussion of Ernest Hemingway in *The Expatriate Perspective: American Novelists and the Idea of America*, Harold T. McCarthy notes that:

> Europe provided Hemingway with a basis for comparative as well as objective analysis of American life ... His was the American artist's typical discovery of individual freedom in Europe—a sense of escape from the relentless pressure for conformity that was possibly the most oppressive feature of American life, a feature singled out for especial comment by all the important European observers of American life since Tocqueville.[27]

Like in Hemingway's own life, in *The Sun Also Rises* Europe becomes a place for the American characters to break free from the constraints of America and American nationalism. Although both Jake and Bill criticize America in their drunken discussion while on the fishing trip, as they do in other scenes of the novel, the two characters' individual viewpoints of America and American nationalism and their actions in response to it are actually quite different. Unlike Jake and Bill, however, Robert Cohn fails to recognize the conformity and bigotry that this nationalism brings with it.

Jake's status as an American expatriate in Europe clearly positions him as an individual alienated by America. While many critics argue this alienation is a result of World War I, Jake's behavior—as do the behaviors of many of the actual expatriates—exhibits a distinct alienation from American social and political life as well. Jake is either constantly drinking or discussing drinking throughout the novel, revealing not only his desire to escape from the effects of the war through alcohol, but also a desire to escape from the effects of American prohibition and its ideologies. Jake makes such comments as "A bottle of wine was good company" (p. 236), and "Bartenders have always been fine" (p. 248); thus, for Jake, drinking serves not merely as a means to an escape, but also serves as a vital social function. In *The Sun Also Rises: A Novel of the Twenties*, Michael S. Reynolds claims that Jake "does not want to think too closely about his moral condition. But then neither did America in 1926, and Jake Barnes is a native son, an American born into a time and place not of his choosing" (p. 62). As exemplified through the historical allusions previously discussed, however, the majority of Americans did seem very focused on their own moral condition—as is evident through prohibition, fundamentalism, and patriotism. While Jake may not be reflecting profusely on his own moral condition, he does seem to reflect on America's moral condition, and, in fact, criticizes the corruption, hypocrisy, and bigotry of that moral condition, in scenes such as on the Burguete fishing trip. Moreover, while still in Paris at a bar, Robert Cohn looks around the bar and says, "This is a good place." Jake agrees, "There's a lot of liquor" (p. 19). Cohn does not comment on the amount of liquor in the bar, but rather he simply says, "This is a good place." Jake assumes that Cohn means, "This is a good place because there's a lot of liquor." For Jake, "a good place" has a lot of liquor; following this logic, for Jake, America was not "a good place," because prohibition was in effect. In fact, in 1924 there were 32,000 permanent American residents in Paris, with 12,000 American tourists visiting Paris in July alone.[28] If the character of Jake can be seen as embodying many of the same opinions of the American expatriates of the 1920s, and presumably other Americans as well, it is not surprising that American expatriates and tourists had raised the prices of alcohol at bars in Paris during this period.[29]

Also, while on the fishing trip, Jake's expatriation and its meaning are satirically addressed by Bill. At breakfast, Bill says to Jake, "You're an expatriate. One of the worst type. Haven't you heard that? Nobody that ever left their own country ever wrote anything worth printing. Not even in the newspapers" (p. 120). Through these words, Bill mimics the voices of such American critics as H. L. Mencken, who scathingly criticized the expatriates and their work. By disregarding the expatriates simply because they left America, these critics propagated the ideologies of self-containment and "purity" that the American nationalism of the 1920s sought to achieve.

Bill goes on to say, "You're an expatriate. You've lost touch with the soil. You get precious. Fake European standards have ruined you. You drink yourself to death. You become obsessed by sex. You spend all your time talking, not working. You are an expatriate, see? You hang around cafés" (p. 120). In this satirical, yet extremely revealing tirade, Bill's arguments against expatriation exemplify the most pertinent ideologies of 1920s American nationalism. The seemingly inconsequential sentence "You've lost touch with the soil" implies that American soil is somehow inherently blessed and different from the soil of any other nation. Likewise, through the focus on the word "soil," this sentence resonates the importance of American agriculture for those middle-class southern and mid-western Americans who created and perpetuated 1920s American nationalism. The sentence "You get precious" criticizes expatriates for being affected and "artsy," rather than being strong, working-class producers. The argument that "Fake European standards have ruined you" registers both American nationalists' disapproval of expatriation as well as their discrimination against Europeans and American immigrants of European descent; the "Fake European standards" certainly encompass such things as alcohol and Catholicism. In light of American prohibition, the criticism of expatriates in the sentence "You drink yourself to death" becomes obvious. Likewise, the strong sexual morality and purity American nationalism attempted to promote becomes clear in the criticism "You become obsessed by sex." The argument against expatriates that "You spend all your time talking, not working" stems from the long-lasting American and Puritan work ethic that pervaded this nationalism. Thus, Jake and the actual expatriates of the 1920s become the antithesis of 1920s American nationalism, for they exemplify all of the fears and evils of this nationalism during their sojourn in Europe.

In *Imagining Paris: Exile, Writing, and American Identity*, J. Gerald Kennedy discusses movement, specifically expatriation, as a means for writers to gain a new perspective on America. Kennedy notes that "Rapid, incessant travel and immediate electronic contact with distant places and cultures broke down provincial perspectives and helped to generate a cosmopolitan consciousness which transcended national themes and issues."[30] The normative values and culture of home, amidst these differing cultures of Europe, become relative, and merely one way of perceiving and experiencing society (p. 28). Ann Douglas suggests that "Hemingway and other American artists lived abroad in the 1920s, less to escape their country than to be able to write more effectively about it" (p. 216). While the concept of expatriate perspective is paramount in both Kennedy's and Douglas's arguments, the negative perspectives of American nationalism as puritanical and discriminatory that Jake, and presumably Hemingway, gains from his expatriate experience implies an equally important emphasis on escape from this American culture. The decision to remain removed from this American culture that Jake (Hemingway) criticizes seems as, if not more, significant than simply criticizing it. And although Kennedy specifically examines Paris as the site for this new perspective of America, in *The Sun Also Rises* this shift of perspective actually occurs more markedly while in the Basque countryside—both during the fishing trip and later in Pamplona. Though provincial in terms of its rural geography, the Basque countryside actually provides a more universal perspective, for its openness to drinking and foreigners diametrically opposes the rigid restrictiveness of the typically rural, American nationalism of the 1920s, and offers an alternative culture to these Americans.

Though Bill recognizes the faults of 1920s American nationalism, unlike Jake, he remains an American resident who chooses to spend only his vacations in Europe. When Bill first arrives in Paris to meet Jake, Jake describes their meeting: "He was cheerful and said the States were wonderful. New York was wonderful" (p. 75). Bill's comment that "New York was wonderful," immediately following his previous comment that "The States were wonderful," seems like a correction. As Douglas explicates in *Terrible Honesty: Mongrel Manhattan in the 1920s*, New York City during this period was considerably different than the rest of the United States and represented what prohibitionists and fundamentalists most despised. Thus, Bill's comment with its "correction" illustrates his dislike of the United States as a whole, but his admiration of urban New York. Similarly, Bill's underlying discontentment with America emerges when Jake introduces Bill to Brett as a taxidermist; Bill remarks, "That was in another country. And besides all the animals were dead" (p. 81). The country Bill mentions is most certainly the United States, and the animals are most certainly the people of the United States; the people of the United States are thus "dead" and hollow, and all of them are merely stuffed with the same filling, perhaps this nationalism, to make them appear to be alive. This comment also implies that while the people of the United States are "dead," the people of Europe are still alive, and thus reiterates Bill's disillusionment with America and attraction to Europe.

Although Bill implies his disapproval of 1920s America and American nationalism through these comments and those during the fishing trip, his character, nevertheless, assumes at times the discriminating language of this nationalism in a way that pushes the boundaries of mimicry and satire. While on the train from France to Spain, Jake and Bill are displaced from eating by a large group of Catholic pilgrims from Dayton, Ohio. Bill encounters one of the priests from the group and asks, "When do us Protestants get a chance to eat, father?" When the priest replies that he is unsure, Bill says, "It's enough to make a man join the Klan" (p. 93). While Bill is joking, Catholicism is still obviously something foreign to Bill. For example, after Jake and Bill's drunken and satirical discussion on the fishing trip about the American political and social figures and their supposed Catholic alma maters, Bill asks Jake if he is "really a Catholic" (p. 128). Jake says, "Technically," and Bill asks what that means. Jake responds, "I don't know" (pp. 128–29). Though Jake is struggling with his own religious identity, and perhaps with the prejudices many Americans had against Catholics, Bill honestly seems to have no idea what being a Catholic means. Perhaps Bill's ignorance of Catholicism stems from the false conceptions of it spread by American nationalism. Although Bill does not maliciously attack Jake for his Catholicism, he does make numerous anti-Semitic comments to or about Cohn throughout the novel. By calling Cohn a "Kike" (p. 168) and describing him as behaving with "Jewish superiority" (p. 166), Bill assumes the anti-Semitic attitudes of 1920s American nationalism. Thus, while Bill satirizes American politics and such nationalist groups as the Anti-Saloon League and the Ku Klux Klan, he nonetheless, at times, takes on their discriminatory attitudes. Bill's dichotomous attitude towards American nationalism and his position as an American intellectual living in New York and visiting Europe on his vacations places him figuratively and literally between American nationalism and American expatriation.

Conversely, Robert Cohn represents a type of American very different from either Jake or Bill; Cohn fails to clearly see the corruption of this American nationalism, and his expatriation has nothing to do with his disapproval of 1920s America. Cohn does not even realize that his Judaism sets him apart from the majority of Americans until he experiences religious discrimination firsthand; but even then, he fails to connect this discrimination to American nationalism. Jake explains Robert's experience with religious discrimination: "No one had ever made him feel he was a Jew, and hence any different from anybody else, until he went to Princeton" (p. 12). Yet, not even this personally directed religious discrimination convinces him to leave America; rather his mistress, Frances, urges him to go to Europe to write. Thus, Cohn's expatriation is not even his own decision, and, in fact, "he would rather have been in America" (p. 13), and would prefer to go to South America on vacation, rather than travel within Europe (p. 19).

Walter Benn Michaels closely examines the character of Robert Cohn in terms of 1920s nationalism, or as he calls it, "nativist modernism." Michaels views Cohn as outside the "race" or "family" because he has no "breeding" or "*afición*," or, more clearly, because he is Jewish (p. 7). Michaels likewise argues that Hemingway's constant comparison and distinction between Jake and Cohn actually links the two, but that Cohn's lack of *afición* is what eventually differentiates these two characters (pp. 27–28). Thus for Michaels, Cohn's attempts to assimilate, and his inability to do so, illustrate the conveyance of this American nationalism to Europe through the characters of Jake and Bill. The problem, however, actually lies in Cohn's attempts to conform to this American nationalism, rather than recognizing its discriminatory nature and attempting to somehow rebel against it—as Jake and Bill seem to do. Jake's reflection that Cohn receives his opinions from books, and specifically from Mencken (p. 49), exemplifies Cohn's conformity and his lack of personal convictions. And although Jake and especially Bill may exclude Cohn because of the American nationalism still ingrained within them, 1920s Europe does not. Cohn is accepted within the Basque community just as quickly as Jake and Bill are, but Cohn cannot appreciate it, for he does not understand how it opposes 1920s America and its nationalism. When Jake reflects that "Cohn was never drunk" (p. 152), Jake is not paying him a compliment. Just as the other characters' drunkenness can be seen as a rebellion against prohibition and its nationalist agendas, Cohn's lack of drunkenness shows his lack of understanding for what prohibition means and his lack of participation in this expatriate rebellion.

Although Jake, Bill, and Cohn all position themselves differently in terms of 1920s American nationalism, their attitudes and behaviors register the effects this nationalism had on different types of Americans. To summarize rather simply, Jake represents the expatriate who rebels against America and its nationalism, Bill typifies the American intellectual tourist who is caught in the middle of American and European culture and their beliefs, and Cohn exemplifies those Americans unable to see the discriminations of this American nationalism. These differences in attitudes towards American nationalism become particularly significant when these three American characters interact with the Basque community during the fishing trip in Burguete, and later during the bullfighting festival in Pamplona.

III

In *The Sun Also Rises*, the Basque village and countryside of Burguete is the setting for Jake and Bill's fishing trip. Many critics contend that the fishing trip is the most restorative section of the novel due to Jake's return to nature, particularly through his ritualistic act of fishing and the male bonding and companionship he experiences with Bill and Harris. While these arguments certainly may be true, the Basque culture that surrounds and interacts with Jake also plays a profound role in Jake's rejuvenation. In the novel, the Basque culture is constructed in such a way as to directly juxtapose 1920s American nationalism. By welcoming foreigners and their "otherness," primarily through the social act of drinking, the Basque culture opposes American nationalism and thus becomes the ideal restorative setting for Jake's expatriation and Bill's vacation.

Historically, the 1920s was an active period for Basque cultural awareness and nationalism, and, although the Spanish Civil War did not officially begin until 1936, the Basque people were already beginning their rebellion against Spain.[31] World War I had increased the industrialization and economy of the Basque region, which both centralized leadership within the Basque territory and increased the bourgeois class, thus allowing for the growth of Basque nationalism.[32] In *Basque Nationalism*, Stanley G. Payne explains the historic and cultural evolution of the Basque people:

> The historic Basque people are evidently an amalgam of several early ethnic groups in the western Pyrenees area; their unity is

based on language and culture rather than biology, even though they exhibit somewhat distinct physical characteristics. Nonetheless, in terms of formally recorded history, the Basque population must be considered fully autochthonous, since neither it nor its language can be traced to any other region or ethnic group. (p. 9)

Thus, while caught between the countries of France and Spain, and ruled by the Spanish government, the Basques possess no cultural allegiance to either country.

Beginning in the late nineteenth century, Basque nationalism developed primarily in opposition to Spanish rule. In 1894, Sabino Arana, a leader of the Basque Nationalist Party, wrote:

Basque nationalists (*Euskerianos nacionalistas*) despise Spain, because it has trampled the laws of their Homeland, profaned and demolished their temple, and delivered their Homeland into the grip of the most infamous enslavement, and it is corrupting their Homeland's blood, which is the Basque race, the Basque language, and will ultimately drive their national feelings from their hearts.[33]

This Basque nationalism described by Arana, and which later flourished in the 1920s, sought to preserve Basque culture from the threat of Spanish cultural and legal domination.

While this historical account of Basque culture and nationalism is significant in that it provides a background for the analysis of the Basque culture in *The Sun Also Rises*, the majority of American readers in the 1920s would not have known the details of the Basque situation. At most, Americans in the 1920s would have known that the Basques sought to gain independence from Spain; and perhaps this information alone serves to link the Basques with the expatriates in terms of their rebellion against a dominating and conforming nation. Nevertheless, the significance of the Basque culture in *The Sun Also Rises* lies in how this culture is constructed as the antithesis of 1920s American nationalism, and how this Basque culture thereby provides a critical commentary on this American nationalism to 1920s American readers.

Hemingway himself felt a special connection to Spain, and of all the Spanish peoples he encountered, he found the Basques the most "straightforward, honest, uncorruptible."[34] In *Hemingway and Spain: A Pursuit*, Edward F. Stanton examines Hemingway's fascination and kinship to Spain and the Spanish peoples: "Those he liked best—the Basque-Navarrese and the Castilians—were not just another venal Mediterranean people. As in all the other European countries he had visited, the aristocracy, the official class, and the laws were bad, yet Spain was 'really a swell country and the people were fine'" (p. 26). Through his experiences in the Basque region, Hemingway came to associate drinking and the acceptance of foreigners with the Basque culture. Stanton notes, "How strange and different from the prim, teetotaling world of the household in Oak Park, where Dr. Hemingway had turned out Ernest's Italian-American friends because they drank and sang too loudly for the neighbors, and how from the serious, joyless religion of the Oak Park Congregational Church! Much more than the Italians, the Basque-Navarrese people knew how to 'really feel things' and to 'live all the way'" (p. 24). Though Hemingway certainly idealized the Basques and their culture, this idealization nevertheless serves an important function in *The Sun Also Rises* in terms of its contrast to 1920s America.

Unlike 1920s American nationalism, the Basque culture of *The Sun Also Rises* embraces foreigners, and employs alcohol as ritualistic in its own culture and as uniting in its interaction with other cultures. On the bus ride to the village of Burguete, Jake and Bill are welcomed into the community of Basques on the bus through the sharing of wine. When Jake and Bill board the bus, one of the Basques offers his wineskin to Jake; when Jake starts to drink from it, the Basque good-naturedly makes a noise like a Klaxon motor horn, causing Jake to spill the wine on himself (pp. 109–10). This humorous act causes everyone on the bus to laugh, and immediately initiates Jake into their group. In a similar gesture of sharing, Bill offers a drink from his bottle of wine to one of the Basques sitting next to him. In his analysis of ritual and landscape in Hemingway's works, David Andersen describes how this Basque wine and the ritual of sharing it becomes a language of its own:

> The offer of wine takes the place of language. When Bill cannot understand the Basque who tries to speak to him, he replies by handing him a bottle of wine. The action seems a *non sequitur* until we see that Bill's offer brings about a counter offer, and, as has been already observed, the reciprocity begins to establish connections and alliances much as language would.[35]

Thus, when Cohn waves goodbye to Jake and Bill, all the Basques wave goodbye back to Cohn (p. 110). Cohn has automatically been accepted into their community because of his association with Jake and Bill, who have both been accepted by the Basques through their shared drinking of wine.

After the bus starts and the group begins their trip, the ritualized drinking between the Basques and Jake and Bill continues. When Bill accepts a drink from the wineskin of one of the Basques, he fails to properly tilt the wineskin and a few drops of wine run down his chin. Jake narrates the Basques' response: "'No! No!' several Basques said. 'Not like that.' One snatched the bottle away from the owner, who was himself about to give a demonstration" (pp. 110–11). This scene is comical to almost everyone aboard the bus, for the Basque who snatches the wineskin to give the demonstration drinks a healthy portion of it, to only the owner's dismay. Though comical, the manner of drinking the wine becomes a serious act that must be taught to outsiders so that they can share in the experience. Later on the trip, when the group stops at a *posada*, Jake describes the reciprocity of the sharing of alcohol: "Two of our Basques came in and insisted on buying a drink. So they bought a drink and then we bought a drink, and then they slapped us on the back and bought another drink. Then we bought, and then we all went out into the sunlight and the heat, and climbed back on top of the bus" (p. 112). The Basques and Jake and Bill are all equal in their payment of drinks, and Jake and Bill, though outsiders, are thus accepted equally into the Basque group. Once back aboard the bus, Jake narrates, "The Basque lying against my knees pointed out the view with the neck of the wine-bottle, and winked at us" (p. 110). The fact that the Basque lies against Jake's knees marks Jake's acceptance within this group and exemplifies the comfort the Basques feel with both Jake and Bill. When the Basque points out the beauty of the landscape with the neck of the wine bottle, wine and drinking become linked with the beauty of the Basque country itself. Finally, the Basque's wink at Jake and Bill signifies a secret understanding and appreciation they have for the landscape, the wine, and the community. Through the ritual of drinking, and without any words, Jake and Bill are thus accepted within the Basque community as equals.

For Hemingway, drinking embodied a participation in a communal delectation as well as a participation in the 1920s literary circle of rebellion against prohibition. Though certainly an alcoholic, as Tom Dardis discusses in *The Thirsty Muse: Alcohol and the American Writer*, Hemingway nevertheless "regarded that immense thirst for spirits not as a sign of addiction but as yet another aspect of his large appetite for the pleasures of life."[36] Hemingway viewed drinking and getting drunk as an initiation rite and an adventure; he reflected in 1923, "I like to see every man drunk. A man does not exist until he is drunk . . . I love getting drunk. Right from the start it is the best feeling."[37] In his short story "The Three-Day Blow," published in 1925 in his collection of stories *In Our Time*, Hemingway reveals this opinion of drinking through his characters of Nick and Bill as they get drunk and converse on a variety of subjects, including baseball, literature, and relationships. While discussing his father, Nick remarks, "He claims he's never taken a drink in his life"; Nick then reflects, "He's missed a lot."[38] Drinking becomes for Nick, as it does for Hemingway, a pleasure of life worthy of participation as well as a means of uniting people.

In addition, alcohol became a form of rebellion for Hemingway and for many of the other literary artists of the 1920s, for when alcohol became forbidden under prohibition, "many independent minds believed it was their moral duty to violate the law on every possible occasion."[39] As Ann Douglas notes, "This was a generation that made the terms 'alcoholic' and 'writer' synonyms" (p. 23); Hemingway was certainly one such writer. Like many alcoholics, Hemingway did not view his excessive drinking as a disease, and he does not present it in *The Sun Also Rises* as such. Rather, drinking in the novel actualizes Hemingway's own views of drinking, and signifies both a communal enjoyment of life and its pleasures and a manner of rebelling against prohibition and its nationalist agendas.

As on the bus trip with the Basques, this communal aspect of drinking appears when Jake and Bill return to Pamplona after their fishing trip in order to enjoy the bullfighting festival and meet up with the rest of their group. They, along with the rest of their group, encounter the same Basque acceptance through shared drinking with the Basque peasants in Pamplona. In fact, when Jake and Bill first arrive in Pamplona, Mike and Brett are wearing Basque berets at the festival (p. 138), illustrating how they, as foreigners, are already somewhat a part of this community. In Pamplona, which is still part of the Basque country, the Basques can be identified by the same black or blue smocks that the Basques on the bus trip wore. During the festival, a group of dancers wearing these blue smocks parade down the street carrying a large banner on which is painted the words, "Hurray for Wine! Hurray for the Foreigners!" (p. 158). The fact that the dancers carry an actual sign cheering the presence of the foreigners, as well as the wine, represents an obvious contrast to American nationalism. Not surprisingly, when the dancers parade down the street, Cohn asks, "Where are the foreigners?" Bill tells Cohn that "We're the foreigners." Just as Cohn fails to recognize himself as different from the majority of America due to his Judaism, and just as he fails to recognize the discrimination of 1920s American nationalism, so Cohn fails to understand that he is the foreigner in this country, and that this Basque brand of nationalism actually welcomes him, even as a foreigner and Jew. Bill, however, does understand what is going on and is able to recognize himself as a foreigner and as the recipient of this welcome, just as he is able to recognize American nationalism and its inability to accept "otherness."

In addition to the wine, dancing becomes a means of welcoming foreigners into this Basque community. While at the festival, Jake describes how they become initiated into the ritualized dance: "They took Bill and me by the arms and put us in the circle. Bill started to dance, too. They were all chanting. Brett wanted to dance but they did not want her to. They wanted her as an image to dance around. When the song ended with the sharp *riau-riau*! They rushed us into a wine-shop" (p. 159). Bill and Jake become a part of the Basque dancing and chanting, and Brett, as a female foreigner, becomes almost an icon to be worshipped. When the ritualized dance is finished, and the foreigners have been accepted into the group, they are, of course, next rushed into the wine shop for the shared drinking that will continue the ritual.

The scene at the wine shop particularly elucidates how the Basque culture willingly invites foreigners into their community. In the wine shop, one of the men at the bar will not let Jake pay for wine, three of the men teach Brett how to drink out of a wineskin, and one man teaches Bill a song. Not only do wine and dancing serve as uniting acts, but the sharing of song and food with the foreigners also brings the community together. Cohn, however, does not share in this meal, because he is asleep in a back room (pp. 160–62). Just as Cohn sleeps during the ride through the beautiful Basque countryside earlier (p. 99), so he again misses the significant moments of their trip. Since Cohn fails to recognize the discrimination of American nationalism, he is unable to appreciate the openness and equality of the Basque culture.

After Jake has bought two wineskins and returned to the bar, he narrates, "Some one at the counter, that I had never seen before, tried to pay for the wine, but I finally paid for it myself. The man who had wanted to pay then bought me a drink. He would not let me buy one in return, but said he would take a rinse of the mouth from the new wine-bag" (p. 161). The issue of reciprocity in drinking again emerges in this scene, but what also arises is the significance of drinking from the wineskins. While on the bus trip with the Basques, Jake has learned the importance of drinking properly out of wine-skins, in the same way that Bill was taught on the bus and Brett was taught in the wine shop. The wineskin becomes a symbolic object in this ritualized drinking, for there is meaning in both drinking out of it properly and taking the first drink from it. By allowing this man to take the first rinse from the wineskin, Jake honors this man and his culture, while simultaneously revealing his understanding of the ritualistic significance of drinking from the wineskin. This ritualized drinking thus serves a particular social function not only within this Basque culture, but also in uniting these different groups of peoples and their different cultures.

In the same way that foreigners and drinking are revered in this Basque community in *The Sun Also Rises*, so is Catholicism. Historically, besides the Basque language, Catholicism was one of the greatest links among the Basque provinces and in the formation of Basque nationalism.[40] In addition, the significance of wine within the Catholic ritualized mass symbolically links Catholicism with the drinking of wine prevalent throughout this section of the novel. Catholicism emerges as restorative in this section of the novel through Jake's decision to enter the Catholic cathedral in Pamplona and to pray. Jake narrates, "At the end of the street I saw the cathedral and walked up toward it. The first time I ever saw it I thought the facade was ugly but I liked it now. I went inside" (p. 102). Jake's original aesthetic judgement of the cathedral as ugly is influenced by the 1920s American nationalism that detested Catholics and their beliefs. His "re-viewing" of the cathedral as something "he likes," and his decision to enter it, demonstrates how he has now cast off the influence of American nationalism by participating in this Basque culture which accepts all of those things that American nationalism rejects. He is now able to embrace his Catholicism in this "open" community. Jake reflects, "I was a little ashamed, and regretted that I was such a rotten Catholic, but realized there was nothing I could do about it, at least for a while, and maybe never, but that anyway it was a grand religion, and I only wished I felt religious and maybe I would next time" (p. 103). Jake regrets being a victim of this American nationalism that has kept him from his religion, but he accepts that Catholicism is really "a grand religion," and hopes that he will be able to be free from the prejudice that has kept him away from it in the past.

Later in the novel, Jake again enters the cathedral with Brett, but it is Brett who wants to leave quickly. Without his previous reservations, Jake enters the church and prays; when Jake and Brett leave the church, Jake is rather reflective. Brett tells Jake that he doesn't look very religious, and Jake says, "I'm pretty religious" (p. 213). While Jake may not be completely serious, and while he certainly has not restructured his entire life around Catholicism, this response is quite different from his earlier response to Bill, in which he claims that he "doesn't know" what it means to be Catholic (p. 129). By absorbing the attitudes of this Basque culture that accepts such things as Catholicism, Jake is able to regain some of his former self that was destroyed by not only the war, but by the American nationalism that emerged with it.

Throughout *The Sun Also Rises* this emerging American nationalism is criticized both through the satirical allusions to American politics and society and through the construction of the Basque culture as the antithesis of this nationalism. Jake and Bill's drunken dialogue while on the fishing trip stands as a particularly key scene in this criticism of American politics, on account of not only their dialogue, but also their drunkenness itself. In addition, the setting of the accepting and "open" Basque culture permits a forum for this critical discussion. While this scene is crucial to the criticism of American nationalism that occurs within the novel, it is not the only scene where prohibition and its ideologies are mentioned; American prohibition is mentioned by Count Mippipopolous early in the novel when speaking with Jake and Brett (p. 63), by the woman from Montana who is traveling with her family on the train (p. 92), and even by the Basque who speaks English on the bus trip to Burguete (p. 113). The ubiquity of this talk of American prohibition in the novel is matched only by the ubiquity of drinking itself. And while the excessive drinking of expatriates such as Jake and intellectuals such as Bill can certainly be analyzed as alcoholic disillusionment due to World War I, this drinking can just as certainly be representative of their disillusionment of American nationalism and of their rebellion to prohibition and its ideologies.

Likewise, while the scenes with the Basques and within the Basque countryside can be considered restorative due to Jake's return to nature, these scenes can also be considered restorative because this Basque culture provides a freedom from 1920s American nationalism. Whether historical Basque nationalism actually accepted foreigners with such openness or not, and whether drinking is actually such a significant part of the Basque culture or not, is unimportant in terms of *The Sun Also Rises*, for the Basque culture that is constructed in the novel presents itself to American readers as a foil for this American nationalism. The welcoming of foreigners, the accepted and important social act of drinking, and the prominence of Catholicism within this Basque culture in the novel all join together to create a culture that distinctly juxtaposes the discriminating, fundamentalist, prohibitionist, Protestant, white middle-class nationalism. In the midst of all these nationalist agendas and ideologies, alcohol becomes the rebellious rallying cry of the expatriates, and when it leaves America, so do they.

NOTES

1. Carol Gelderman, "Hemingway's Drinking Fixation," *Lost Generation Journal* 6 (1979): 12–14.

2. Matts Djos, "Alcoholism in Ernest Hemingway's *The Sun Also Rises*: A Wine and Roses Perspective on the Lost Generation," *The Hemingway Review* 14 (2):65 (1995).

3. Ernest Hemingway, *The Sun Also Rises* (New York: Scribner, 1926), p. 128. Subsequent references to *The Sun Also Rises* will be parenthetically cited by page number.

4. Thomas M. Coffey, *The Long Thirst: Prohibition in America, 1920–1933* (New York: Norton, 1975), p. 8.

5. Ann Douglas, *Terrible Honesty: Mongrel Manhattan in the 1920s* (New York: Farrar, Straus and Giroux, 1995), p. 4.

6. Ibid., p. 304.

7. Walter Benn Michaels, *Our America: Nativism, Modernism, and Pluralism* (Durham: Duke Univ. Press, 1995), pp. 136–37.

8. Douglas, *Terrible Honesty*, p. 306.

9. Marc Dolan, *Modern Lives: A Cultural Re-reading of "The Lost Generation"* (West Lafayette: Purdue Univ. Press, 1996), p. 92.

10. Michael S. Reynolds, *The Sun Also Rises: A Novel of the Twenties* (Boston: Twayne, 1988), p. 87.

11. John Higham, *Strangers in the Land: Patterns of American Nativism, 1860–1925* (New Brunswick: Rutgers Univ. Press, 1955), p. 271.

12. Michaels, *Our America*, pp. 28–30.

13. Ernest Hemingway, *The Torrents of Spring: A Romantic Novel in Honor of the Passing of a Great Race* (New York: Scribner, 1998), p. 81.

14. Michaels, *Our America*, p. 95.

15. Edward Behr, *Prohibition: Thirteen Years that Changed America* (New York: Arcade, 1996), pp. 73–74.

16. Ibid., p. 73.

17. Ibid., p. 238.

18. Michael S. Reynolds, "*The Sun* in Its Time: Recovering the Historical Context," in *New Essays on The Sun Also Rises*, ed. Linda Wagner-Martin (Cambridge: Cambridge Univ. Press, 1987), p. 62.

19. Mike Shatzkin, ed., *The Ballplayers: Baseball's Ultimate Biographical Reference* (New York: Arbor House/William Morrow, 1990), s.v. "Frisch, Frankie."

20. Harold Seymour, *Baseball: The Golden Age*, 2 vols. (Oxford: Oxford Univ. Press, 1989), 2: 378–79.

21. Frederic Joseph Svoboda, *Hemingway & The Sun Also Rises: The Crafting of a Style* (Lawrence: Univ. Press of Kansas, 1983), p. 17.

22. William T. Manning, "How a Nation May Lose Its Soul," *New York Times*, 29 May 1916.

23. W.D.F. Hughes, *Prudently with Power: William Thomas Manning, Tenth Bishop of New York* (West Park: Holy Cross Publications, 1960), p. 92.

24. Coffey, *The Long Thirst*, p. 143.

25. William Jennings Bryan, *William Jennings Bryan: Selections*, ed. Ray Ginger (Indianapolis: Bobbs-Merrill, 1967), p. 217.

26. Austin K. Kerr, *Organized for Prohibition: A New History of the Anti-Saloon League* (New Haven: Yale Univ. Press, 1985), p. 230.

27. Harold T. McCarthy, *The Expatriate Perspective: American Novelists and the Idea of America* (Rutherford: Fairleigh Dickinson Univ. Press, 1974), pp. 146–47.

28. Douglas, *Terrible Honesty*, p. 108.

29. Reynolds, *The Sun Also Rises: A Novel of the Twenties*, p. 62.

30. Gerald J. Kennedy, *Imagining Paris: Exile, Writing, and American Identity* (New Haven: Yale Univ. Press, 1993), p. 188.

31. Stanley G. Payne, *Basque Nationalism* (Reno: Univ. of Nevada Press, 1975), p. 104.

32. Ibid., pp. 93–94.

33. Juan Diez Medrano, *Divided Nations: Class, Politics, and Nationalism in the Basque Country and Catalonia* (Ithaca: Cornell Univ. Press, 1995), p. 80.

34. Edward F. Stanton, *Hemingway and Spain: A Pursuit* (Seattle: Univ. of Washington Press, 1989), p. 24.

35. David M. Andersen, "Basque Wine, Arkansas Chawin' Tobacco: Landscape and Ritual in Ernest Hemingway and Mark Twain," *Mark Twain Journal* 16 (1972): 4.

36. Tom Dardis, *The Thirsty Muse: Alcohol and the American Writer* (New York: Ticknor & Fields, 1989), p. 157.

37. Ibid., p. 158.

38. Ernest Hemingway, "The Three-Day Blow," in *In Our Time* (New York: Scribner, 1996), p. 44.

39. Dardis, *The Thirsty Muse*, p. 11.

40. Payne, *Basque Nationalism*, pp. 88–89.

DONALD A. DAIKER

The Pedagogy of The Sun Also Rises

"Pain is the teaching emotion."

—Edward Albee, *The Zoo Story*

"When you teach, you learn so much."

—Paavo Jaarvi, Music Director, Cincinnati Symphony Orchestra

"He who teaches others, teaches himself," wrote the great Moravian educator and reformer John Amos Comenius almost four centuries ago. Comenius believed that teachers learn in the very act of teaching because "the process of teaching in itself gives a deeper insight into the subject taught" (47).

Educators past and present agree with Comenius that teachers learn by teaching. The sixteenth century encyclopaedist Joachim Fortius believed that "if a student wished to make progress, he should arrange to give lessons daily in the subjects which he was studying, *even if he had to hire pupils*" (Gartner 15, ital. mine). The 19th century English educator Andrew Bell writes, "That the teacher profits far more by teaching than the scholar does by learning, is a maxim of antiquity, which all experience confirms—'*Docemur docento*'—'He who teaches learns'" (75). The American psychologist Jerome Bruner tells this story of teaching quantum theory to college students:

From *The Hemingway Review* 27, no.1 (Fall 2007): 74–88. Copyright © 2007 by the Ernest Hemingway Foundation.

I went through it once and looked up only to find the class full of blank faces—they had obviously not understood. I went through it a second time and they still did not understand it. And so I went through it a third time, and that time I understood it." (88)

Sandra Cisneros agrees that turning students into teachers is one of the best ways of enhancing their learning. When asked to identify an appropriate writing assignment for students reading her award-winning novel *The House on Mango Street*, Cisneros replied, "My assignment as a teacher would be to have the students write the Cliffs Notes. When you teach is when you have to look at the text deeply" (7).

Ernest Hemingway's brilliant novel *The Sun Also Rises* (1926) demonstrates that teaching can be a powerful source of learning for the teacher. Jake Barnes, the novel's narrator and protagonist, tries to teach Lady Brett Ashley, the woman he loves but cannot have, the importance and significance of bullfighting. Brett fails to understand the lesson, but in teaching Brett Jake himself becomes the learner. In the novel's closing pages, most clearly in the final Madrid sequence, Jake puts into practice the knowledge he has internalized from teaching Brett, becomes the metaphorical bullfighter, and thereby ends forever his mutually destructive relationship with Lady Brett.

That *The Sun Also Rises* is a novel about teaching and learning[1]—what Terrence Doody calls "a novel of education" (217)—is established in its opening paragraph when Jake Barnes tells us that Robert Cohn disliked boxing but "learned it painfully and thoroughly to counteract the feeling of inferiority and shyness he had felt on being treated as a Jew at Princeton." Jake adds that Cohn had been a "star pupil" of boxing coach Spider Kelly, who "taught all his young gentlemen to box like featherweights" (*SAR* 11).[2]

But the importance of teaching and learning in *The Sun Also Rises* extends well beyond the boxing ring. Learning is the key to the philosophy of life that Jake articulates, and Hemingway endorses, in the novel's central chapter XIV:

You paid some way for everything that was any good. I paid my way into enough things that I liked, so that I had a good time. Either you paid by learning about them, or by experience, or by taking chances, or by money. Enjoying living was learning to get your money's worth and knowing when you had it. You could get your money's worth. The world was a good place to buy in. (*SAR* 152)

Jake asserts in this passage that "learning" is one of the major sources of enjoyment in life. By learning about food and drink, books and travel, languages like French and Spanish, and sports like boxing and fishing, Jake gets his money's worth of life's pleasures. Jake's goal in life, he explains, is "learning to get your money's worth and knowing when you had it."

Aside from friendship, Jake derives most pleasure from bullfighting, which he has learned about thoroughly if not yet painfully. Jake carefully reads bull-fight newspapers like *Le Toril* (38), he travels to Pamplona and other venues to watch bull-fights "every year" (*SAR* 102), and he "often" (137) talks about bulls and bull-fighters with Montoya, the hotel proprietor, and other *aficionados*, those who are "passionate about the bull-fights" (136). Jake has learned bull-fighting so well that Montoya places "his hand on [Jake's] shoulder" in recognition of a fellow *aficionado* (136).

Jake has learned to get his money's worth of enjoyment from bullfighting, and through the central portions of the novel he teaches his friends about it. Even before the bullfights begin, he teaches Bill Gorton about the unloading of the bulls and the role of the steers in quieting them down (*SAR* 138). He later helps Bill, Mike Campbell, Robert Cohn, and Brett Ashley see that bulls use their horns like boxers, with a left and a right (144). He explains that bulls are "only dangerous when they're alone, or only two or three of them together" (145).

But Jake's teaching focuses on Lady Brett Ashley. During the second day of bull fights, Jake completely ignores Mike Campbell beside him in order to become Brett's teacher: "I sat beside Brett and explained to Brett what it was all about" (*SAR* 171). Significantly, Jake and Brett are seated in barreras, according to *Death in the Afternoon* the location most conducive to teaching and learning: "If you are going [to a bullfight] with some one who really knows bullfighting and want to learn to understand it and have no qualms about details a barrera is the best seat ..." (33). "I had her watch Romero," Jake says (171), and in so doing he helps Brett try to understand how close the young bullfighter always works to the bull and how his bullfighting gives real emotion. Brett had earlier called the bullfight a "spectacle" (169), but with Jake's instruction it becomes "more something that was going on with a definite end, and less of a spectacle with unexplained horrors" (171). Above all, Jake tries to teach Brett to understand Romero's importance and his greatness: "Romero had the old thing, the holding of his purity of line through the maximum of exposure, while he dominated the bull ..." (172). Jake at first believes that his teaching of Brett is successful—he uses the key phrase "she saw" no fewer than four times in a single paragraph to indicate his conviction that Brett is learning from his instruction and Romero's example. "I do not think Brett saw any other bullfighter," Jake says (171).

But Jake's teaching fails. Although Brett sees the purity of Romero's cape work, she misses his larger importance—symbolically represented by the bull's ear that, along with "a number of Muratti cigarette-stubs," Brett shoves "far back" into her hotel drawer in Pamplona (*SAR* 203). Brett's leaving behind the ear presented by popular acclamation to Romero, and then by Romero to her, shows that she is like the American tourists who "don't know what he's worth . . . , don't know what he means" (176). Interested primarily in Romero's "looks" (172), Brett manipulates Jake into introducing her to the bullfighter so that she can go to bed with him. Their affair causes bloody fights between Cohn and Jake and then between Cohn and Romero, as well as pain and anguish for Cohn, Mike, Jake, Romero, and finally Brett herself.

But Jake eventually learns the lessons that Brett misses. During the final bullfight of the fiesta, Jake makes no attempt to teach Brett. He speaks to her only to answer procedural questions, not to instruct. Instead, Jake concentrates on the personal relevance of Romero's work in the bullring, especially Romero's capacity for erasing the hurt of Cohn's beating: "He was wiping all that out now. Each thing he did with this bull wiped that out a little cleaner" (*SAR* 223). What Jake learns from Romero's "course in bull-fighting" (223) is that it is possible to clean up the messes in our lives. To this new knowledge he can now apply the earlier lesson he sought to teach Brett: it is through maximum exposure that you dominate the bull or any other force that, like Brett,[3] threatens to destroy you. Jake is beginning to internalize his own teaching, to apply to his own life what he has tried but failed to teach Lady Brett.[4]

When at the end of the novel he travels to Madrid to answer Brett's calls for help—Romero has left her, not the other way around—Jake has so well internalized the lessons he had earlier tried to teach Brett that he lives them. That is, in ending once and for all a relationship that drives Brett into other men's arms and prompts Jake himself to commit acts he acknowledges to be immoral, Jake puts into practice the wisdom that he has learned from Romero's bullfighting and that Brett has failed to learn. Jake the teacher has become Jake the learner.

First, Jake follows Romero's example of maximum exposure in two major ways: by leaving the safety of France, "the simplest country to live in" because "everything is on such a clear financial basis," for the complexities of Spain, where people become your friend for "obscure" reasons and where "you could not tell about anything" (*SAR* 237); and then by responding to Lady Brett's cry for help—"COULD YOU COME HOTEL MONTANA MADRID AM RATHER IN TROUBLE" (242, 243)—with an immediate and unequivocal *YES*. Jake is always most exposed when he is alone with Brett—like the bulls she becomes most dangerous when detached from the herd (145)—especially when they are alone together in a bedroom. During the early bedroom scene in Paris Jake becomes so "low" and so obviously dispirited by Brett's refusal to live with him that Brett says, "Don't look like that, darling" (63). In agreeing to meet Brett at her Madrid hotel room, in moving from "the terrain of the bull-fighter" to "the terrain of the bull" (217), Jake is knowingly—and courageously—exposing himself to another potentially debilitating bedroom scene.[5]

Even within the terrain of the bull, Romero controls virtually every element of the bullfight. During the final day of bullfighting, after Romero has begun his affair with Brett, "Everything of which he could control the locality he did in front of her all that afternoon" (*SAR* 220). All of Romero's movements were "so slow and so controlled" (221). Jake exerts the same control over Brett when the two meet in Madrid, although his control is evinced in more subtle ways than Romero's. For instance, it is Jake—and not Brett—who chooses Botin's restaurant for lunch and later decides on a taxi ride through town. Jake's control, even dominance, is further manifest in his understated sense of humor, a trait notably absent from the Paris bedroom scene. When Brett claims that Romero wanted to marry her, Jake responds with skeptical humor: "Maybe he thought that would make him Lord Ashley" (246). When Brett later invites Jake to think about Romero's comparative youth, Jake again replies with humor: "Anything you want me to think about it?" (248).

Jake's full control of the situation and himself as well as his dominance of Brett is shown in several other ways during the Madrid sequence. When they embrace for the first time, Jake is not swept away by passion but fully in control of his thoughts and sensations: "I could feel she was thinking of something else. She was trembling in my arms. She felt very small" (*SAR* 245). Later, as Brett and Jake are about to leave the Hotel Montana, Jake is still fully in control of the situation and of Brett: "I could feel her crying," Jake says at one point and, moments later, "I could feel her shaking" (247). Jake's dominance is also reflected in Brett's echoing his words. Moments after Jake tells Brett that she "ought to feel set up," Brett says, "I feel rather set up" (247, 248).[6] Still later, at the Palace Hotel bar, Jake separates himself from Brett theologically as he had earlier distanced himself emotionally. Thus when Brett asserts that "deciding not to be a bitch" is "sort of what we have instead of God," Jake challenges her use of the inclusive plural pronoun: "'Some people have God,' I said. 'Quite a lot'" (249).

Jake remains in control of Brett during the novel's penultimate scene in Botin's restaurant. There Jake eats "a very big meal" accompanied by four bottles of *rioja alta* (249), prompting many readers of *The Sun Also Rises* to conclude that Jake, still in thrall to Brett, is getting drunk to drown his sorrows.[7] Nothing could be further from the truth. Although Brett is convinced that Jake is getting drunk, her perspective is no more to be trusted here than her earlier thinking that going off with Cohn would be "good for him" (89).

When Brett tells Jake not to get drunk because "You don't have to," she has no idea what she is talking about; preoccupied with herself as ever, she has not bothered to learn anything about Jake since he set her up with Romero. Brett has not the slightest knowledge, for instance, of Jake's swimming, diving, and self-restoration in San Sebastian, which is indeed one reason why he doesn't have to get drunk.[8]

Mistaken though she may be, Brett's belief that Jake is trying to get drunk is understandable. After all, she has seen him drink three martinis at the Palace bar in addition to three bottles of wine plus two glasses of wine from a fourth bottle at Botin's. That's probably enough alcohol to make even an inveterate drinker like Jake legally "drunk": it's likely that his blood-alcohol content exceeds legal limits and that he could not pass a breathalyzer test. But Jake's words and actions make clear that both at Botin's and afterwards he has achieved an emotional sobriety that enables him to control his relationship with Brett.

If Jake had been actually trying to get drunk instead of merely drinking a good deal, he would not have eaten "a very big meal" of roast young suckling pig—"My God! What a meal you've eaten," Brett exclaims (*SAR* 248)—because food slows the absorption of alcohol into the blood stream.[9] And he would not be drinking *rioja alta*, one of the lightest and most delicate (and finest) of the world's wines.[10] Instead, as at the end of Book II, when Jake acknowledges that he has gotten "drunker than I ever remembered having been" (227), he would be drinking a potent brew like absinthe.

If Jake had become not only legally drunk but functionally intoxicated by drinking *rioja alta* with Brett, his vision would have been affected, as it was earlier in Pamplona when he had drunk not only wine but "much too much brandy" and his hotel room had started to "go round and round" (*SAR* 151, 153). Similarly, when Jake purposely got drunk on absinthe, he saw his bed go "sailing off" before that "wheeling" sensation subsided and his world seemed only "to blur at the edges" (228). But in Madrid, Jake's emotional sobriety is underscored by his clarity of vision: "the houses looked sharply white" (251).

Whereas Brett's word is often not to be trusted, especially in the Madrid sequence, Jake tells the truth here as he does throughout the novel.[11] Thus when Jake denies that he is getting drunk, we should take him at his word—especially since he has freely acknowledged earlier instances when he had been in various stages of inebriation. For example, Jake admits to being "a little drunk" (*SAR* 29) in Paris, and "quite drunk," "very drunk" (151), and then "drunker than I ever remembered having been" (227) in Pamplona. The common Latin expression "*in vino veritas*" applies to Jake in two ways: he utters truth when he is drinking wine, and he tells the truth about the effects of the wine or alcohol he is drinking.

Jake's denial that he is getting drunk takes on even greater force and persuasiveness because of its syntactic form—one of Hemingway's *trios*, three crisp consecutive assertions that essentially repeat each other. A trio is Hemingway's most powerful means of syntactic emphasis, to be taken at face value without irony or qualification. Thus when Hemingway's "Hills Like White Elephants" concludes with the trio, "'I feel fine,' she said. 'There's nothing wrong with me. I feel fine'" (*CSS* 214), we can be certain that, even when confronted by her lover's lies and evasions, even in the midst of pain and rejection, Jig will maintain her values, independence, and self-control. By the same token, the response of Count Mippipopolous to Brett's calling him dead—"No, my dear. You're not right. I'm not dead at all" (*SAR* 68)—makes clear that Brett is badly mistaken. Significantly, the scene at Botin's restaurant closes with a trio of Jake's: "'I'm not getting drunk,' I said. 'I'm just drinking a little wine. I like to drink wine'" (250). Jake's trio tells us to believe him when he rejects Brett's accusation that he is getting drunk. It is another sign of Jake's control of the situation and his domination of Brett.

But the novel's most significant trio occurs earlier as Jake's train from San Sebastian arrives in Madrid: "The Norte station in Madrid is the end of the line. All trains finish there. They don't go on anywhere." (*SAR* 244). This trio takes on special importance because Jake echoes it in his next-to-last spoken utterance. "I'll finish this" (250), Jake declares, the moment before leaving Botin's for a taxi ride through Madrid with Brett. Jake's determination to "finish this"—remember that Count Mippipopolous tells Brett, "you never finish your sentences at all" (65), and Brett admits, "I can't stop things" (187)—is a clear assertion of his control and dominance, and carries three-fold significance. First, Jake's statement suggests his resolve to get his money's worth from the wine he has paid for (Brett, like Mike Campbell, is penniless, a metaphor for her/their emotional bankruptcy); he has now learned how to get his money's worth of life's pleasures. Second, by finishing "this," Jake will not be leaving a mess behind for others to clean up, as he had earlier in Pamplona when, after he had made it possible for Brett and Romero to go off together, "A waiter came with a cloth and picked up the glasses and mopped up the table" (191). Finally, and most significantly, Jake's "I'll finish this" announces his determination to end, once and for all, his romance with Lady Brett Ashley.

The novel's final four paragraphs—Hemingway at his richest and best—show that Jake has internalized the lessons of life implicit in Romero's bull-fighting, the lessons Jake has learned from his attempts to teach them to Brett. Like Romero in the bullring, Jake fully controls everything that transpires in the "very hot and bright" Madrid sunshine. It is Jake, not Brett, who tells the taxi driver "where to drive," in contrast to the earlier cab ride in Paris where he had asked Brett, "Where should I tell him" to drive? (*SAR* 32). But the key word in this paragraph is "comfortably." For the first time in the novel, Jake feels comfortable when alone with Brett. In Paris Brett had made Jake cry and beg, in Pamplona she had made him act immorally, but in Madrid Brett no longer exerts control over Jake. Even when they are seated "close against each other" and when his arm is around her, Jake tells us that Brett "rested against me *comfortably*" (251, my emphasis). Unlike the Paris cab ride, where Jake stares at Brett ("I saw her face in the lights from the open shops ... then I saw her face clearly.... Brett's face was white" [33]) and kisses her on the lips, during the Madrid cab ride Jake is not even looking at Brett. He most certainly is not after a kiss, but is focused instead on their surroundings (the white houses), the weather (hot), and their route (the Gran Via).

However comfortable Jake now feels with Brett beside him, Brett herself is tense and miserable. For probably the first time in her life she has been rejected by a lover. Although she wants to believe—and wants Jake to believe—that it is she who has made Romero go, her words and acts gradually reveal to both Jake and the reader that Romero has left Brett, not the other way around.[12] Although Brett tells Jake that Romero "really" wanted to marry her after she had "gotten more womanly" (*SAR* 246), her behavior—throughout the hotel scene she cries, shakes, trembles, cries some more, and constantly looks away[13]—shows how depressed Romero's desertion has left her. So do her words. Perhaps the most telling index of Brett's emotional state is her decision to go back to Mike Campbell: "He's so damned nice and he's so awful. He's my sort of thing" (247).

Brett's equating herself to a "thing" shows just how badly she feels about herself, how far her self-esteem has fallen because of Romero's rejection. The depth of self-loathing reflected in Brett's seeing herself as a "thing" echoes Belmonte's disparagement of the bullfighter Marcial as "the sort of thing he knew all about" (*SAR* 219). Because Brett already feels so low, she no longer cares that Romero's having paid the bill at the Hotel Montana makes her a prostitute: "It doesn't matter now," she tells Jake[14] (247). It is a combination of Brett's depression and self-pity that leads her to reach out romantically to Jake for what proves to be the final time. In Paris, dancing with Jake, she had asked if he was "bored" before suggesting that they "get out of here" together (31); in Pamplona Brett had asked, "Do you still love me, Jake?" (187) before persuading him to introduce her to Romero; and now in Madrid Brett once again tries to tap into Jake's love for her, this time by evoking the might-have-been: "'Oh, Jake,' Brett said, 'we could have had such a damned good time together'" (251).

What makes Brett's come-on to Jake different this time is Jake's response. Significantly, Jake does not respond immediately. At first he says nothing. He does not turn to face Brett, and he certainly does not stare at her as earlier.

Rather, he is looking straight ahead to see "a mounted policeman in khaki directing traffic." That Jake takes his time in responding shows that he has taught himself the lessons of Pedro Romero, whose work in the bullring is "so slow and so controlled" (*SAR* 221) and whose passes are "all slow, templed and smooth" (223). That Jake does not look at Brett also recalls Romero's work in the bullring: "Never once did he look up" (220).

The richly complex final image of the novel—the raised baton of the khaki-clad policeman, slowing the taxi and "suddenly pressing" Brett and Jake together—underscores in multiple ways the lessons Jake has learned through teaching Brett about Romero's bullfighting. The policeman's "khaki" suggests war, as had the "very military" (*SAR* 242) appearance of the postman delivering Brett's second telegram; each is a forceful reminder of the origin of Jake's injury as well as a sign of his current vulnerability. Like Romero in the center of the ring, Jake is fully exposed because he locates himself wholly within the terrain of his bull—Lady Brett.

Brett's enticing "we could have had such a damned good time together" is the emotional equivalent for Jake of the bull's final charge. Unaware of Jake's self-teachings, Brett of course expects Jake to share her nostalgia and to embrace her self-pity. But she is badly mistaken. Earl Rovit is right in asserting that the raised baton of the policeman is "symbolic of the new command" that Jake has gained over himself and his relationship with Brett (158). But there is more here. The raising of the policeman's baton recalls Romero's drawn sword as he is about to kill. At the moment of the killing, "for just an instant" (222), Romero and the bull "were one," in the same way that Jake and Brett come together briefly when the taxi's sudden slowing momentarily presses them against each other. What happens in the bullring—"There was a little jolt as Romero came clear" (222)—exactly parallels what occurs in the taxi, what Hemingway in *Death in the Afternoon* calls "the moment of truth" (174): "'Yes,' I said. 'Isn't it pretty to think so?'" (*SAR* 251). Brett has to be taken aback—jolted, if you will—by Jake's refusal to indulge in her fantasies, but Jake has cleared himself of future romantic involvement by asserting that under no circumstances could he and Brett have lived happily ever after. As someone who "had been having Brett for a friend" (152), and as someone who knows that she "can't go anywhere alone" (107), Jake will not leave Brett stranded and penniless in Madrid; he arranges and pays for "berths on the Sud Express for the night" (247) so that he can return her to Michael,[15] her "sort of thing."

Jake's full control of his relationship with Brett, suggested by his choosing when and how they will leave Madrid, is manifest in the novel's famous final line. Spoken only after a deliberate pause following Brett's *cri de coeur*, Jake's words reveal through humor and irony the emotional distance he has achieved from Brett. Jake's initial "Yes" seems to imply his agreement with Brett, but it is an ironic affirmative immediately negated with "Isn't it pretty to think so?" Jake's control here is demonstrated not simply through what he says but how he says it. For example, his using the word "pretty" to mean not *pleasing*, *attractive*, or *good* but rather *foolish*, *silly*, or *ridiculous* deliberately echoes Brett's earlier equally ironic question, "Hasn't he [Mike] been pretty?" (*SAR* 185). Jake is subtly reminding Brett that it is her inability to remain faithful to Mike—and perhaps to any one man—that makes "a damned good time" for her unlikely.

Hemingway's late manuscript changes—two major additions and one important revision—help reinforce Jake's full control at the close of the novel[16] (Hemingway, *SAR Facsimile* II: 615–616). One key addition to the manuscript first draft is Jake's line, "I'll finish this," an unequivocal assertion that Jake is in charge and knows exactly what he must do. A second major addition is the sentence "He raised his baton" to the novel's penultimate paragraph. The raised baton also suggests Jake's power and authority. The important revision concerns the novel's final line, which apparently went through three stages:

> "Yes," I said. "It's nice as hell to think so."
> "Yes," I said. "Isn't it nice to think so"
> "Yes," I said. "Isn't it pretty to think so?"

Each revision shows Jake in firmer control. Hemingway may have eliminated the profanity in the first version above because Jake's swearing earlier in the novel almost always indicates his anger and at least a partial loss of control.[17] He may have gradually changed the form of Jake's utterance from a statement to a question—including a question mark in the final version—to achieve the sense of understatement that often characterizes Hemingway's most important utterances.[18] Finally, by substituting "pretty" for "nice," Hemingway allowed Jake to appropriate Brett's earlier term to make clear that he is the one now in charge of their relationship.[19] Significantly, the last words in the novel are Jake's.

The control that Jake evinces from the moment he arrives at Madrid's Norte Station until the moment he dismisses Brett's fantasies as "pretty" is clear evidence that in trying to teach others, especially Brett, about bullfighting he has in fact succeeded in teaching himself. By teaching others, he has taught himself that, like Romero with his final bull, it is possible to move beyond and even erase past mistakes and misdeeds:

> The fight with Cohn had not touched his spirit but his face had been smashed and his body hurt. He was wiping all that out now. Each thing that he did with this bull wiped that out a little cleaner. (*SAR* 223)

Following Romero's example, Jake wipes out his past emotional beatings in Paris and Pamplona. In the sunshine of Madrid's Gran Via, he becomes the metaphorical bullfighter who, fully exposed, "Out in the centre of the ring, all alone" (222), controls and dominates the force that threatens to destroy him by making Brett "realize he was unattainable . . ." (172). Jake the teacher has evolved fully into Jake the learner.

Notes

1. A number of commentators on *The Sun Also Rises* have recognized its educational theme although no one I've read has identified Jake as simultaneous teacher and learner. Earl Rovit, for example, calls *Sun* an "epistemological" novel and speaks of Jake's "painful lessons in learning how to live" (149). Linda Wagner refers to Jake's "initiation" and "education" (69), and Lawrence Broer to the "self-study course in emotional pragmatism" that Romero provides Jake (137). Ernest Lockridge notes that under "Barnes's tutelage," Brett receives a "bullfight-appreciation lesson" (80), while Robert Fleming focuses on the "lessons" that Jake learns first from Count Mippipopolous and then from Pedro Romero ("Importance of Count Mippipopolous" 144).

2. All quotations from *The Sun Also Rises* are from Scribner's 2003 edition and are cited parenthetically in the text.

3. Carl Eby is right in asserting that although Robert Cohn and Jake Barnes are each by turns a steer and a bull, Brett "is invariably a 'bull'" (308). For especially insightful discussions of the role of bullfighting in *The Sun Also Rises*, see Ganzel and Josephs.

4. For critical readings of *The Sun Also Rises* that focus on Jake's growth and the novel's positive ending, see Baskett, Benson, Budick, Daiker, Ganzel, Petite, and especially Vopat.

5. Jake rescues Brett, H. R. Stoneback writes, because he "places great importance on 'the values'—and one of the values is loyalty, generously assisting old friends who are 'in trouble'" (286).

6. Earlier, by contrast, it had been the other way around: it was Jake who had echoed Brett's words, who had gotten "into the habit of using English expressions in [his] thinking" (*SAR* 153).

7. See for example Balassi (115), Reynolds (62), and Svoboda (94). For an opposing view, see Vopat (103).

8. Vopat refers to San Sebastian as "Jake's Rest and Recuperation leave," convincingly arguing that its "lessons are still with him" when he arrives in Madrid (100–101). For detailed and sensitive discussions of the San Sebastian episode, see Knodt and Steinke.

9. In *Death in the Afternoon*, Hemingway speaks of dining "on suckling pig at Botin's" as one of life's highest pleasures (104), clearly an experience that would be diminished if one were drunk.

10. In *Death in the Afternoon*, which offers many insights into *Sun*, Hemingway describes Rioja Alta and Rioja Clarete as "the lightest and pleasantest of the red wines" (461).

11. That Jake characteristically tells the truth is underscored by his admitting to the rare occasion when he doesn't: "I lied," he confesses, in telling Romero that he had seen two of his bullfights when he had in fact seen only one (*SAR* 178).

12. Hemingway readers are close to unanimous in rejecting my assertion that it is Romero who leaves Brett. See for example Gladstein, Comley and Scholes, Lewis, and Spilka. The latter refers to Brett's "charitable withdrawing of her devastating love" for Romero (179).

13. In Hemingway, a person's looking away usually signals either dishonesty or reluctance to accept an pleasant truth. In the Paris bedroom scene Jake lies "face down on the bed" (*SAR* 61) because he would rather not accept the impossibility of his relationship with Brett. Later Robert Cohn is "lying, face down, on the bed in the dark" (197), a sign of his unwillingness to acknowledge Brett's indifference. The innkeeper in Burguete, who knows she is over-charging Jake and Bill for their room, "put her hands under her apron and looked away. . . ." When Jake protests, she "just took off her glasses and wiped them on her apron" (115).

14. Earlier it was important for Brett's self-esteem that she not think of herself as a prostitute. That's why she rejected the Count's extravagant offer of "ten thousand dollars"—not because she "knew too many people" in Biarritz, Cannes, or Monte Carlo (*SAR* 41). The latter explanation is only what Brett "told him," not the real reason for her preferring to go off instead with Cohn, who offers not money but love. That Brett no longer cares that she has traded sex for money illustrates her deep despair.

15. In Hemingway's unfinished sequel to *The Sun Also Rises*, Brett has in fact returned to Michael. Probably written in 1927 and catalogued under the title "Jimmy the Bartender," this nine-page afterword to *The Sun Also Rises* shows Jake Barnes drinking at the Dingo Bar in Paris when Mike Campbell and Brett Ashley walk in together. See Fleming, "Second Thoughts."

16. Frederic Svoboda's study of the textual evolution of *The Sun Also Rises* supports my contention that Hemingway's late revisions to the novel's final chapter portray a more controlled and dominant Jake Barnes: "Jake's statements near the end of the first draft seem to project a protagonist who is more bitter and less in control of himself than the Jake Barnes of the completed novel" (40).

17. Jake usually swears only when he is angry, as when Bill Gorton asks about his relationship to Brett ("I'd a hell of a lot rather not talk about it" [*SAR* 128] or when he receives Brett's telegram, "Well, that meant San Sebastian all shot to hell" (243).

18. After announcing his own central philosophy of life in Chapter XIV, Hemingway has Jake undercut it with "It seemed like a fine philosophy. In five years, I thought, it will seem just as silly as all the other fine philosophies I've had" (*SAR* 152).

19. For Svoboda, the novel's final sentence evolves from a "petulant and aggrieved" statement to "a wearier, yet more peaceful" one to "an even more appropriate expression of Jake's realistic, weary, yet essentially healthy accommodation to the realities of his relationship with Brett" (95).

Works Cited

Albee, Edward. *The American Dream and The Zoo Story.* 1959. New York: Penguin Books, 1997.

Balassi, William. "The Writing of the Manuscript of *The Sun Also Rises.*" In Nagel. 106–125.

Baskett, Sam S. "Brett and Her Lovers." *Centennial Review* 22 (1978): 45–49.

Bell, Andrew. *Bell's Mutual Tuition and Moral Discipline*. London: C.J.G. & F. Livingston, 1832.

Bloom, Harold ed. *Brett Ashley*. New York: Chelsea House, 1991.

Benson, Jackson J. *Hemingway: The Writer's Art of Self-Defense*. Minneapolis: Minnesota UP, 1969.

Brenner, Gerry. *Concealments in Hemingway's Works*. Columbus: Ohio State UP, 1983.

Broer, Lawrence R. "Intertextual Approach to *The Sun Also Rises*." In *Teaching Hemingway's The Sun Also Rises*. Ed. Peter L. Hays. Moscow: U of Idaho P, 2003. 127–146.

Bruner, Jerome. *The Process of Education*. New York: Vintage Books, 1963.

Budick, E. Miller. "*The Sun Also Rises*: Hemingway and the Art of Repetition." *University of Toronto Quarterly* 56 (1986–87): 319–337.

Cisneros, Sandra. "Study Guides: The Reviews Are In." Education Life. *The New York Times* 4 August 2002: 7.

Comenius, John Amos. *The Great Didactic*, Part II. Trans. M. W. Keatinge. London: A. and C. Black, Ltd., 1921.

Comley, Nancy R. and Robert Scholes. *Hemingway's Genders: Rereading the Hemingway Text*. New Haven: Yale UP, 1994.

Daiker, Donald A. "The Affirmative Conclusion of *The Sun Also Rises*." 1974. Rptd. in Nagel 74–88.

Doody, Terrence. "Hemingway's Style and Jake's Narration." 1974. Rptd. in *Ernest Hemingway: Seven Decades of Criticism*. Ed. Linda Wagner-Martin. East Lansing: Michigan State UP, 1998. 103–117.

Eby, Carl P. *Hemingway's Fetishism: Psychoanalysis and the Mirror of Manhood*. Albany: State U of New York P, 1999.

Fleming, Robert E. "The Importance of Count Mippipopolous: Creating the Code Hero." 1988. In Nagel. 141–145.

———. "Second Thoughts: Hemingway's Postscript to *The Sun Also Rises*." In Nagel. 163–169.

Ganzel, Dewey. "*Cabestro* and *Vaquilla*: The Symbolic Structure of *The Sun Also Rises*." *Sewanee Review* 76 (1968): 26–48.

Gartner, Alan, Mary Conway Kohler, and Frank Reissman. *Children Teach Children: Learning by Teaching*. New York: Harper & Row, 1971.

Gladstein, Mimi Reisel. *The Indestructible Woman in Faulkner, Hemingway, and Steinbeck*. Ann Arbor: UMI Research P, 1986.

Hemingway, Ernest. *The Complete Short Stories of Ernest Hemingway: The Finca Vigía Edition*. New York: Scribner's, 1987.

———. *Death in the Afternoon*. New York: Scribner's, 1932.

———. "Jimmy the Bartender." Item 530. Hemingway Collection. John F. Kennedy Library. Boston, MA.

———. *Ernest Hemingway: Selected Letters, 1917–1961*. Ed. Carlos Baker. New York: Scribner's, 1981.

———. *The Sun Also Rises*. 1926. New York: Scribner's, 2003.

———. *The Sun Also Rises: A Facsimile Edition*. Ed. Matthew J. Bruccoli. Detroit, MI: Archive of Literary Documents, 1990.

Jaarvi, Paavo. Comments during a Cincinnati Symphony Orchestra Donors' Choice Concert. 5 September 2005.

Josephs, Allen. "*Toreo*: The Moral Axis of *The Sun Also Rises*." 1986. In Nagel. 126–140.

Knodt, Ellen Andrews. "Diving Deep: Jake's Moment of Truth at San Sebastian." *The Hemingway Review* 17 (Fall 1997): 28–37.

Lewis, Robert W. "Tristan or Jacob?" 1965. Rptd. in Bloom. 63–75.

Lockridge, Ernest. "The Primitive Emotion that Drives Jake Barnes." 1990. In *Readings on The Sun Also Rises*. Ed. Kelly Wand. San Diego, CA: Greenhaven, 2002. 79–93.

Nagel, James ed. *Critical Essays on Ernest Hemingway's The Sun Also Rises*. New York: G. K. Hall, 1995.

Petite, Joseph. "Hemingway and Existential Education." *Journal of Evolutionary Psychology* 12 (1991): 152–164.

Reynolds, Michael S. *The Sun Also Rises: A Novel of the Twenties*. Boston: Twayne, 1988.

Rovit, Earl. *Ernest Hemingway*. New Haven, CT: College and University P by special arrangement with Twayne, 1963.

Spilka, Mark. *Hemingway's Quarrel with Androgyny*. Lincoln: Nebraska UP, 1990. 175–183.

Steinke, Jim. "Brett and Jake in Spain: Hemingway's Ending for *The Sun Also Rises*." *Spectrum* 27 (1985): 131–141.

Stoneback, H. R. *Reading Hemingway's The Sun Also Rises: Glossary and Commentary*. Kent, OH: Kent State UP, 2007.

Svoboda, Frederic Joseph. *Hemingway and The Sun Also Rises: The Crafting of a Style*. Lawrence: Kansas UP, 1983.

Vopat, Carole Gottlieb. "The End of *The Sun Also Rises*: A New Beginning." 1972. Rptd. in Bloom. 96–105.

Wagner, Linda W. "*The Sun Also Rises*: One Debt to Imagism." 1972. In Nagel. 63–73.

Chronology

1899	Born Ernest Miller Hemingway on July 21 in Oak Park, Illinois.
1917	Graduates from Oak Park High School; works as a reporter for the *Kansas City Star*.
1918	Enlists in Red Cross Ambulance Corps; wounded in Italy on July 8.
1920	Begins writing for the *Toronto Star* newspapers.
1921	Marries Elizabeth Hadley Richardson; moves to Paris.
1923	Attends first bullfight in Spain; publishes *Three Stories and Ten Poems*; moves to Toronto; son John (Bumby) is born.
1924	Returns to Paris; publishes *In Our Time* in Europe.
1925	Publishes *In Our Time*, which adds fourteen short stories to the earlier vignettes, in America.
1926	Publishes *The Torrents of Spring* and *The Sun Also Rises*.
1927	Divorces Hadley Richardson; marries Pauline Pfeiffer; publishes *Men Without Women*.
1928	Moves to Key West, Florida; son Patrick is born.
1929	Publishes *A Farewell to Arms*.
1931	Son Gregory is born.

1932   Publishes *Death in the Afternoon*.

1933   Publishes *Winner Take Nothing*; begins first African safari.

1935   Publishes *Green Hills of Africa*.

1937   Begins covering the Spanish Civil War for the North American Newspaper Alliance; publishes *To Have and Have Not*.

1938   Publishes *The Fifth Column and the First Forty-nine Stories*.

1940   Publishes *For Whom the Bell Tolls*; divorces Pauline Pfeiffer; marries Martha Gellhorn; buys Finca Vigía estate in Cuba.

1944   Serves as war correspondent in Europe; suffers concussion in serious auto accident.

1945   Divorces Martha Gellhorn.

1946   Marries Mary Welsh.

1950   Publishes *Across the River and into the Trees*.

1952   Publishes *The Old Man and the Sea*.

1953   Awarded Pulitzer Prize for *The Old Man and the Sea*; begins second African safari.

1954   Suffers major injuries in two plane crashes in Africa; receives Nobel Prize for Literature and Award of Merit from the American Academy of Arts & Letters.

1961   Commits suicide in Ketchum, Idaho, on July 2.

1964   *A Moveable Feast* is published.

1970   *Islands in the Stream* is published.

1986   *The Garden of Eden* is published.

1999   *True at First Light: A Fictional Memoir* is published.

2005   *Under Kilimanjaro*, first unabridged version of *True at First Light*, is published.

Contributors

HAROLD BLOOM is Sterling Professor of the Humanities at Yale University. Educated at Cornell and Yale universities, he is the author of more than 30 books, including *Shelley's Mythmaking* (1959), *The Visionary Company* (1961), *Blake's Apocalypse* (1963), *Yeats* (1970), *The Anxiety of Influence* (1973), *A Map of Misreading* (1975), *Kabbalah and Criticism* (1975), *Agon: Toward a Theory of Revisionism* (1982), *The American Religion* (1992), *The Western Canon* (1994), *Omens of Millennium: The Gnosis of Angels, Dreams, and Resurrection* (1996), *Shakespeare: The Invention of the Human* (1998), *How to Read and Why* (2000), *Genius: A Mosaic of One Hundred Exemplary Creative Minds* (2002), *Hamlet: Poem Unlimited* (2003), *Where Shall Wisdom Be Found?* (2004), and *Jesus and Yahweh: The Names Divine* (2005). In addition, he is the author of hundreds of articles, reviews, and editorial introductions. In 1999, Professor Bloom received the American Academy of Arts and Letters' Gold Medal for Criticism. He has also received the International Prize of Catalonia, the Alfonso Reyes Prize of Mexico, and the Hans Christian Andersen Bicentennial Prize of Denmark.

H. R. STONEBACK is a distinguished professor in the English department at the State University of New York at New Paltz, where he has also been director of graduate studies. He is the author or editor of many books. One of his newest volumes of literary criticism is *Reading Hemingway's* The Sun Also Rises.

WOLFGANG E. H. RUDAT was a professor in the English department at the University of Houston. In addition to his text on tragicomedy in *The Sun Also Rises*, he published *Alchemy in* The Sun Also Rises: *Hidden Gold in Hemingway's Narrative* and other titles.

181

PAUL CIVELLO is the author of a piece on Hemingway's "Big Two-Hearted River," has published on Frank Norris, and has contributed a chapter on Don DeLillo to *American Novelists since World War II*.

JAMES NAGEL is a distinguished professor at the University of Georgia. He has published many titles, including *Ernest Hemingway: The Writer in Context*, *Ernest Hemingway: The Oak Park Legacy*, and *Hemingway in Love and War*. He is a past president of the Ernest Hemingway Society and the founder of the journal *Studies in American Fiction*. He is also the general editor of the *Critical Essays on American Literature* series, which now contains more than 150 volumes.

RON BERMAN is professor emeritus at the University of California, San Diego. He is the author of *Fitzgerald, Hemingway, and the Twenties* and *Translating Modernism: Fitzgerald and Hemingway* among other titles.

ADRIAN BOND is on the faculty at George Brown College in Toronto, where he teaches classes in communication. In addition to academic publication in both the humanities and the sciences, he has published other works of nonfiction, fiction, and poetry, and editorial cartoons as well.

DANIEL S. TRABER is an associate professor of English at Texas A&M University, Galveston. He is the author of *Whiteness, Otherness, and the Individualism Paradox from Huck to Punk*.

JEFFREY A. SCHWARZ received a Ph.D. in English from St. Louis University. In addition to his work on *The Sun Also Rises*, he has published on *A Farewell to Arms* and other works.

DONALD A. DAIKER is professor emeritus at Miami University in Ohio. He has published essays on *The Sun Also Rises* and several books on writing as well.

Bibliography

Auchincloss, Louis. *Writers and Personality*. Columbia: University of South Carolina, 2005.

Bak, John S. *Homo Americanus: Ernest Hemingway, Tennessee Williams, and Queer Masculinities*. Madison, N.J.: Fairleigh Dickinson University Press, 2010.

Baldwin, Marc D. *Reading* The Sun Also Rises: *Hemingway's Political Unconscious*. New York: P. Lang, 1997.

Berman, Ronald. *Fitzgerald, Hemingway, and the Twenties*. Tuscaloosa: University of Alabama Press, 2001.

———. *Modernity and Progress: Fitzgerald, Hemingway, Orwell*. Tuscaloosa: University of Alabama Press, 2005.

———. *Translating Modernism: Fitzgerald and Hemingway*. Tuscaloosa: University of Alabama Press, 2009.

Blackmore, David. "'In New York It'd Mean I Was a . . .': Masculinity Anxiety and Period Discourses of Sexuality in *The Sun Also Rises*." *Hemingway Review* 18, no. 1 (Fall 1998): 49–67.

Broer, Lawrence R., and Gloria Holland, ed. *Hemingway and Women: Female Critics and the Female Voice*. Tuscaloosa: University of Alabama Press, 2002.

Bruccoli, Matthew J. *Classes on Ernest Hemingway*. Columbia: Thomas Cooper Library, University of South Carolina, 2002.

Clifford, Stephen P. *Beyond the Heroic "I": Reading Lawrence, Hemingway, and "Masculinity."* Lewisburg, Pa.: Bucknell University Press, 1998.

Comley, Nancy R., and Robert Scholes. *Hemingway's Genders: Rereading the Hemingway Text*. New Haven: Yale University Press, 1994.

183

De Koster, Katie, ed. *Readings on Ernest Hemingway*. San Diego: Greenhaven Press, 1997.

Donaldson, Scott. *Fitzgerald & Hemingway: Works and Days*. New York: Columbia University Press, 2009.

Donaldson, Scott, ed. *The Cambridge Companion to Hemingway*. Cambridge; New York: Cambridge University Press, 1996.

Earle, David M. *All Man!: Hemingway, 1950s Men's Magazines, and the Masculine Persona*. Kent, Ohio: Kent State University Press, 2009.

Field, Allyson Nadia. "Expatriate Lifestyle as Tourist Destination: *The Sun Also Rises* and Experiential Travelogues of the Twenties." *Hemingway Review* 25, no. 2 (Spring 2006): 29–43.

Forter, Greg. "Melancholy Modernism: Gender and the Politics of Mourning in *The Sun Also Rises*." *Hemingway Review* 21, no. 1 (Fall 2001): 22–37.

Fulton, Lorie Watkins. "Reading around Jake's Narration: Brett Ashley and *The Sun Also Rises*." *Hemingway Review* 24, no. 1 (Fall 2004): 61–80.

Gajdusek, Robert E. *Hemingway in His Own Country*. Notre Dame, Ind.: University of Notre Dame Press, 2002.

Gandal, Keith. *The Gun and the Pen: Hemingway, Fitzgerald, Faulkner, and the Fiction of Mobilization*. Oxford, England; New York: Oxford University Press, 2008.

Helbig, Doris A. "Confession, Charity, and Community in *The Sun Also Rises*." *South Atlantic Review* 58, no. 2 (May 1993): 85–110.

Justice, Hilary K. *The Bones of the Others: The Hemingway Text from the Lost Manuscripts to the Posthumous Novels*. Kent, Ohio: Kent State University Press, 2006.

Leff, Leonard J. "The Sun Almost Rises: Hemingway and the Hollywood Marketplace of Depression America." *Arizona Quarterly: A Journal of American Literature, Culture, and Theory* 51, no. 4 (Winter 1995): 45–67.

Meyers, Jeffrey, ed. *Ernest Hemingway: The Critical Heritage*. London; New York: Routledge, 1997, 1982.

Moddelmog, Debra A. *Reading Desire: In Pursuit of Ernest Hemingway*. Ithaca, N.Y.: Cornell University Press, 1999.

Nagel, James, ed. *Critical Essays on Ernest Hemingway's* The Sun Also Rises. New York: G.K. Hall; London: Prentice Hall International, 1995.

Oates, Joyce Carol. *Uncensored: Views & (re)views*. New York: Ecco, 2005.

Pavloska, Susanna. *Modern Primitives: Race and Language in Gertrude Stein, Ernest Hemingway and Zora Neale Hurston*. New York; London: Garland, 2000.

Reynolds, Michael S. The Sun Also Rises, *a Novel of the Twenties*. Boston: Twayne Publishers, 1988.

Rosen, Kenneth, ed. *Hemingway Repossessed*. Westport, Conn.: Praeger, 1994.

Rovit, Earl, and Arthur Waldron, ed. *Hemingway and Faulkner in Their Time*. New York: Continuum, 2005.

Rudat, Wolfgang E. H. *Alchemy in* The Sun Also Rises: *Hidden Gold in Hemingway's Narrative*. Lewiston, N.Y.: Mellen, 1992.

———. "Anti-Semitism in *The Sun Also Rises*: Traumas, Jealousies, and the Genesis of Cohn." *American Imago: Studies in Psychoanalysis and Culture* 49, no. 2 (Summer 1992): 263–75.

———. Jake's Wound and Hemingway's War Trauma Once More: Allusions to *Tristram Shandy* and Other Jokes in *The Sun also Rises*. *Journal of Evolutionary Psychology* 12, nos. 3–4 (August 1991): 188–206.

Scafella, Frank, ed. *Hemingway: Essays of Reassessment*. New York: Oxford University Press, 1991.

Schmigalle, Günther. "'How People Go to Hell': Pessimism, Tragedy, and Affinity to Schopenhauer in *The Sun Also Rises*." *Hemingway Review* 25, no. 1 (Fall 2005): 7–21.

Stoltzfus, Ben. *Hemingway and French Writers*. Kent, Ohio: Kent State University Press, 2010.

Strong, Amy L. *Race and Identity in Hemingway's Fiction*. New York: Palgrave Macmillan, 2008.

Svoboda, Frederic Joseph. *Hemingway and* The Sun Also Rises: *The Crafting of a Style*. Lawrence, Kan.: University Press of Kansas, 1983.

Tomkins, David. "The 'Lost Generation' and the Generation of Loss: Ernest Hemingway's Materiality of Absence and *The Sun Also Rises*." *MFS: Modern Fiction Studies* 54, no. 4 (Winter 2008): 744–65.

Tyler, Lisa. *Student Companion to Ernest Hemingway*. Westport, Conn.: Greenwood Press, 2001.

Wagner-Martin, Linda. *Ernest Hemingway: A Literary Life*. Basingstoke; New York: Palgrave Macmillan, 2007.

Wagner-Martin, Linda, ed. *Ernest Hemingway's* The Sun Also Rises: *A Casebook*. Oxford, England; New York: Oxford University Press, 2002.

———. *Hemingway: Seven Decades of Criticism*. East Lansing: Michigan State University Press, 1998.

———. *A Historical Guide to Ernest Hemingway*. New York: Oxford University Press, 2000.

———. *New Essays on* The Sun Also Rises. Cambridge, England; New York: Cambridge University Press, 1987.

Acknowledgments

H. R. Stoneback, "From the rue Saint-Jacques to the Pass of Roland to the 'Unfinished Church on the Edge of the Cliff.'" From *The Hemingway Review* 6, no. 1 (Fall 1986): 2–29. Copyright © 1986 by the Ernest Hemingway Foundation.

Wolfgang E. H. Rudat, "Bill Gorton, Jake's Wounded Preacher: The Therapeutic Nature of Jokes." From *A Rotten Way to Be Wounded: The Tragicomedy of The Sun Also Rises*. Copyright © 1990 by Peter Lang.

Paul Civello, "*The Sun Also Rises*: Learning to Live in a Naturalistic World." From *American Literary Naturalism and Its Twentieth-Century Transformations: Frank Norris, Ernest Hemingway, Don DeLillo*. Copyright © 1994 by the University of Georgia Press.

James Nagel, "Narrational Values and Robert Cohn in *The Sun Also Rises*." From *Hemingway: Up in Michigan Perspectives*, edited by Frederic J. Svoboda and Joseph J. Waldmeir. Copyright © 1995 by Michigan State University Press.

Ron Berman, "Protestant, Catholic, Jew: *The Sun Also Rises*." From *The Hemingway Review* 18, no. 1 (Fall 1998): 33–48. Copyright © 1998 by the Ernest Hemingway Foundation.

Adrian Bond, "The Way It Wasn't in Hemingway's *The Sun Also Rises*." From *The Journal of Narrative Technique* 28, no. 1 (Spring 1998): 56–74. Copyright © 1994 by *The Journal of Narrative Technique*.

187

Daniel S. Traber, "Whiteness and the Rejected Other in *The Sun Also Rises*." From *Studies in American Fiction* 28, no. 2 (Autumn 2000): 235–53. Copyright © 2000 by Northeastern University.

Jeffrey A. Schwarz, "'The Saloon Must Go, and I Will Take It with Me': American Prohibition, Nationalism, and Expatriation in *The Sun Also Rises*." From *Studies in the Novel* 33, no. 2 (Summer 2001): 180–201. Copyright © 2001 by the University of North Texas.

Donald A. Daiker, "The Pedagogy of *The Sun Also Rises*." From *The Hemingway Review* 27, no. 1 (Fall 2007): 74–88. Copyright © 2007 by the Ernest Hemingway Foundation.

Index

Characters in literary works are indexed by first name (if any), followed by the name of the work in parentheses